MACHINE AGE ARMIES

Machine Age Armies

by John Wheldon

ABELARD-SCHUMAN

LONDON   NEW YORK   TORONTO

LONDON
Abelard-Schuman
Limited
8 King Street WC2

NEW YORK
Abelard-Schuman
Limited
6 West 57 Street

TORONTO
Abelard-Schuman
Canada Limited
896 Queen Street West

To my dear wife

Contents

Contents

Acknowledgements

I wish to acknowledge my gratitude to Sir B. H. Liddell Hart, D.Litt., who patiently answered my queries about his ideas and work, found time to comment on my interpretation of it, and gave permission to quote from his writing and correspondence. Also to the late Major-General J. F. C. Fuller, C.B., C.B.E., D.S.O., who gave me very full answers to all questions concerning the growth of his ideas about armoured forces, and permission to quote them.

Also to Mr. J. E. Christie, of Florida, U.S.A., who gave me a valuable outline of the aims and methods of his father, the late J. W. Christie, tank designer; to Lieutenant-Colonel Philip Johnson, C.B.E., D.S.O., M.I.Mech.E., who gave me full access to his records of the development of the Medium D tank; to Colonel R. J. Icks, U.S. Army (retired), who proved a mine of information about the onset of mechanization in the U.S. Army; to the Curator of the Tank Museum, Royal Armoured Corps; and to the Curator of the Ordnance Museum, U.S. Army.

For information concerning very recent history I am indebted to Mr. Arie Hashavia, journalist, of Tel Aviv, Israel (but I wish I could read the Hebrew on his maps!), and to the Office of the Chief of Information, U.S. Army. Needless to say, all this help was with factual material. Interpretations which may, who knows, be heretical are all my own.

Lastly, I am indebted to Sir Julian Huxley, not only for permission to quote material from one of his essays, but for the very idea of making a study of military ideas as evolving forces. For this book was to have been a comparatively simple study of armoured vehicles—it was after reading some Huxley essays that I switched from the artifacts to the ideas behind them.

List of Maps

List of Illustrations

Preface

Distaste for war has grown in this country ever since World War I proved to be something other than an autumn picnic. When the spate of destruction ceased in 1918, there was a general awareness that European armies were functioning inefficiently, in that their losses, and the devastation they caused, were not in proportion to their achievements; but there was little or no public interest in their reorganization and modernization, and virtually no official research was undertaken to make them more efficient. It was as though the experiences of World War I were emotionally so damaging as to prevent rational examination of their causes. As though the new, mechanical form of total war loomed horrifically as something too dreadful to be tampered with—a Frankenstein monster that surgery would only make more insanely destructive. It was not seen, by the majority of professional soldiers or by the majority of politicians, let alone the general public, that greater efficiency in mechanized armies could possibly result in a reduction of the scope of their sheer destructive powers—if efficiency were measured in speed of operation.

The reform of mechanized warfare became the concern of a minority of military thinkers, whose ideas were in general poorly received, and in certain instances rejected outright. Consequently, the industrial powers of Europe and the U.S.A. entered World War II with armies, and ideas about the use of armies, that were largely pre-industrial age in character with a few modern elements grafted onto them; and perhaps because of this, the further searing experiences of destruction, loss, and frustration made us, when they were past, push armies and armaments to the furthest recesses of our consciousness, and accept willingly and with relief the absurd idea that the West's unilateral possession of nuclear weapons could usher in an era of world peace. Irrational distaste for war and ostrich-like refusal to contemplate its sociological origins could go no further. Or could they?

For, even after the U.S.A. ceased to be the only power in possession of nuclear weapons, and the need for an alternative to nuclear warfare became urgent, the prevailing attitudes to war remained negative; the Western army of 1967, was still essentially, the cold leavings of 1944, with a thin nuclear encrustation. Revision of aims, organization, and method remains scarcely touched upon by the armies of the Western powers after half a century of machine-powered armour and transportation, and is a closed book to the public in general, who appear to exchange only expressions of fear and hopelessness, and futile pleas for general, partial, or even unilateral disarmament.

It is particularly curious that our country lost its enthusiasm for war so abruptly and dramatically. Britain had looked outward, militantly and aggressively, for seven hundred years, and had revelled unashamed in the most extreme forms of jingoism. From Saxon times to 1916, war was a normal, necessary, and inevitable aspect of life, and no one could afford to ignore it. Throughout the nineteenth century and up to 1914, our national enthusiasm for it swelled tremendously, and it was our greatest pride that our flag flew and our bugles rang the world around. And then, as it were overnight, this national extroversion was abandoned; flag-waving patriotism was replaced by disillusionment, cynicism, and fear of absolute disaster.

Now these latter attitudes are merely the reverse of imperialistic fervour. They are moral attitudes, not reasoned ones. It is no more reasonable to be hostile to the idea of war than to be enthusiastic for it. A man who tries to banish war like a bad dream, as by pleading for world disarmament, is behaving as irrationally as an early Moslem volunteering for a suicide mission in the hope of attaining paradise.

It is curious that our schools do not teach human psychology and ecology, even to our most intelligent children. If they did, perhaps we should enlarge our understanding of the historical development of war as a social activity. During our formative years we encounter war as it were episodically, or as an aspect of religious instruction. We do not come to appreciate it, in this important phase of our mental development, as part of our basic human behaviour. We do not learn the facts of competitive and predatory life at a suitably early age. Quite the reverse. Children are taught untrue and non-sensical ideas concerning basic human and animal relationships, and they come to think of war as an exceptional and abnormal state of affairs, associated with evil and treachery and shattering a supposedly normal condition of harmony, peace, and plenty. This concept is sometimes at variance with the image of history, but the differences are falsely explained in terms of human change. We are supposed to be less gullible, less ignorant, less bloodthirsty than our ancestors.

If this were really the case, we should not be so depressed at the thought of all-out war, and we should not be apprehensive about "controlled escalation". We should feel ourselves quite confident, as rational creatures fully in control of our activities, to manage armed disputes competently as they arise. As it is, we are not at all confident that even "limited" wars can be kept to their original objectives by the people who start them. Most people imagine that every local campaign is in immediate danger of expanding into a world-wide nuclear holocaust; their own politicians tell them so. Far from being more knowledgeable about war than our ancestors were, it is quite possible that we are very much the reverse; we may be just as appallingly ignorant concerning the psychology of group competitive behaviour, the roles of armed competition in national societies, and the evolution of military technique, at the very time when our exploding technology renders ignorance of them supremely dangerous.

Although armed group conflict is one of the most important aspects of human life, and our second oldest trade, it has not been overhauled and examined as a basic human activity since the New Stone Age. Trained psychologists have been slow to accord it the investigation it deserves. You can read about war as fiction, as memoirs (which often are for all practical purposes fiction), as historical scholarship (usually taking one no later than World War I, because modern weapon technology baffles the scholar who is not also a soldier), as propaganda, or as professional study. But you cannot read about it as an aspect of behaviour. It is a danger-ously undeveloped area in the growing body of knowledge about ourselves. The aim of this book, in describing the onset of machine warfare, the ways in which humanity in general tried to cope with it, the few original ideas which were put forward to help us, and the receptions they were accorded, is to contribute usefully to what we must hope will become a major field of enquiry and understanding.

Chapter One

The Confusion of Mars

Machine warfare, like other ramifications of the Industrial Revolution, may be said to have its roots in the Renaissance, and no doubt one could cite Leonardo da Vinci as the progenitor of every mechanical weapon from the atomic bomb to the tank. To explore their ultimate sources, however, might distract us from the present. Machine warfare is with us now, fantastically expensive, and dangerous on so vast a scale that we can scarcely grasp to the full its dysgenic possibilities. We will do well to limit our researches in the present volume to the immediate past, and so we may accord the honour of having set our species fairly upon the path of machine warfare to one Alexander Forsyth (1769–1843), a Scottish Presbyterian minister who in 1807 patented the use of mercuric fulminates as priming for firearms, and so created the possibility of applying automation to the discharge of lethal projectiles. Before Forsyth, all guns great and small were fired by a priming charge of fine powder, which was ignited by a sometimes unreliable and always weather-conscious apparatus, such as a burning wick or a flint and steel, outside the gun breech. Forsyth's fulminates did not need fire to set them off. They detonated when struck a smart blow, and a gun fitted with a device for placing a small quantity of fulminate over the fire hole, and a simple trigger-controlled hammer with which to strike it, could be re-loaded and fired more rapidly than a flintlock and was reliable in all weathers. Muzzle-loading rifles fired this way were in general service in armies and pioneering colonial societies everywhere by 1850, their efficiency being further increased by the use of a novel bullet of French design, the "Minié", which contained an iron plug in its base and was cast to a diameter smaller than the gun bore. When inserted at the gun muzzle, the bullet slid easily down the bore. When the gun fired, the bullet was expanded by its base plug, gripped the bore, and so flew accurately. This kind of rifle was used in the Crimean campaign.

The immediate success of Forsyth's invention encouraged gun-makers to attempt the design of breech-loading guns of a kind which could be mass-produced. Hitherto, breech-loaders had been generally unsuccessful, because of the difficulty of sealing the breech against escape of gases when the gun fired; this in turn had been due partly to easy tolerances in manufacturing standards, but mostly to the inescapable use of a loose propellant charge—a measure of powder—in conjunction with the flint-and-steel method of firing. While it was known that perfect sealing would be obtained if the charge were contained in a metal case, and while these had been made by highly skilled craftsmen to the orders of princes ever since the time of Henry VIII, it had hitherto proved impossible to mass-produce an expendable case of precise dimensions incorporating the means of admitting fire from the priming to the propellant charge. Hand-made cartridge cases, tailored to the gun so that their fire port matched the one drilled through the gun breech, were expensive, and had to be carefully retrieved for re-charging. Forsyth's invention led to the solution of this problem, because it did away with the necessity of striking fire outside the gun: the percussion cap could be incorporated in a cartridge with both pro-pellant and missile, and a hinged-block or bolt opening made in the breech to allow the cartridge's admittance there. The percussion cap, at the base of the cartridge, would then be detonated by a steel pin, which would be jabbed into it as the trigger was pulled. The rifleman need no longer remove the butt from his shoulder as he fought; he need only aim, fire, flip open the breech (this action automatically extracting the spent cartridge), insert another cart-ridge, and fire again. His rate of fire would be enormously increased, and he would be able to fire comfortably from kneeling or lying positions. This kind of gun was becoming commonplace by the 1860s, and was used by the Prussians at Sadowa against the Austrians, with powerful effect. By the seventies, the breech-loader had a magazine attached to it, from which rounds could be fed to the breech as fast as the marksman could aim, fire, and work the re-loading mechanism, which was designed to eject the spent case, feed a fresh round into the breech, and cock the firing mechanism with one manual operation, by bolt or lever action. This was the gun which destroyed the Red Indian and brought about the complete colonization of North America by Europeans. Clearly, this was semi-automation of a high order, and it was applied to cannon foundry too. In conjunction with the sliding carriage recoil absorption system, it led to the "quick-firing" cannon which could plaster a battlefield with bursting shell in a way that certainly would have amazed the artilleryman of Napoleonic times. But better, or worse, was yet to come: full automation.

This was attained as a consequence of three major inventions by French and Swiss government employees of the eighties: the smokeless propellant, the solid-drawn brass cartridge case, and the hard-jacketed bullet. The first reduced fouling, the chief obstacle to efficiency in small and complex mechanisms built to fine limits. The second, being precisely dimensioned, was ideally suited to fast and continuous mechanical loading and extraction. The third would joggle its way slickly through the loading apparatus and leave less of itself in the bore, important considerations in a weapon designed to fire 240 rounds a minute.

Two hundred and forty bullets fired successively by one small gun in one minute! Such is the superiority of the machine to the mechanically employed workman, that one machine-gun firing at this rate gives a sustained firepower superior to that of 500 marksmen armed with magazine rifles! The American Hiram Maxim, aided by the British firm of Vickers, had his machine-gun working efficiently before the eighties were out, and the unfortunate Matabele in Rhodesia provided the first evidence of its powers in 1893. The Pathans confirmed this two years later at the Malakand Pass, while at Omdurman in 1898 the Dervishes fell in such numbers before the Maxim battery on Kitchener's right flank that the German military attaché, witnessing their slaughter, wrote at once to his Imperial employer recommending the new weapon to his attention and suggesting that the German army could not afford to be without it. In this way was automation applied to missile throwing and a new era in human redundancy begun. Maxim was knighted by Queen Victoria for his services to humanity.

The practical development of mass-produced machine weapons confronted the war leaders of Europe, and their armies of warriors trained in hand-to-hand killing techniques, with an evolutionary impasse and therefore a choice of ways: successful adaptation, or hostile reaction involving frustration, heavy loss, and possible extinction. The former was quite direct, being the immediate renunciation of war ideas based on the fighting performance of animals and the equally immediate development of fighting machines armed with machine weapons. The only way to beat the machine is to employ a better machine. The military application of this axiom is apparent to us now, because we have half a century's experience of advanced machine weapons.

They have given us an expensive education. It was not so easy for soldiers in the first decade of the present century to evaluate their powers, because their development in the nineteenth century, while quite prolonged—eighty years passed between Forsyth and Maxim—was sudden in its maturation. Their approach was stealthy; their final pounce, a surprise. For example, the last major clash in the nineteenth century between industrial powers was that between France and Germany (Prussia) in 1870, and it was decided at close quarters by the co-ordinated efforts of fighting men, of whom the Germans with 400,000 were 100,000 the more numerous. The Germans were also the better served in matters of organization, being arrayed in the right strength in the right place at the right time by their generals. The Franco-Prussian War was settled by the mental and physical exertion of manpower. Moreover, each side had expected much of certain new weapons, and each was disappointed. The French were disappointed with their "Mitrailleuse" (grape shooter), a breech-loading multi-barrelled heavy rifle mounted on a stand and operated by a crank handle to deliver sustained rapid fire from a large magazine. The Prussians likewise were not satisfied with the performance of their Dreyse "Zundnagelgewehr" (needle gun), a breech-loading rifle supplied to several infantry formations. More had been expected of these weapons in the attack than they were capable of achieving, and the conclusion inevitably drawn, and as inevitably welcomed all over Europe and America, was that machinery could not master the fighting European-type male human. Unfortunately, it was unfounded. The Mitrailleuse had been handicapped by inferior organization, for it was used offensively as a substitute for artillery when it should have been used defensively to augment direct infantry fire. The needle gun was merely an inferior type of breech-loader, which had been designed in the twenties and was really out of date in 1870. Its cartridge being made of cloth, the gas sealing at the breech was inadequate. After firing a few aimed rounds from the shoulder, the German soldiers fired it from the hip, where the escaping gases could not burn their faces and endanger their eyes; every modern soldier who has fired a machine-gun from the hip while running with it, and has seen the bullets kick up fountains of earth and stones only a few yards ahead, knows how inaccurate that sort of shooting usually is. In defence, as it was used at Sadowa against the Austrians, the Dreyse needle gun was much more deadly, for unlike a muzzle-loader, it could be fired from the prone position. This made its user difficult to see, and improved his aim.

But by and large the European battlefield of 1870 was not fully integrated with the growing European machine age environment, and this was the last lesson in large-scale European war before 1914. Its value was only that of a description of human battle-power within one rapidly changing phase of industrial development. Unfortunately, it was not viewed in this way, but was taken as a long-term precedent, as late as 1914.

On the other hand, the experiences of the British army in colonial war during the same period pointed another lesson, namely that a smallish regular army could be highly successful in defensive-offensive operations if it held superiority of modern weapons, which permitted it to destroy vast hordes of warriors charging to the attack. Unfortunately the lesson was not understood; colonial war was set aside as something qualitatively different from European war, and its demonstration of the inhibitory effect of modern fire-power was accepted as relevant only to "primitive" conditions. We might imagine that the machine-gun featured so conspicuously in these, as to have forcibly obtruded itself across all contemporary military thought, but this was not so. There can be little doubt that the machine-gun became associated all too closely with only a narrow range of military activities—colonial war against comparatively ill-armed peoples. In the eyes of British military leaders, it existed outside the great European war traditions. In consequence, they required only the most junior of officers to receive instruction in its capabilities, and allowed it, relatively speaking, little more than a passing mention in the training manuals.

The few officers seconded to work with machine-guns soon developed the techniques for mass-producing death. Years before World War I, they had constructed libraries of fire charts and distribution patterns to cope with every imaginable situation, interlocking patterns of horizontal and vertical cones of fire that would catch and kill any number of men moving in any formation over any ground contour. Soon, they brought about a bizarre situation whereby one young colonel—and they were very young—in charge of 64 machine-guns commanded a sustained small-arms firepower considerably greater, and far more mobile, than that commanded by a brigadier with nearly 2500 riflemen.

Yet very few people reasoned ahead to discover what would happen when machine-weaponed European armies clashed on the grand scale. The military leaders of Europe and America certainly did not. They seemed unaware that they were trapped in an evolutionary cul-de-sac, and when World War I commenced, they set their manpowered armies to fight in the manner of 1870. As the latter were as unfairly matched against mass-produced machine weapons and field fortification material, particularly barbed wire, as a team of longhand clerks would be if matched against an electric typewriter and a battery of calculating machines, their casualties were enormous and their attainment nil, for their efforts could not decide the issue of the conflict. The fighting demonstrated only that machine age missile throwing was so far advanced as to prevent fighting human animals from closing with their enemy in the concentrations necessary for achievement of their aims. Automation had been applied to yet another trade, and the consequence was serious redundancy among manual operatives.

By 1914, small numbers of machine weapons could destroy the concentrations of men required to overwhelm a given number of their enemy faster than they could be moved across the battlefield. To permit the attacking infantry to advance, the attacking artillery had first to smash the defenders' fieldworks, barbed wire, machine-gun nests, and artillery defences. This meant that the attainment of the fighting men conformed to that of their own missile projectors. They could advance to the limits of the protective bombardment, a depth of 3000 yards or so, but relatively small reserves of weapons and barbed wire still in the possession of the defending forces stopped further movement beyond this "permissive" zone. In any case, infantry were morally and physically exhausted after advancing this distance over fire-swept ground. The attacking gun batteries delivered their permissive blow in the form of prolonged bombardments sometimes lasting several weeks; inevitably this was at the expense of basic army mobility, because vast quantities of shells had first to be accumulated—a procedure which choked the somewhat inflexible transport system behind the front, which was largely made up of narrow-gauge railway tracks on which the trains had to be run carefully lest their steam and smoke betray offensive preparations. Moreover, even the heaviest prolonged bombardments were unable to eliminate every enemy machine-gun and cannon, and so could not save the attacking infantrymen from enormous casualties which, together with disease and moral exhaustion, weakened the attacking forces at a rate that could not be matched by the supply of fresh replacements. Finally, even were the enemy front to be seriously cracked by these ponderous blows, proper advantage could not be taken of the fact, since cavalry, the traditional exploiting arm, was hopelessly vulnerable to stray machine-guns and coils of barbed wire, while the destruction to the ground caused by the preliminary bombardment prevented the rapid advancement of essential stores. War had become primarily a conflict of industrial resources and only secondarily one of manpower.[1]

As an evolutionary crisis, this situation offered a choice of responses:

a) to cease from large-scale offensive movement and to hide from missile fire behind fortifications, permitting the enemy to waste himself upon them;

b) to persist in conventional "manpower" attacks in the hope that their sheer weight would eventually overwhelm the defences;

c) to adapt successfully to the situation through technology, by devising machine or chemical weapons to overcome the machine defences.

[1] For a perfect analysis and summary of this situation, see J. F. C. Fuller, *Memoirs of an Unconventional Soldier*, p. 106.

Although it is obvious to us that the first and third alternatives were the appropriate ones, it was not at all obvious to the average European civilian or soldier at that time—presumably because of heightened emotion. The first choice was entirely neglected except by the Germans, who were fighting on two fronts and found it necessary to rest on the defensive on one of them. The British and French General Staffs seemed to consider the preparation of permanent defences ignoble, the implication presumably being that this would be a tacit admission of their inability to eject the invader. It is possible that some Allied generals would have rested on a logical defensive system had they been allowed to do so. But no general with a career and pension at stake was prepared to risk accusations of defeatism and failure to "prosecute the offensive". Thus, sentiment triumphed over sense, and in keeping the lamps of offensive ardour alight, our generals extinguished many lives. For the same emotional reasons, the second choice, continuation of conventional attacks, was persevered with beyond all reason. Despite all the evidence before them, the governments of Britain and France, Germany and later the U.S.A., were certain that the war would be decided by bayonet thrusts. And so were their responsible military authorities, the troops in general, and the civilian populations. They thought only of killing enemy soldiers in battle. Millions and millions of humans believed that their prodigious national war efforts were directed to one aim: a successful and decisive bayonet charge.

Persistence in this belief led to a peculiar perversion of strategy, based on the exaltation of inefficiency. For the artillery-bombardment-and-bayonet-charge offensive was inherently inefficient. As the expenditure of hundreds of thousands of tons of war material and tens of thousands of lives was required for even the most minor offensive, for the seizure of a few hundred yards of enemy held territory, so this reduced attainment became accepted as normal, and an assault which at fearful cost succeeded in bending a ten-mile stretch of enemy line to a maximum depth of five miles was hailed as a great victory. It was in truth a tragic absurdity, the relationship of effort to attainment being entirely unreasonable. Worse, the immense destruction of life and war gear persuaded some war leaders that this process of attrition was itself a strategic aim, the idea being that the side coming first to the bottom of the barrel would be the loser. But as the killing of men was essentially an irrelevancy on a machine-dominated battlefield, and because the machine weapons fed on the very industrial roots of modern urban civilization, in the long term there could be no real winner to such a contest—only two losers, one more bankrupt than the other.

By and large, the human species quite failed to recognize that it was trapped in an evolutionary cul-de-sac. It persisted with a form of behaviour so irrelevant to the prevailing situation as to be almost suicidal. There was no question of humans being unable to devise the means of dealing successfully with their war environment; that was not the difficulty at all. The difficulty was that the prevailing beliefs and attitudes about war, and the dominating pitch of mass emotion, quite prevented people in general, and their leader groups in particular, from sizing up the situation as a situation, and from evolving appropriate new responses. That was half a century ago, when we entered the cul-de-sac of machine war.

The logical way out of the cul-de-sac was, of course, the development of machines or chemical weapons which could dissolve the state of siege and restore the contest to a state of fluidity in which decision would be achieved through generalship. This was perceived by very few people indeed—only a microscopic fraction of Europe's population. This, I think, is a matter of great importance to us today. A novel development was urgently needed, but the need was not generally perceived by either the responsible governments or by the peoples they governed.

Asphyxiant gases were developed by German scientists during 1914–15, but the German General Staff declined to use them on a scale great enough to ensure complete and overwhelming success. As a result, the Allies developed gases too, both sides developed breathing apparatus, and stalemate resulted. Later, vesicant (blister) gases were introduced, but these did not have the quality of overwhelming destruction inherent in the mass-asphyxiants of 1915.

Self-propelled machines for fighting in were developed independently and simultaneously in France and Britain during the period

1915–16, and it is a measure of their failure to understand the forces shaping their environment that the General Staffs of the two Allies did not even think it necessary to inform each other that this work was being attempted, let alone seek to collaborate upon it. No directives indicating the roles and employment of these machines emanated from the General Staffs of either Britain or France. As a result, the machines proposed were of quite varied types: armoured rollers to clear paths for infantry assaults; armoured personnel carriers to carry infantry storming parties to the enemy trenches; self-propelled field artillery mounts; and all-round armoured fighting vehicles carrying both infantry and artillery weapons and capable of fighting in their own right. Eventually, the types put into production were, on the British side, all-round fighting machines, and on the French side, self-propelled guns.

In general, French ideas were conservative, even among the most advanced supporters of the "char d'assaut". The French tended to think of it only as a support weapon, not as a machine destined to change the face of war. On the other hand, the leading British armoured vehicle protagonist, Colonel E. D. Swinton, suggested that the tank, as he named it, constituted a new and dominant weapon through its combination of mobility with protection and fighting power, and should entirely reshape tactical thinking. Far from merely supporting and elaborating and reducing the cost of the existing infantry-artillery attack system, it was in his view a means of terminating the war in a few strokes.

It appeared to him that in its first manifestation the tank was a form of siege engine. Such an engine, he argued, could achieve decisive results quickly and cheaply, if massed secretly and used in ways that achieved surprise. To use it in any other way would be to forfeit its advantages and add to the overall complexity of war.

He drafted a scheme whereby it would be possible to shatter decisively the German defence system as it then existed. Its main points[2] were as follows:

1) Tanks would be built in great numbers, and massed secretly at a point where the front should be decisively broken.
2) The customary preliminary bombardment would not be used,

_____
[2] See E. D. Swinton, *Eyewitness*, p. 198 et seq.

(a) because it would alert the Germans, and (b) because the tanks had no need of it.

3) The tank attack would begin at dawn, with tanks leading the infantry. Artillery would then be used for counter-battery work to prevent enemy artillery from engaging tanks and the British infantry, which would be about to follow the tanks.

4) The first day would see the German positions completely breached, and their artillery and command zones in retirement. The ground being almost entirely undamaged, and ammunition expenditure and casualties relatively light, it would be possible to extend communications forward with great rapidity, so that the attack could be resumed the next day, or the day after. As the Germans would not be able to evolve appropriate anti-tank tactics in the time available, this pattern of offensive would quickly prove decisive, when a salient was made deep enough to permit lateral expansion behind the untouched portions of the enemy line.

Today, this project seems eminently reasonable, and one sees at once that it would be improved if some tanks were modified to serve as cross-country transports for men, guns, and supplies, as if some smaller, lighter, faster ones could be built with a view to penetrating deeper into enemy territory and thus accelerating his collapse.

But at the time, such ideas were unacceptable to the average military mind, which was probably unaware that the combat situation which it accepted as "normal" was in fact one of impasse. Rather than being hailed as the rational solution to a difficult problem, Swinton's scheme was condemned as wildly outlandish. Lord Kitchener, an engineer who in the nineties had made imaginative offensive use of mechanical transport in conjunction with a tactical defence, condemned the tank as a "pretty mechanical toy", and Field Marshal Sir John French, then Commander-in-Chief of the British armies in France, would go no further than to state cautiously that if engineers could produce fighting machines and tell him what he could do with them, he, as Commander in the field, would try to do it.[3] Apparently it did not occur to Sir John that this was also a confession of bankruptcy in professional thought. Other generals were less forthcoming. Similar responses were made

[3] See E. D. Swinton, *Eyewitness,* p. 149.

in France, where the employment concepts held by the French inventors were far less clear, and opposition to the tank idea was complicated by bitter intrigue over rival designs and contracts.

By the summer of 1915 both Britain and France were building tanks, Britain to a contract for 150 machines, France to 400; this was due almost entirely to determined behind-the-scenes activity on the part of persistent minority groups. Meanwhile, bayonet-charge attacks continued unabated on every front, and no schemes were put forward by either War Cabinet or General Staff to conserve military strength until mechanized forces could be built and trained. And when in 1916 tanks were first used in battle, it was not in any way connected with Swinton's proposals of the previous year.

The new Commander-in-Chief of the British Expeditionary Force, Field Marshal Sir Douglas Haig, asked for tank support as soon as his offensive in the Somme Valley showed signs of failure and undue cost. He mendaciously stated that even a few of the new machines would be sufficient to "tip the scales". Swinton resisted this pressure as well as a Colonel could resist a Field Marshal— especially when the latter made it appear almost that the successful ending of the war hung in the balance—but was overruled, and 40-odd tanks were sent to France. Their commander was replaced by a man chosen by Haig's staff, and in England, Swinton was replaced by a. more acceptable figure—an unsuccessful infantry brigadier.[4] Meanwhile, the small number of tanks sent to France were used as infantry support weapons. They achieved some local surprise and success but were quite unable to affect the total situation, being dispersed over an area of many square miles and used to no preconceived general plan. Their isolated and unrelated actions resulted only in newspaper headlines—and in giving the Germans the opportunity to prepare anti-tank defences. French authorities later asserted that, had not the British Commander-in-Chief revealed the secret of tanks in this way, they would have staged a large-scale surprise assault in 1917. However, as the French tank forces were regarded and used only as mobile artillery and no overall scheme existed for integrating infantry with tank training, and as the French infantry were ordered to pursue their attacks without in any way relying on tank support (the spiritual solution

[4] F. G. Anley.

of a practical problem), one may wonder how the French surprise attack would have fared.

Thus, we see that by midsummer 1916, warring Europe was far from solving the problem set by the impasse of machine warfare. Tanks which had promised a way through the deadlock were now, like gas, merely incorporated within it, as an added complexity and expense.

We can see that machine warfare promised to overwhelm European man before he could learn how to adapt himself to it. More than a quarter of a century had passed since Maxim had perfected his machine-gun and Armstrong his sliding gun-carriage and hydraulic recoil absorption system, but no progress whatever had been made towards gaining a general recognition of the essential nature of the problems set by these weapons, let alone towards producing appropriate organizations and movements. Government, public, and soldiers alike made unquestioning acceptance of the most novel and deadly guns and cannon, and produced thousands of miles of barbed wire to make field fortifications, yet at the same time continued to exhibit military behaviour that had been evolved during the eighteenth century. Faced with a crisis that exhibited absolutely unprecedented characteristics, mankind in general was totally unable to produce the appropriate responses. Gas was rejected as "monstrous" and "evil" (actually, non-asphyxiant gas is very humane, relative to high-explosive and fragments of metal). Tanks were seen only as "mechanical toys", or at best, as unreliable novelties to be used occasionally as support weapons. This was, and is, the first lesson of machine age warfare: that mankind in general is very slow to adapt to it. We shall see that it is a repeating lesson; mankind is still not fully adapted to it, and is repeatedly confused when it exhibits novel characteristics.

Chapter Two

The Triumph of Vulcan

At the end of Chapter One we left machine warfare weltering in the Somme battles of 1916. Colonel Swinton's intelligent and humane "Notes on the Employment of Tanks", which he submitted to the War Office in March 1916, had been disregarded and suppressed. These Notes were submitted more than three months before the onset of the Somme offensive, which cost 20,000 lives on the first day alone. Their value was completely unrecognized by the military leaders of this nation. British army behaviour was still essentially eighteenth-century in character; such mechanization as was accepted served only to transport men and horses to the scene of battle. Arrived there, they discharged their weapons and ran at each other in the manner of Waterloo.

In the air, flying machines attempted to observe the fighting and the disposition of enemy artillery and reserves. Some aircraft served as flying machine-gun mounts for the purpose of shooting down the enemy's observation machines. Others were equipped to drop bombs, but were unable to achieve anything approximating to even a small well laid-on artillery bombardment. There was no question whatever of "air power" offering an immediate solution to the impasse of machine warfare. The only hope lay in motorized, self-propelled, gun-carrying armour—in the tanks—and the first few tank units had just been squandered, and were in danger of being labelled as a "support" weapon. This fate had already overtaken the French chars d'assaut, which were grouped with artillery, under artillery command. The British tanks were likewise split up among infantry divisions for combat control purposes, but for administrative and training purposes they were made into a Corps. This was to prove their ideological salvation, and ultimately was to create a crisis in machine warfare destined to have the most far-reaching political effect.

BREAKDOWN OF OLD METHOD

Above: Animal transport can no longer maintain the impetus of the offensive. (Ypres.) *Courtesy: Imperial War Museum.*

Below: To maintain supplies and movement, light railways are laid up to the front line. Result: shellfire; break in supply; attack loses momentum. (Arras.) *Courtesy: Imperial War Museum.*

ARCHITECTS OF NEW METHOD

(From left to right): J. F. C. Fuller at Tank Corps H.Q. in 1917 with T. J. Uzielli (Head of "Q") and H. J. Elles (Commanding Tank Corps). *Courtesy: R.A.C. Tank Museum.*

NEW MATERIAL

"Mother"—the first cross-country fighting machine. *Courtesy: Imperial War Museum.*

As 1916 ended and another year of Europe at war began, the British Tank Headquarters in France was given a radical overhaul, and was fortunate in receiving a young, able, and imaginative staff; there were at least two officers, Major G. le Q. Martel and Colonel J. F. C. Fuller, who saw clearly that the tank was capable of rapid evolution and was potentially a dominant arm, and who worked out numerous schemes for its more decisive employment.

Martel envisaged a "tank army",[1] but his scheme was entirely futuristic and not in any way related to immediate needs. Fuller likewise recognized that the power of the tank lay in its potential for unrestricted movement; however, he saw clearly that "tank armies" were of the distant future, and therefore argued that Tank Corps planning should be based upon surprise, speed, and co-ordination of the movements of tanks, infantry, and artillery. He first worked out a project closely resembling Swinton's (which he had not seen), and then, when this failed to gain acceptance, recognized that propaganda on the home front was a vital first requirement.[2] His subsequent schemes were therefore always framed with "education" in mind. He realized that a fully mechanized army could not be built quickly, and might not be built at all unless the possibilities of armoured mobility could be demonstrated in a really spectacular show; the tank force's main problem was a psychological, rather than an engineering one. Fuller therefore produced a scheme which he called tank raiding,[3] whereby a massed tank force, its component units supported by and co-operating with infantry and artillery groups, would travel secretly by rail behind the entrenched front to deliver surprise attacks against unsuspecting German positions. These attacks would last no more than twenty-four hours, the assault forces then retiring without attempting to hold ground. In this way, the mechanized mobility then available to the British army could be fully exploited, the brief endurance range of slow tanks and infantry on foot being extended laterally through secret railway movements behind the front, from which sudden forward movements could be made wherever it was desired to strike a psychological blow against the enemy. Tank raiding, Fuller

---

[1] See G. le Q. Martel, *Our Armoured Forces*, p. 396.
[2] See J. F. C. Fuller, *Memoirs of an Unconventional Soldier*, p. 123.
[3] See Fuller, op. cit., pp. 170–75.

reckoned, would attain several important goals simultaneously, in British as well as in German minds.

The first, of course, would be an unanswerable demonstration of tank power, giving the staff of the Tank Corps (as it was now designated) the ideological authority they sought. Others would be the maintenance of a defensive-offensive cheap for Britain and costly for Germany, and matched to the abilities of a non-mechanical army. Such an operation could be expanded at will when the means to conduct fully mobile operations were developed; it would provide essential data on which they could be based.

Fuller considered that the German defences guarding the town of Cambrai, then the headquarters of Crown Prince Rupprecht, would constitute an ideal venue for the first great tank raid. Cambrai, on the River Scheldt, 100 miles NNE. of Paris, is situated on a main strategic route between France and Germany, and was a most important communications centre behind the great salient in the German lines threatening Paris. The defences before the town were considered almost impregnable to conventional assault. Hence, if the tanks succeeded here, their attainment would be irrefutable, and this would be apparent to the British and French, as well as to the German military leaders. Fuller believed that the Cambrai defences could be breached by a massed tank assault sprung upon the defenders as a complete surprise. The British artillery would not be allowed to fire its usual prolonged preliminary bombardment, and its activities during the battle would be dictated by the immediate requirements of the tanks and infantry. The tanks would carry special apparatus for crossing the wide German trenches. Certain tanks would be detailed to destroy barbed wire entanglements; others would be specially equipped to relay wireless messages, and others would be adapted to haul supplies across country.

As already remarked, schemes of this nature could not be implemented without the sanction of the commander-in-chief, and the goodwill and co-operation of the army commanders with and under whom the tank forces would operate; in the summer of 1917 sanction was not forthcoming. The commander-in-chief, Sir Douglas Haig, was preoccupied with his infantry-artillery offensive at Ypres, in which he repeated the pattern of 1915 and 1916 on a greater scale, and at even greater cost. He was so far indifferent to the tanks as to recommend reduction of their strength in order to procure more infantry recruits, and wrote to the War Office on August 20, 1917, recommending that all transfers to the Tank Corps, including those from cavalry regiments, should be postponed; that no civilian personnel other than those now employed should be allocated to the manufacture of tanks; and that manufacture of aircraft, guns, ammunitions, mechanized transport, spare parts, and railway locomotives should take priority over that of tanks. Thus, there could be no hope of directly implementing the tank raid project by persuading Field Marshal Haig of its potentialities as a variant of the main offensive. Its only hope lay in the possibility of support from an army commander who might wish to incorporate it in a local offensive.

The third battle of Ypres was one of the most futile main offensives, and one of the most costly relative to achievement, that Britain has ever fought. It occurred intermittently between July and October 1917 over reclaimed marshland, like that near the Wash in Lincolnshire, for no clearly defined reasons; it was described sometimes as a break-through attempt, sometimes as a means of assisting the French, and sometimes even as a crude attempt to drain German fighting strength by prolonged attrition. It cost at least a quarter of a million casualties and an incalculable quantity of industrial resources, and the gain accruing from it was a tiny salient in a morass, some four miles deep at the furthest point. The reasoning behind it was fundamentally weak, uninformed, and unimaginative, in that it was supposed by Haig and his staff that the conventional infantry-artillery attack could be made successfully if the strength of supporting artillery were greatly increased. In fact, the increase in artillery fire merely ensured that no great depth of advance would be possible. Among the reasons for this which Haig and his staff failed to see or recognize were the probable condition of reclaimed marshland after prolonged artillery fire; the probability of heavy seasonal rain following shortly after the proposed date for opening the battle; and the effect upon the attacking infantry of the German regrouping of their defensive positions— aerial reconnaissance showed that the Germans were greatly deepening their defensive zone, moving the main line of resistance

beyond the range of the greater part of the British artillery. The
sum of these conditions meant that the prolonged British artillery
bombardment would destroy the ground surface and the drainage
system, and the rain would then turn the meal-like soil into a quagmire, all without harming the Germans' final line of resistance. The
attacking infantry would then have to fight their way through five
miles of bog against a flexible resistance of strong-points and fox-
holes, with every round of reserve ammunition, every scrap of food,
and every evacuated wounded man carried on the backs of men or
mules, under a continuous fire from the German artillery—which
could not be reached by British fire. Seen as a problem in forward
motion against defined resistances, third Ypres was insoluble by
the techniques known to Haig and his staff. As can be seen from
Haig's letter to the War Office of August 20, 1917, the British
Commander-in-Chief had no concept whatsoever of the new type
of mobile warfare fought by tanks; the only solution he could
advance for the problem of third Ypres was the procurement of
still more cannons and cannon fodder.

This is emphasized because of an entirely novel turn of events
which took place as third Ypres slowly and painfully petered out.

During August 1917, Fuller discussed the idea of tank raiding in
the Cambrai–St. Quentin area with General Hugh Elles, commanding the Tank Corps, who further discussed it with General Sir
Julian Byng, commanding the British Third Army which manned
the front in the vicinity of Cambrai. Byng then approached Haig
to canvass the idea of an attack on the Third Army front led by
tanks en masse, and Elles wrote to Haig requesting permission to
withdraw five battalions of tanks from their current piecemeal
deployment, and asking for a decision on "the use of tanks in raids,
which rests on a matter of policy on which a ruling is asked". Elles
went on to point out that on good going, tanks could be used en
masse replacing infantry as the main attacking force. These representations to the British High Command evoked nothing but a
reaffirmation of the official doctrine that tanks would remain "an
adjunct to the infantry attack", and would stay low on the list
of war production priorities.

Yet within a month, official attitudes were suddenly reversed. On
October 15, General Elles was summoned to Haig's headquarters to

discuss tank-led operations on the Third Army front. Nothing was settled for more than a week, but on October 24, Haig abruptly made up his mind, and told Byng and Elles to go ahead with a limited offensive at Cambrai, based upon the draft outline of a massed tank assault worked out by Fuller to illustrate his raiding project. No change of attitude could have been more dramatic, or more absurd. For Haig ordered this wholly novel attack to take place on November 20, that is, in less than four weeks' time.

Now Haig had vacillated over tank employment from the summer of 1916 to the autumn of 1917. He could not identify the problem from which they derived their being. He was possibly incapable of grasping Colonel Fuller's ideas concerning tank domination; indeed, he approved the reduction, in scope and size, of all tank activities. Moreover, he was to continue this negative behaviour into 1918. On August 27, 1917, Haig had replied to Sir E. H. W. Tennyson D'Eyncourt (Tank Supply Committee), who had written to him on the subject of Fuller's project, "the tank, at any rate in its present state of development, can only be regarded as a minor factor ... the tank is an adjunct to infantry and guns ..." Now, only fifty-eight days later, he proposed seizing in one swoop an area of German-held territory much larger than that disputed for three months at Ypres, and fortified so heavily as to be considered virtually impregnable to the type of assault he invariably approved —that of men and horses. Moreover, he proposed doing this with tanks supported by a relatively small army of tired infantry, entirely lacking the mobility required to persevere with an advance for longer than twenty-four hours.

The Cambrai battle of 1917 was not based on the raid project in any except the most superficial sense. Its purpose was defined as the seizure and holding of a prescribed quadrilateral area of ground, and the massed tank force was to be used only as a device for initiating the attack. Thus, what had been conceived as a one-day raid was now mounted onto an attack of indefinite duration, and no attempt was made to reason out the consequences of such a casual mating of cross-purposes. Haig actually hoped to pass cavalry through the gap made in the German lines by the initial tank assault, but this again was an absurd idea when measured in terms of supply (in November vast quantities of horse food were needed), communication difficulties, and above all the helplessness of horsed troops against modern small-arms and machine-guns.

In this light, Cambrai 1917 appears a curious hotch-potch of a battle: Fuller demonstrating the mechanism of a tank raid; Byng unrealistically looking for a break-through; Haig trying to seize territory undeterred by his armies' experiences in Flanders; and possibly, Haig and his advisers aware that a massed tank attack might yield newspaper headlines which, cleverly written by the propaganda service, could provide a "successful" ending to the third battle of Ypres.

Cambrai certainly produced the headlines; the tank attack of November 20, 1917, gave to Britain the cheapest advance of the war and caused the church bells to be rung in gladness all over the land.

At 6.20 a.m. on November 20, 1917, the Germans before Cambrai were startled by the onset of a brief artillery bombardment, and stood to their arms only to be horrified and dismayed by the sight of 350 tanks advancing upon them through the dawn mists. These tanks were not groping about a battlefield on piecemeal commitments. They were working to a closely reasoned system. Some of them were ripping up the barbed wire with grapnels. Others, in groups of three, manoeuvred like ships at sea, taking turns to attack their allocated section of the German triple-trench system, which they crossed after depositing huge bundles of brushwood to serve as stepping stones, the trenches being too wide for tanks to cross without special equipment. The German defences before Cambrai were considered tank-proof and impregnable, but the British Tank Corps H.Q. had demonstrated that a mobile offensive can beat the most formidable static defence if the planning is both realistic and imaginative.

Tank groups with their infantry teams moved in rehearsed patterns through the German defences, rapidly eliminating opposition on the surface and clearing out deep trenches and dugouts. By the time darkness fell on the same day, as much enemy territory had been seized as had been taken during the whole three months of Third Ypres, at less than one-sixtieth of the casualties, and at a much smaller fraction of the cost in munitions. Four thousand prisoners and one hundred guns were captured.

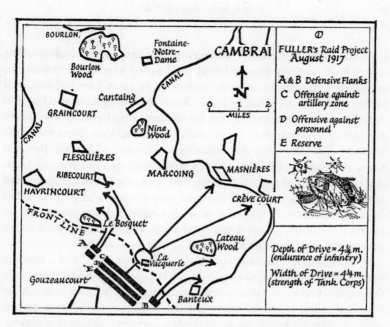

BOURLON

Bourlon
Wood

GRAINCOURT

Cantaing

FLESQUIÈRES

RIBECOURT

HAVRINCOURT

FRONT LINE

Le Bosquet

A

E

Gouzeaucourt

B

La Vacquerie

Fontaine-
Notre-
Dame

Nine
Wood

MARCOING

Lateau
Wood

Banteux

CAMBRAI

CANAL

CANAL

0   1   2
MILES

N

MASNIÈRES

CRÈVE COURT

FULLER's Raid Project
August 1917

A & B Defensive Flanks
C Offensive against
    artillery zone
D Offensive against
    personnel
E Reserve

Depth of Drive = 4¼ m.
(endurance of infantry)

Width of Drive = 4¼ m.
(strength of Tank Corps)

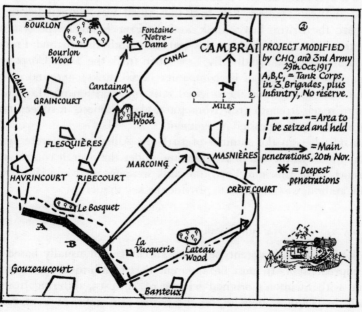

BOURLON

Bourlon
Wood

GRAINCOURT

Cantaing

FLESQUIÈRES

HAVRINCOURT   RIBECOURT

Le Bosquet

A

B

Gouzeaucourt

C

La
Vacquerie

Fontaine-
Notre-
Dame

Nine
Wood

MARCOING

Lateau
Wood

Banteux

CAMBRAI

CANAL

CANAL

0   1
MILES

N

MASNIÈRES

CRÈVE COURT

PROJECT MODIFIED
by CHQ and 3rd Army
29th Oct, 1917
A, B, C, = Tank Corps,
in 3 Brigades, plus
Infantry. No reserve.

= Area to
be seized and held

= Main
penetrations, 20th Nov.

= Deepest
penetrations

What happened after those startling ten hours was another story. With the pre-planned raid used up on the initial assault, no planning remained. The tanks wore out or were knocked out, and were returned to Tank Corps Base Workshops, and Cambrai rapidly deteriorated into a chaotic infantry dog-fight outside which the army commanders could only stand helpless, watching the casualty lists soar and the reinforced Germans (who, for the first time, used aircraft in close co-operation with ground troops) beating back the tired infantry. They had been unable to grasp, or had never read, those aspects of the tank raid project which stressed the importance of matching the scope of such actions to the cross-country mobility of all arms, and of stopping them by dynamic intervention of the high command at the peak of their success.

But although Cambrai dragged on for ten days and ended in utter failure, its first twenty-four hours, its tank hours, were not forgotten. Cambrai became the name for mechanized war. After Cambrai, most soldiers recognized the power of tanks to penetrate defence systems based on barbed wire, trenches, infantry weapons, and indirect artillery fire, and the Allied war council began to regard the British heavy tank, and the French small type of tank, as the ideal machines for this purpose. Both British and French tank forces grew rapidly. By November 1918, the Tank Corps was to reach a strength of 63 companies (2268 tanks), ten and a half times the strength of the original tank organization of May 1916. The French strength grew from 400 tanks organized in sixteen tank groups to 5400 organized in regiments.

And when in the summer of 1918 the Allied armies were again committed to the offensive, this time under the overall control of a French Generalissimo, Foch, the tank weapon, used in a stereotype of Cambrai, was expected to provide the key to success.

A PATTERN OF MACHINE WAR

Unfortunately, stereotype acceptances are not usually based on comprehension. It must be apparent that Cambrai was essentially one with Swinton's original scheme of 1914–15, differing from it only in technical details. But the battle of Cambrai was staged a year after Swinton wrote his "Notes on the Employment of Tanks", thanks to the muddle and misuse of the first tanks. Now, nine months later still, the Cambrai stereotype was to be put into general service. It was a stereotype nearly two years old, which quite failed to take in the basic lesson taught by both Swinton and Fuller: namely, that decisive operations in the machine age should be psychological ones, based on surprise. By 1918 the tank surprise was gone.

The Allied war leaders were not alone in belatedly recognizing the power of the tank in line-breaking operations; the Germans had appreciated it also, and in consequence had systematically developed the technique of anti-tank defence in passive and active aspects. The former consisted of natural and artificial obstacles: streams, marshes, woods, clumps of trees felled to mask their tank-bellying stumps, iron and concrete obstacles, and camouflaged pits. Trench systems were designed around these to offer angles of slope and crossing beyond the attainment of tanks, and were further protected by minefields. Active defence was comprehensive. There were mutually supporting groups of artillery, both specifically anti-tank giving direct fire from motorized or fixed mounts, and field artillery on special call giving indirect fire, this latter frequently in the form of gas concentrations. There were heavy machine-guns and rifles (the latter unpopular because of the ferocious kick), and mortars adapted to give flat-trajectory fire. An important role of the passive aspect was to create defiles within which the tanks would fall ready victims to the active operators. Ideally, the passive and active defences were constructed together as anti-tank forts, mutually supporting, distributed to a depth of about two and a half miles.

And those early heavy tanks moved very, very slowly and could be penetrated by the lightest artillery missile.

It is doubtful if the tardiness of their acceptance of tanks was appreciated by the Allied war leaders. The Battle of Amiens, the first of a series of actions aimed at smashing and levering the German forces out of France, was launched at first light on August 8, 1918, in the style of Cambrai. About 580 tanks were made available for the task: 462 fighting tanks and 118 armoured supply carriers. Of the fighting tanks, 42 were held in reserve, and 420 actually detailed to the attack. Five of these were prevented by mechanical breakdown from participating in it. All the Cambrai arrangements had been made: secrecy; specific objects; infantry-tank rehearsals; the tanks scheduled to lead the affair; silence from the waiting artillery. The battle started well. The air was still and the ground covered with a thick mist, and when their moment came the tank-men, infantry, artillerymen, and sappers all swung into well rehearsed action unhindered by it. One can say that the mist gave them their victory. So long as it lasted the teams worked hard and fast together, cleared out the German defences, and covered mile after mile with relatively few casualties to men or machines. When the tanks were held up or destroyed, it was due largely to the passive aspect of the German anti-tank defences. Then, around midday, the sun began to disperse the mist, and the advance immediately slowed and stopped as the active anti-tank defences saw their enemy and rapidly put scores of tanks out of action. The maximum advance on that day was seven and a half miles, and nearly all of it was accomplished before the mist rose. The total number of tanks knocked out by enemy fire was 100 (21.6%). Next day, again in a dawn mist, the attack continued, with 145 tanks leading it; and again, as soon as the mist cleared, the tanks rapidly fell victim to anti-tank gunfire—39 of them (26.9%) perished this way. The next day, August 10, only 67 tanks could be mustered, and of these 30 (44.7%) were knocked out. On August 11, the momentum of the attack was gone completely, despite its reinforcement with a further 85 tanks. The Tank Corps reported that having in four days suffered casualties from all causes, including accident and breakdown, totalling 72.1%, their reserves were now used up, and the only machines available, 38 in number, were being used in local piecemeal affairs. Thus, in four days of action, the entire Tank Corps, the principal means whereby the British army could hope to prevail against the enemy by land, was temporarily eliminated from the battlefield. And in war, temporary circumstances can have enduring consequences. An advance of twelve miles had been made, but the German army was not des-troyed, and it is almost certain that the advance would have been negligible but for the fortuitous appearance of heavy morning mist upon the battlefield.

The Tank Corps repaired its own machines in France, and all cases of mechanical failure, and of incomplete enemy destruction, were salved, repaired, and sent back to the front. Also, a steady trickle of new machines came from the factories in England. Losses in personnel were not so severe as losses in machines, because the tank is essentially a man-saver; unless it takes fire and blows up very quickly, at least some of the crew stand a chance of escaping when it is destroyed. This work of repair and replacement enabled the British command to resume the offensive on August 21, 1918, in a different place—further to the north at Bapaume. During the ten days intervening between the halt at Amiens and the onset at Bapaume, 280 tanks were prepared for action, 190 actually going into battle on August 21. Three days later, only 53 of these remained! Casualties were thus 81%, and this figure would have been greater had not the R.A.F. begun to take an interest in tank operations, No. 8 Squadron being attached to the Tank Corps for co-operation and experiment. The idea behind this co-operation had been to assist in offensive operations by the identification of targets from the air and the piloting of tanks towards them, experiments being conducted in wireless and other forms of ground-air communication, but this work was soon abandoned in favour of defensive co-operation whereby the R.A.F. flew advance guards before the tanks to locate lurking German anti-tank guns, drop smoke bombs in front of them, and attack them with machine-gun fire. This was done at Amiens, Bapaume, and all the remaining tank actions of World War I, and accurately foreshadowed developments of World War II. Meanwhile, they prevented the heavy tank from becoming entirely extinct before November 11, 1918.

After Bapaume, an interlude of nine days permitted Tank Corps Base Workshops to produce 81 machines. These were used on September 2 at Arras, a few miles north of Bapaume, and when they were gone a recuperation period of a fortnight allowed hardworking fitters to repair 20 in time for an action at Epehy. A later consignment of new machines brought the total up to 175 in time for the battle at Bellicourt; here losses totalled about 112, and, the Tank Corps announcing itself to be destitute of reserves, the advance stopped. Since the offensive begun at Amiens some sixty-four days earlier, 819 machines had been knocked out in battle—41.4% of the total British production of fighting tanks for the entire war period. This may seem a very high casualty rate for a relatively short period of battle, the rate of tank loss being considerably higher than the rate of new tank production, despite increases in the latter through 1918. In fact this is an under-estimate, inasmuch as the fighting tank production includes those tanks which were used exclusively for training purposes in England and those which were still unbuilt, but contracted for, during the autumn of 1918. Of course a tank knocked out is not always a tank destroyed, but the fact remains that the Germans knocked them out of battle faster than the British could replace them.

For the last offensive actions of the war, at the River Selle and Maubeuge, the British were never able to muster more than 48 tanks:

Selle	October 12, 1918	48 tanks
	October 20, 1918	4 tanks
Maubeuge	November 2, 1918	3 tanks
	November 4, 1918	37 tanks, scraped together from 4 battalions (A battalion in full strength should have had 36 tanks.)
	November 5, 1918	8 medium tanks.

The Tank Corps then announced itself to be "at the end of its resources".

Similar fortunes had attended the French forces. The machines built to the first tank production programmes were largely destroyed, worn out, or converted to serve as cross-country supply carriers by the summer of 1918, and the brunt of the fighting was done by small two-man Renault machines. Only 453 of these had been produced by March 1918, and in general they were committed to action in batches, as they came off the assembly line and were assembled in battalions. The French army began its summer offensive at Soissons on July 18, and of the 223 tanks employed on this day, tank casualties owing to enemy fire totalled 27% in machines and 25% in men. After this first day, tank participation in the battle became increasingly piecemeal as the German anti-tank defence became more capable, and the attack petered out within four days. French tanks were subsequently used in some thirty operations between July 23 and November 11, as machines became available. Casualties were frequently severe: personnel losses usually between 25% and 30%, and tank losses often up to 50%. Frequently, German anti-tank defences succeeded in virtually annihilating individual sections of Renault tanks. Only the fact that the small two-man French tank could be manufactured relatively quickly saved the French tank forces from complete exhaustion. As it was, the French army was unable to build up overwhelming reserves of tanks; it had to commit all machines as they became available, because, as with the British forces, the infantry attacks rarely succeeded unless backed up by tanks.

Fortunately, at this juncture the German economic system collapsed under the combined effects of four years of attrition warfare and an extremely efficient British naval blockade. Threatened with starvation and rebellion, morally weakened by the defection of their Austrian and Bulgarian allies, and dismayed by the entry of the powerful U.S.A. on the British and French side, the German government sued for peace, and an armistice was declared. The policy to which the Allied war leaders now subscribed, of continuing a land war by slow thin-skinned heavy tanks used in Cambrai-type assaults against highly developed German anti-tank organizations, was thus never put to further test. Allied propaganda services, making the most of a 20-mile advance over the past ninety-six days—an unprecedented distance on that front but actually an average daily move of a little over one and a half furlongs over a quarter of a year—persuaded the nation to believe that peace had been brought about by battlefield success. The true situation, that machine war of the twentieth century had slipped further into a condition of stalemate, and that such victory as the Western Allies could claim was actually due to the fortuitous existence of mineral deposits, was not generally perceived. But it was so.

The story of machine age armour thus throws some interesting light on the human species' adaptability, or lack of adaptability, to a suddenly changed environment. Advanced by a minority as the means of rapidly terminating an unpleasant situation, it was first received with hostility and disdain, and then actually incorporated within the unwanted situation, increasing the latter's cost and adding to its complexity. When average homo sapiens recognized the utility of the new device, it was too late to draw any profit from it.

But the greatest impact of modern armour on modern military thought was yet to come. Just as a tiny minority of thinking soldiers had foreseen its possibilities for resolving the cul-de-sac of 1914, so an equally tiny minority saw new possibilities in it for banishing the deadlier deadlock of 1918. It is with the theories advanced by this second minority, and their tremendous impact upon warring humanity, that the greater part of this book is concerned.

Chapter Three

Out of the Impasse?

During the latter part of 1917, when Colonel Fuller was Chief of Staff to the Tank Corps in France, he came to believe that the heavy tank as it then existed was not a suitable means of achieving or maintaining combat mobility, because it was too slow and its range of action too short. Its role was limited to line-breaking, and in its existing thin-skinned form it was rapidly losing its power in this; direct fire anti-tank artillery was making it dependent on fog, smoke, or aircraft co-operation for protection. These views underwent further development when Tank Corps H.Q. in France received the first examples of a new medium tank, known as the Medium A or "Whippet". This machine derived from an imagined need for a faster tank with longer range to work with cavalry, to complement the heavy tank working with infantry. It was crewed by three men and could move on good going at 8 mph over a range of 80 miles. It was not a very satisfactory design, as its range and speed were little superior to those of the heavy tank, while its obstacle-crossing ability was markedly inferior. Moreover, it was uncommonly difficult to drive. It could not co-operate with cavalry, because on the road the horses trotted faster than the tank, while under machine-gun fire the horses died and the Whippets had no one to co-operate with. To the Tank Corps H.Q. it appeared that a fast machine for long-range operations must be designed by themselves, and more important still, that these operations should be specifically tank-based and free from cavalry limitations. Experiments were undertaken at the nearby Tank Corps Base Workshops, with a view to modifying existing tanks with sprung suspension and higher power-weight ratios. The results were most encouraging: a Whippet was made to travel at 30 mph, and a modified heavy tank at 20 mph. These were speeds hitherto undreamt of in connection with the tactical deployment of fighting troops. Even the slow tanks had moved farther and faster than the non-mechanized armies which they served. If tanks capable of 30 mph and a circuit of action of 100 miles were to become available, how should they be incorporated within the horse-and-foot armies? The situation was staggeringly unprecedented. Never in the entire history of human conflict have such wide possibilities opened so suddenly. Cavalry could attain perhaps 20 mph and hold it for a charge of a few hundred yards on level ground, but no army had ever been given the opportunity to move shock troops at this speed, over almost any kind of terrain, over a circuit of 100 miles— with the added possibility of maintaining a rolling supply train in vehicles with equal performance. The concept of a new, fast, long-range medium tank promised to give the British army almost the same advantage over its horse-and-foot contemporaries that medieval mounted knights held over a rabble of unhorsed, unarmoured peasantry. Should this new mobility be used as it were defensively, merely to give better chances of survival in trench warfare? Or should it be used for new offensive purposes? If so, what would be the tank's objective? Should it attack the enemy's infantry? His cavalry? Or both? Or what?

Fuller later said that the answer to these questions flashed through his mind one day in March 1918, at the height of the German spring offensive, as he watched confusion develop in the retreating British army. Effective two-way communications between some headquarters and their fighting troops had broken down, with the result that an army which had successfully withstood three years of frontal hammering now was in danger of sudden demoralization, through breakdown in command. The German successes derived largely from infiltration tactics which took the attacking troops around centres of resistance to menace vulnerable rearward objectives. This upset the British command system and precipitated withdrawals.

But the German attack was not mechanized; its supply lines were animal-powered, and the attacking forces were infantry, with a very few slow tanks. Supply difficulties and head-on clashes instead of infiltration occurred, and eventually the offensive lost its impetus and position war was resumed.

NEW METHOD

Preparations for the first battle to be based on mechanisation. (Cambrai, 1917.) *Courtesy: R.A.C. Tank Museum.*

THE WORLD'S FIRST FAST TANK: THE MEDIUM D

A turning point in the evolution of modern mobile warfare. *Courtesy: R.A.C. Tank Museum.*

Left: General Heinz Guderian, foun-
der of the German Armoured Forces.
(Picture taken in France in May,
1940.) *Courtesy: Imperial War Museum.*

Below: Capt. B. H. Liddell Hart
(*right*) discusses mobile operations
with Brig. P. C. S. Hobart, R.T.C.
(*centre*), and his adjutant, Bill Yeo.
Behind, the first type of fast tank to
enter service. *Courtesy: Cassell & Co.
Ltd.*

It occurred to Fuller that if an infiltration attack were made at the speed of fast tanks over a hundred-mile circuit of action, a very different result would follow. And the British could have fast tanks and fast cross-country supply vehicles by the thousand in 1919. What if they were launched directly at the German command system? Attacking before dawn, and moving at 20 mph across country, they would not need to fight their way through the front-line positions. In a little over an hour they could reach German Army Headquarters, situated some 20 miles to the rear. In an army, only one "will" exists per many thousand "bodies". What if this will were to be surprised—overtaken by a wholly novel and fast-moving fighting vehicle—and suddenly extinguished? What would happen to the enemy armies, when their controlling brain was shot? Trained to function in response to orders issued by type-writer and telephone, would they not become demoralized as soon as the command system disintegrated? Any fast tank operation aimed at demoralization instead of annihilation might well yield decisive results in a matter of days instead of weeks, and at a tiny fraction of the cost of a conventional attack.

Fuller called a Tank Corps Headquarters conference to discuss the development of fast tanks that had already taken place in Tank Corps Base Workshops; and as a result of this conference, Colonel Philip Johnson, a Tank Corps engineer officer who had been a main agent in the spring-suspension and high-speed experiments, was sent to England to design a 20 mph, 200-mile range machine embodying a number of the features that had already been developed at Base Workshops. Fuller, certain that this machine could be developed quickly, set to work to draft a scheme for its employment. He completed it by May 24, 1918, and entitled it "The Tactics of the Attack as Affected by the Speed and Circuit of the Medium D Tank". This work far transcended tactics, how-ever, and was soon renamed "Strategic Paralysis as the Object of the Decisive Attack". Here, Fuller had declared himself; he was offering a new strategic policy based on the psychological, as opposed to the physical, destruction of enemy forces. It was under these sober titles that he launched his ideas at the minds of the Allied war leaders. But he quickly realized that psychological war-fare—for this is what the paralysis idea amounts to—has to be

waged against reaction in one's own camp as well as against the
enemy, and so when he had completed a redraft of his theory, he
called it "Plan 1919".

In Plan 1919 he argued that as all armies moved in battle at the
speeds of men and horses, and as they were confined, strategically,
to roads and railways, so perforce they had to come to battle to
decide their differences. Marching and counter-marching could
decide the issue of a battle, but could not obviate it. The superior
mobility of the Medium D fast tank, on the other hand, enabled
it to transcend "battle" and drive straight against the enemy command. Conventional fighting, in which an army tries to destroy
another piecemeal, is like battering a man slowly to death. Plan
1919, by contrast, is a shot through the brain. The fast tank does
not need roads; it can roam everywhere. It can be modified for
swimming. The aeroplane can escort it, guide it, give it secrecy.
Together at dawn, they can penetrate the enemy's frontier, by-
passing the entrenched and hostile men, leaving them behind without stopping to indulge in destructive fighting. Together they will
race onward through the enemy's land and together they will reach
the enemy's brain. They will surprise and destroy his headquarters,
communication centres, and supply depots. With no orders to tell
them what to do and no supplies to refill their bellies or their guns,
possessed by mounting doubts and fears because of the threats and
confusion to their rear, bewildered front-line soldiers will be lost;
they will continue to fight awhile, answering their latest orders, but
will surrender, or panic, or both, as soon as their opponents press
them, for they will receive no guidance from their commanders to
help them in the new situation. And with that, everyone can go
home in peace and a sane solution can be found to the difficulties
that provoked the original conflict.

That was Plan 1919: a year and a half of objective thought, some
energetic work at Tank Corps Base Workshops, and a few thousand
words in typescript; and the nub and centre of it, the substitution
of "paralysis" for "killing", a complete inversion of established
thought and behaviour. Fuller was convinced that Plan 1919 would
be the means of effecting the collapse of Germany in that year,
but the Armistice of November 1918 saved the Allied General
Staffs from the necessity of getting to grips with the idea. Plan

1919 thus had no place in World War I. It was reserved for the future.

During the early twenties another military theorist rose to prominence with ideas on army reform, envisaged as based upon an improved mobility compounded of armour, general mechanization, improved signalling, and indirect operations. This was Capt. B. H. Liddell Hart, K.O.Y.L.I., who as a very young officer had first seen action in the Somme battles of 1916. Liddell Hart was unconnected with tank development during World War I, but like Fuller he had come to suspect the military teaching of his time as basically unsound. By 1918 he was arguing that as formal attacks against machine defences were quite unable to yield any result that could be called profitable, soldiers should cultivate intelligence and mobility above mere brute courage; they should avoid hitting the enemy wherever he could effectively resist, and instead, should percolate around and through his positions, eating away at the foundations as a rushing torrent eats away soil—always indirectly. The greater the depth at which this indirect offensive could be practised, he said, the greater the psychological effect on the enemy, the greater his confusion, and the more rapid his collapse. He recognized, however, that drastic modernization of signalling and cross-country supply methods were essential to the development of such a policy. The impasse on the World War I battlefields likewise encouraged him to look back into the history of human conflict with a view to finding common experience there of the frequency with which the military impasse occurred in pre-industrial ages, and of the strategic devices of past times by which long-term advantages were gained. Soon he came to regard as basically erroneous the widely held belief that an enemy can be defeated only on the field of battle, and likewise its corollary that the purpose of war is victory through the physical destruction of an enemy's armies. Arguing that the long-term purpose of war should be neither victory for one nor defeat for another, but a secure peace deriving from the merging of interests, he drew evidence from history and everyday behaviour to show a need for psychological weapons that would persuade an enemy or rival to submit or agree to a policy, and he concluded that military strength should be developed primarily in ways that would facilitate dealing psychological blows.

By 1920 he had related this concept of strategic purpose to his earlier one of indirect tactics, by enlarging the scope of the latter far beyond the confines of the battlefield. He envisaged indirect action being aimed at the demoralization not merely of the front-line troops, but at the generals who thought for them, and at the government which employed the generals. He called this continuous spreading of disorganization and demoralization the "Expanding Torrent".

Soon after this, Liddell Hart read Plan 1919, which had been printed in a Tank Corps periodical pamphlet called "Weekly Tank Notes", designed to encourage military thought in the direction of mechanization and mobility. He was fascinated by its logic, and recognized at once its relationship to his own concept of psychological war. Here, in the fast tank, with its 200-mile circuit of action so thoughtfully provided by Fuller and Johnson, was the main force of the Expanding Torrent. Use the same chassis to carry infantry, artillery, and supplies; link the air arm to the movements of these vehicles; use parachute drops, radio, every modern aid; and the Expanding Torrent, moving at 20 mph across country, diverging here, concentrating there, would be too much for any conventional army to stop. Its scope was illimitable.

We can see, then, that towards the end of World War I both Fuller and Liddell Hart, unknown to each other, had come to think in terms of the paralysis of opposition as distinct from the killing of enemies. If we wish to compare their early achievement, we can remark that whereas Fuller, with Colonel Philip Johnson's engineering assistance, had conceived of a machine which would implement his ideas, Liddell Hart had as yet thought of no detailed applications of engineering technology with which to further his Expanding Torrent. On the other hand, Fuller had drafted Plan 1919 for the specific purpose of striking the army, corps, and divisional headquarters of the German forces in the field, and thus had set a limit of about 20 miles to the initial depth of penetration; and while in Plan 1919 he anticipated that the armies thus beheaded would fall rapidly into confusion and rout, he conceived the development of the Plan as first a lateral movement behind the front, and subsequently a general frontal pressure and pursuit. Plan 1919 was an immense step forward—immense in its decisive renunciation of killing as the purpose of war, and immense in its introduction of that strange vehicle, the fast tank. But it was still just a step, after which came a pause.

Liddell Hart's contribution was to turn the defined span of this step into a movement of unlimited scope: the flow of an expanding torrent, carrying the means of inflicting a multiplicity of psychological blows aimed at successive nerve centres, which would not merely precipitate the collapse of one section of an enemy's army in the field, but would numb with shock every fibre of a network of command, political as well as military, and paralyse a nation. And the mechanical key-piece of this work was—the fast tank of Plan 1919, with its 200-mile radius of action.

The work of Fuller and Liddell Hart cannot be said to have been unified or even co-ordinated, although each was aware of the other's activities. They met and corresponded, and a certain amount of cross-influencing of ideas probably occurred. Certainly they influenced each other's careers. We have seen how Liddell Hart responded to Plan 1919. In 1925 his book, *The Future of War*, so captivated the imagination of the C.I.G.S. nominate, Sir George Milne, as to lead to a series of meetings between general and writer; these resulted in the former being prompted to elect Fuller as his Military Assistant, and in his rapid "conversion" to a policy of radical modernization—a policy which, unfortunately, he failed to implement during his terms of office.

Fuller had been working in the War Office since August 1918, at first to expedite the wartime enlargement of the Tank Corps after the Allied War Council's recommendation. After the Armistice he was given the task of reorganizing training schedules; (curiously, at the same time, Liddell Hart was given the task of redrafting the official Infantry Training Manuals). Then in August 1921, he was appointed Senior Instructor at the Staff College at Camberley. He became Milne's Assistant in February 1926. It is probably accurate to say that his increasing concern with the task of persuading a backward-looking army to see the true continuation of its traditions in modernization and mechanization caused him to lose touch with the immediate and practical extension of Plan 1919. Army mechanization assumed two distinct aspects for him: the contemporary requirements of empire administration, and the possible future development of machine weapons in another continental war. He certainly argued the case for mechanization on two separate levels simultaneously; for example, in his essay of 1919, which won the Royal United Services Institution's Gold Medal, he outlined a new type of division which would hold an independent fast tank battalion, besides a tank company within each infantry battalion, and which would use motor traction in some of the artillery units. As a step towards overall mechanization, this today seems quite unadventurous. But at the time it was so adventurous as to be professionally dangerous. It provoked a tremendous furore, and was considered in some quarters to be outrageously revolutionary, despite the fact that Fuller also included some horse-mounted cavalry and horse-drawn artillery to please the traditionalists. Yet at the same time, in *Tanks in the Great War*, which was to be published the next year, he was setting down his belief that in the next major war the principle of Plan 1919—the paralysis of an enemy through a blow struck at its head—would be so generally accepted that campaigns would become vast duels fought by contending commanders through the agency of armoured land-fleets. Later, in his lectures and publications, he repeatedly stressed the importance of building land-fleets (he saw no need for dismounted action except for certain defensive roles); and this over-emphasis on armour, and playing down of other arms, was a prime cause of the hostility with which his ideas were received in some influential circles. Fuller saw the land-fleet developing ultimately to another impasse, from which the "deterrent" weapon would emerge to frighten populations into demanding peace. For him, this was the logical development of psychological war, and he looked ahead to the coming of deterrent weapons—"mechanical and chemical weapons ... replaced by others still more terrible ..."—in the belief that they would persuade nations to "cease to demand" war. He then drew a dangerous analogy between the evolution of weapons and that of human social attitudes, from which he concluded that the latter would grow more mature, so to speak, with the former—a serious over-estimation of our species' power to conduct its inter-group competition on rational terms.

However up-to-date our technological inheritance, our psychological outfit is still palaeolithic, or at best neolithic, and our uses and abuses of technology, including weapons, must depend upon the responses evoked by our emotions. (Motivation to action must be through the emotions; there is no direct biological link between rational thoughts and actions.) All the evidence of machine age war so far goes to show that despite full awareness of its disastrous, indeed dysgenic nature, we can still be motivated quite easily into a state of warlike excitement. Therefore, we should beware of "reform" through a single aspect of technology. Such influences invariably produce unlooked-for and unwanted results. But if increased understanding of the workings of human behaviour can overtake weapon development, the end envisaged by Fuller in 1919 may come about through the construction of environmental conditions which never demand war response, the motivation for such reconstruction of our entire economic and social existence being, of course, fear of dangerous weapons.

Liddell Hart, on the other hand, although sometimes arguing that psychological effect could be gained by "external" activities analagous to those advanced by Fuller, notably blockade, air-raid, and use of gas, came more and more to the conclusion that "internal" psychological warfare was the main line to take, and soon concentrated his attention on devising methods of achieving striking psychological successes through the agency of existing military organizations which could be improved in detail. Early in the twenties he was advocating the employment of composite aircraft-tank-artillery-infantry formations, the last two being carried in armoured and tracked cross-country vehicles. He called the infantry "tank marines" and envisaged several roles for them, recognizing that many jobs, both offensive and defensive, simply could not be done from within vehicles, and that the circumstances of their work would be less likely to resemble an armoured duel between highly intelligent commanders than a shrewd paralysis blow from one such against the conventionally arrayed troops of a conventionally minded mediocrity. Hence, he advocated the use of compound formations in unlimited depth, arguing that the faster and farther they travelled, and the less predictable their course, the safer they would be and the less difficult it would be to supply them

with their needs. This last idea, of supply within controlled confusion, was the one which his critics found the most difficult to
accept.

Thus we see that Liddell Hart tended to concentrate less on the
evolution of weapons than on the creation, through high-speed
use of cross-country vehicles carrying commonplace weapons, of
extremely novel and therefore alarming environmental conditions,
which, although ephemeral, would serve to paralyse an enemy's
organized resistance.

Fuller's New Model Army was based on the concept of an
armoured land-fleet. It was a high aim, but its author was aware
that overstatement of the case for mechanization was essential to
assure it some measure of fulfilment. Liddell Hart's New Model
Army was essentially a contemporary army made highly mobile,
with a strong fast tank arm; but it had an entirely new purpose—
that of paralysing instead of killing an enemy, through attack on
his most sensitive strategic centres.

It would not be easy to define "official" British, French, or
American army doctrine of the twenties. On the one hand there
existed revulsion against "trench warfare"; but on the other, professional soldiers were strongly motivated towards extreme conservatism by strong social and economic influences, which resulted
from reductions in military expenditure acting upon the *laissez-
faire* attitude to structural reform held by many higher members
of the military hierarchy. In general, the expressed official and
popular views of "modern war" made much of "future" needs
for "modernization" and "mobility", but were sadly lacking in
detailed structure; and they co-existed with an acceptance of pre-
1914 organizations, and with an absence of practical experiment
and will to change.

Upon an amorphous military world the words of Fuller and
Liddell Hart, in lectures, journals, and books, fell with dramatic
effect. Their writings were published widely in the twenties and
early thirties, and were translated into several foreign languages.[1]

---

[1] Fuller wrote twenty-five books and Liddell Hart about ten up to
1936. Fuller's book on *Armoured Warfare* was translated by Soviet
authorities and distributed (30,000 copies) in the Red Army.

Together with the works of other "modern" military writers such as G. le Q. Martel and Charles de Gaulle, who advocated general mechanization as distinct from novel concepts of employment, they became centres of dispute concerning tanks, horses, vehicular mobility, the education of officers, and progress-versus-reaction generally. They gained firm adherents from minority groups of young officers in several countries, but they gained no official recognition whatever in the British, French, or U.S. armies.

Nevertheless, their indirect influences were very great indeed, and undoubtedly played very important parts in pre-shaping important events of World War II. In the first place, Fuller was largely responsible for Britain's sudden abandonment in 1918 of slow tanks. After 1918, the only surviving specifications approved by the General Staff were for fast "D" types. There were specifications for a large "Medium" (the original specification), and for a "Light Infantry" which had the same powers of mobility as the Medium (including flotation) but was of a smaller size. A very few proto-type D vehicles were built by Colonel Johnson to these specifications, and in the period 1921–22 Messrs. Vickers entered the field with rival designs originating from the department of the Master General of Ordnance. The Vickers machine, later re-designated Vickers Medium, was accepted for quantity production, not because it was superior to the D (its performance was much inferior, though its mechanical reliability was greater), but probably because it was considered politic in General Staff circles, and especially by the Master General of Ordnance, to get rid of Philip Johnson's inconveniently independent tank design establishment—after the contract was awarded to Vickers, the D experiments were dropped. But although true experiment was abandoned, Vickers' fulfilment of their contract made the British army the owners of 200 fast tanks—the only ones in the world—and therefore branded it with modernity. Incidentally, the Master General of Ordnance, Sir Noel Birch, was later given a place on Vickers' board. To the watching military world it must have appeared that the British General Staff thought so highly of Fuller and Liddell Hart as to build fast tanks especially to prove their theories. Actually, of

---

Up to 1962 Liddell Hart's works have been translated into 31 languages and published in 42 countries.

course, the British army was decidedly backward-looking; it had
been given fast tanks because a fast tank specification was the only
one available, and the General Staff lacked the wit to devise
another. And it was not until 1926–27 that overall mechanization
was faced up to, and an experimental armoured and mobile force
considered for experiments on Salisbury Plain. There can be little
doubt that these decisions were made only with great reluctance.
It seems difficult, at a time when all motorized armies have a quite
venerable look, to appreciate that even after a whole quarter of
the twentieth century had passed, this mechanization had scarcely
commenced. It would have been possible for a soldier to enlist in
1920, two years after World War I, and to leave the army seven
years later, without once participating in what we consider
"modern" war training—without even seeing a tank, or a chemical
warfare unit, or a motorized unit, or a military radio set, or an
example of ground-air co-operation. It seems incredible that after
its horrible experiences in World War I, the British army did not
rush to modernize itself. But it did not, and moreover the agents of
modernization met with tremendous hostility when they pressed for
experiment.

The trouble was that the situation which brought the tank into
existence was not generally understood, and the tank itself was still
largely regarded as a casual extra to the forces of man, the fighting
animal, rather than a foundation member of a new military order.
The experiences of World War I were not of themselves enough to
change this popular concept, because our attitudes and responses to
war are reflective less of immediate circumstances than of thousands
of years of bygone circumstances. By far the greater number of
Europeans and Americans in 1914–18 were unaware that a crisis in
human competitive behaviour was at hand; they accounted for the
total danger and loss of the war period in terms of local human
error, which could be rectified by the replacement of one stereotype
public figure by another bearing a different group label.

This was quite understandable: people then were educated to
evaluate environmental circumstances in this way. Indeed, they still
are. Ignorance of biological mechanism, and certitude of political
and religious teaching, persuade many people to this day to believe
that all human behaviour is conducted rationally on a basis of in-

sight into self-decided goals. In 1918, an important result of this was the widespread belief that World War I was the "war to end wars". Another equally widespread idea posited trench warfare as an early twentieth-century accident which could never happen again, its corollary being that the "tank era" was therefore past history as well. The subscribers to this belief felt that the tank's only remaining use was in colonial administration, where light tanks or armoured cars could usefully supplement the work of police and troops in times of civil disturbance. Many arguments were thrown about on this topic of the tank's strictly limited utility, some of them absurdly fallacious. One of the commonest stated that as the development of anti-tank missiles was likely to exceed that of armour protection, so the anti-tank gun would prevent the tank's effectual movement on the battlefield, and the fighting man would have to rely again upon the horse for decisive mobility in combat. Absurd though this argument may be, it obtained very wide acceptance through the entire period between the wars, and was actually repeated in Parliament in 1935 by Duff Cooper, then Parliamentary Secretary for War.

Thus, military thinkers who advocated radical reform of military organization and purpose were in a dangerous situation. Their military society was generally unaware how urgent was the need for reform, and worse still, in Britain, France, and the U.S.A. was an inflated condition of war establishments. Lacking positive direction from above, they could be guaranteed to fight, department against department, for survival. At such a time, with promotion slow and uncertain, it is waste of time to tell a man well advanced on the seniority list owing to his understanding of horse troops that he should start at the bottom of the ladder again, this time with tanks. A man in such a position will find it easy to rationalize convincingly the essential nature of his own services, and the uselessness of anything threatening to replace him. And he will believe his own arguments.

Therefore, military reformers in the years following World War I badly needed patronage. Unhappily, among the highest in the British military hierarchy there appeared to be a grave lack of men who could both accept the need for reform and push its case.

The first C.I.G.S. after World War I was Sir Henry Wilson, who seems to have recoiled from the prospect of reorganization as from something beyond his powers, and to have taken refuge in irony and quasi-humour. His successor, in 1922, was Lord Cavan, who was quite incapable of relating the experiences of World War I to the general world situation of rapidly developing industrialization and technology. Being unaware of the forces shaping his environment, he imagined he could preserve it in archaic form by act of will, and regarded would-be reformers as agents of destruction. He tried to prevent serving soldiers from publicly expressing their ideas on military reform, no matter how mild, and inevitably his policy of repression drove progressive forces underground and encouraged sectarianism. In 1926, Lord Cavan was succeeded by Sir George Milne. At last it seemed that a forward-looking patron of military science had come to office, for he consulted with Captain B. H. Liddell Hart, who had acquired a reputation for advanced military thinking with his novel infantry training schemes and his publications discussing the future of war; further, he appointed Fuller his personal adviser. But alas, behind the façade of brisk determination was a lack of basic knowledge and understanding which, on encountering well argued opposition, turned to irresolution. Sir George Milne never confessed to apostasy, but he soon came to give only token acknowledgment to the need for modernization, and in all practical considerations he yielded to the pressure of his reactionary peers. He reconciled words with acts by advocating an ultra-Fabian conversion to modernization, in which a five-year plan was an unthinkable hurry and ultimate achievement was reserved for an unborn generation.

We can see that at this most critical period in British history, the military leaders were unable to grasp the opportunities that were theirs, through what limitations of intellect or education we can only guess. All we can say with certainty is that the system of preferment in the British officer corps failed to produce in the General Staff, and particularly in the latter's Chief, the type of man most necessary in his day for achieving the full integration of the army with its environment.

Lacking patronage, would-be reformers had to preach directly to the multitudes, and so became not reformers, but rebels. And this in turn unleashed other subjective factors connected with the circulation of ideas. Absence of positive guidance from the most senior members of the hierarchy meant that the bulk of the army had to form their attitudes by the lowest common denominator of subjective reasoning: "Hang you, Jack, I'm all right." From 1918 onward, jungle warfare between departments characterized the administrative life of the War Office, as sections within establishments grossly inflated by wartime needs now fought one another for survival. The reforms which will presently be described would have achieved the cure of this painful disorder, had they been acted upon. As it was, they succeeded merely in inflaming it.

This situation was paralleled in other countries. Control of air and tank forces was a matter for contention in the American, French, and Soviet armies. Both France and the U.S.A. soon put tanks under control of infantry. It was said that the American move was dictated by "West Pointer" policy. All Corps appointments under the 1920 National Defence Act of Congress went to West Point graduates, and as the U.S. Tank Corps was then commanded by a non-West Pointer, the U.S. Tank Corps therefore ceased to exist; on the other hand, the Chemical Warfare Department, which was commanded by a West Pointer, was enlarged to corps status, although the U.S. government did not for a moment contemplate engaging in large-scale chemical or bacteriological warfare.

But it was particularly tragic that the British army was unable to maintain an objective approach to mechanization, because, while this was discussed in all technologically advanced countries, and while many minor reforms contributed in varying measure to their general army mechanization, only two major theories of mobile machine age war emerged during the inter-war years, and both were British.

By 1926 the General Staff had done nothing towards organizing an Armoured Force, beyond authorizing Fuller to collate military opinion on the nature of its constitution. Fuller carried out his task, but at the end of the year, the force's constitution was still not settled, nor was any charter prepared to define its activities if it were settled. Yet early in 1927, the General Staff announced that Fuller would be the commander of an Armoured Force with which the British army would experiment that year on Salisbury Plain.

Actually, no such force was raised. Fuller was appointed to the command of an infantry brigade within the area chosen as the scene of the "experiment", and was placed under the orders of the overall Divisional Commander. He was also made garrison commander.

Fuller had been placed in a most difficult situation. While publicly identified as an experimenter, in reality he had nothing with which to experiment, and neither time nor liberty to do so should material belatedly arrive. Any experiments he attempted under these conditions would inevitably fail, and thus he would effectively discredit his own ideas. Forgetting his own teaching on the psychological approach, Fuller tried to blow down the façade of pretence in the most direct way, by firing his offer of resignation at it. But the defences were too deep, too well dug in, and too well prepared. First, the force of his blow was dissipated in a pocket of kind understanding: he was persuaded to rescind his offer. Then while he was pinned down in these paper entanglements, the enemy counter-attacked by infiltrating forward past both flanks, and isolated him from both his bases by appointing first a "safe" man to fill the Armoured Force post, and then another to fill that of Military Assistant to the C.I.G.S. In the latter case the defences were barred as well as bolted against his return, by lowering the grade of the post. Paradoxically, in this brief engagement between the forces of progress and reaction, it was the latter which made proper and successful use of indirect action, profiting by the discipline of the service which isolated the struggle over real policy from the public announcements of the Secretary of State for War.

At this point, Liddell Hart entered the conflict in his capacity as Military Correspondent of the *Daily Telegraph*, making it clear to the public that the show as advertised by the Secretary of State for War bore no resemblance to the show actually prepared by the Army General Staff. This precipitated some awkward questions in the House of Commons, raised public opinion against procrastinating generals, and made the Secretary of State for War a very angry man. Within a week the Armoured Force was properly raised and constituted. Another week, and its commander was given a properly experimental charter of action. But at a price: Liddell Hart, then on half pay, was quickly retired, and Fuller was out, never again to be given a post anywhere near the formative centres of military development.

Chapter Four

New Model Armies

The new commander of the Armoured Force, an infantryman named Collins, unfortunately had little concept of the essential mobility of his charge. The latter experimented for two years. It consisted of two battalions of tanks; a brigade of medium artillery and a battery of light artillery, with a variety of gun tractors and a few Vickers self-propelled guns; a battalion of lorried infantry; and an engineer company. Various units of the Royal Air Force co-operated with it from time to time, but unfortunately sectarianism was rife here also; many senior officers of the R.A.F. were uninterested in combined operations, possibly because they feared that close involvement with army work could lead to a loss of R.A.F. independence.

The novelty of the force was greater than its operational achievement, the latter being truly progressive only in some details, such as the engineer group led by G. le Q. Martel, which made some notable obstacle-crossing experiments, and the reconnaissance element commanded by Frederick Pile, which gave a preview of an armoured force's latent power to paralyse opposition.

By and large, the Armoured Force spent much of its time learning to travel about in an orderly column of march, and relatively little of it in the exploitation of operational possibilities. The widely varying road and cross-country speeds to be found within a heterogeneous assemblage of fighting and carrying vehicles offer serious organizational problems to the commander of an armoured force, and these are especially challenging when the force has but the most rudimentary radio communications, as was the case in 1927 and 1928. But there are two basic ways of responding to such a challenge. The simpler is to impose a basic "mobility standard" by obliging all units to conform their rate of progress to that of the least mobile one; the other is to encourage each unit to move as fast as it can along its own path of advancement while directing each activity towards the attainment of a common purpose.

The first was the method chosen by Collins, and suggests strongly that he found the mechanical aspect of his force almost an inconvenience; he wanted to array his troops for frontal fighting, to line them up for volley firing so to speak. The psychology of this approach gives us a glimpse of the tremendous gulf, in thought and understanding, between the advocates of armoured mobility and the more conventional soldiers. To Collins, and the school of thought he represented, an armoured force was a phalanx on wheels. He could not see that true mass, or density, is relative, being a ratio between weight (strength of blow) and volume (extent of mobility), and that three tanks five miles apart could possess greater mass than a thousand Macedonian phalanxes herded together into a sweating conglomerate. That is to say, he was not capable of recognizing that as all force derives from movement, so the most advantageous use of mechanical forces must derive from the proper exploitation of mechanical mobility. This in turn blinded him to the possibilities of psychological warfare. He was unable to see his problem in the perspectives of history and science.

Later in 1927, the exercises took a livelier turn, and the Armoured Force was given the task of checking the advance of an infantry division and a cavalry brigade, which had been ordered to advance to a point thirty miles away. It succeeded and the old-style forces were very badly mauled. It was possible to argue that the mauling would not have been so severe, had the old-style units possessed adequate anti-tank equipment. But although anti-tank weapons would have enabled them to fend off the tanks, it could not have restored their unmechanized mobility, for as soon as they left their bases the infantry and cavalry became besieged troops, their communications cut to ribbons by the motorized forces.

In 1928 the Armoured Force was given the task of delivering frontal assaults against conventional forces in defensive positions. Unfortunately, the method of command adopted by Collins did not allow them to succeed fully. He was not imaginative or flexible enough to operate Plan 1919 or the Expanding Torrent. Subjected to rigid uniformity of marching speed, the Armoured Force was unable to exploit its unique powers of cross-country locomobility.

But at all times, its intrinsically superior powers of movement gave it the initiative, and taught a plain lesson to the watching world: machine warfare had come to stay, and was already developing far beyond its boundaries of 1918.

Coincidentally with the Armoured Force demonstrations, and powerfully reinforcing them, came a surprise from the U.S.A., where J. W. Christie, an inventor who had perfected steam traversing gear for the naval gun turret and who had built highly advanced self-propelled gun-carriages during 1916–18, turned to armoured warfare and built highly novel fast tanks.[1] In 1928 he demonstrated his "Model 1940" tank which, with a power-weight ratio of 40 to 1, was capable of 70 mph on the road and 40 mph across country. It could cross a foot-high obstacle without slackening speed, leap a 12-foot gap, cross marshes which baulked conventional tanks, and range 1000 miles in a couple of days. Although far ahead of popular military acceptance, it was enough to make even the most reactionary soldier sense that change was in the air. The world-wide creation of new mechanized forces was imminent, come peace, come war. And the change was not too soon. A full thirteen years had elapsed since 1915, when Swinton wrote his scheme for the mass employment of fighting machines. Nor was the first sign of change too great. In the British army's small and heterogeneous experimental mechanized force, only eleven units had some measure of cross-country mobility, and of these, only a few had some measure of armoured protection. Considering the rate of technological advancement in Europe and North America, it was a very lame effort indeed. Yet even so, it was far ahead of anything in any other nation's army. In 1927, when the Armoured Force burst upon the world, the U.S.A., the U.S.S.R., France, Italy, and Japan were still getting used to the idea of using slow tanks to support infantry and cavalry, and of creating small tank and armoured car establishments for these obsolete roles. For all practical purposes the U.S. army was still organized on a 1915 footing of infantry and cavalry, with but a few old tanks, the latter being shared among infantry divisions on a fixed scale with no allowance for circumstances of varying difficulty. In France, the latest reorganization of 1926 (which was not in fact implemented) allowed for:

[1] See Appendix C.

1) "13-ton tanks" to operate independently against enemy machine-guns before a general attack, and also to support infantry;
2) "main battle tanks" of 22 tons to fight enemy tanks, hold flanks, and also support infantry;
3) 70-ton "rupture" tanks to destroy strong enemy positions.

In this programme we see but the vaguest hint of independent mobile operations. French military thought circled endlessly around the central and obsolete theme: physical destruction of the enemy on the field of battle, through headlong assault.

In the U.S.S.R., as late as 1928, the policy laid down in the "Preliminary Correct Line for the War Doctrine of Tanks" followed this French pattern, with modifications apparently derived from Fuller's arguments. It prescribed the use of tanks:

1) to lead the assault wave, and to penetrate the enemy's artillery and reserve zone;
2) to give immediate support to infantry.

They were to be organized for role (1) as independent army troops, and for role (2) as allocations to infantry, in varying strengths as dictated by local requirements.

Italy and Japan used tanks only for the immediate support of infantry, both favouring the Renault Light Tank for this role.

Then came the Armoured Force on Salisbury Plain, and Christie's Model 1940, focussing world-wide attention on army mechanization. Change followed at once. The same year, 1928, the British General Staff recommended that overall army mechanization should be undertaken. Within two years, General Douglas MacArthur had persuaded the U.S. General Staff to adopt a similar policy. Other countries followed suit. Around 1930, the Italian army dropped Renault-type infantry support tanks in favour of fast Vickers machines, and reorganized their tank units within motorized formations. By 1931, France was using Vickers-type vehicles to mechanize the cavalry, and was working out establishments for various types of mechanized formation. In the U.S.S.R., the idea of "Tanks with Motorized Troops" gained rapid support from 1928 onward, its strongest advocate being Colonel Kalinowski, who later commanded the first Soviet "Mechanized Experimental Force". In Germany, where by the terms of the Treaty of Versailles the army was not permitted to possess tanks, a young light infantry officer named Heinz Guderian, who was already an enthusiastic reader of Fuller, Liddell Hart, and Martel, became seized with a burning desire to equip the German army with powerful motorized formations. Given the task of developing motorized supply troops, he took the opportunity to experiment with them as motorized combat units. On a less exuberant plane, the German General Staff secretly requested the firm of Rheinmetall-Borsig to build a few tanks based on Vickers designs, to be tested in Poland.

The general idea of mechanizing military forces had existed, here and there, vague and nebulous, in all European armies during the period immediately after World War I. But it fell to Fuller and Liddell Hart to give this idea assimilable and practical forms, and to Christie to build the machine most adaptable to its expression. Christie's own concepts on the employment of fast motorized units had no influence on army development, but the machines he built most certainly had: they effectively underlined MacArthur's wisdom in the U.S.A., and they were seized upon overseas, first in the U.S.S.R. and later in Britain, as basic material for the construction of highly mobile forces. And the Experimental Armoured Force on Salisbury Plain was the catalyst which precipitated action out of contemplation.

But as soon as the industrial nations moved towards mechanization, they encountered two related areas of indecision. One was the question of overall cost. Complete modernization of a large army would require astronomical sums; there would be no end to the expenditure, for the technological improvement of fighting vehicles would—or should—involve regular scrapping and replacement. Fuller and Liddell Hart, concerned primarily with the British case, had sensibly argued that this cost would be considerably reduced if "quality" was rated far higher than "quantity". A small, élite, highly trained, and excellently equipped force, functioning in ways aimed at bringing rapid decision to a conflict, would be ideally suited to British needs, though not to those of large nations with vast land frontiers. Unfortunately, many British statesmen and soldiers believed that the British army should follow continental patterns, and could not see that these were alien to British requirements.

This problem in turn led to the second quagmire of inaction: if existing armies were to be scrapped, then who would survive the shake-up of the Establishment? If military forces were to be re-shaped according to the dictates of tanks and motor transport, then the oily, parvenu tankman would displace the cavalryman, the horse artilleryman and the guardsman from their exalted places in the military hierarchy. And even if the army were to be only partly reshaped, the limited amount of money available would mean that expansion of tanks and motors could only take place at the expense of older arms.

Mechanization within the industrial nations' armies was in fact shaped by these forces. In a period of world slump and war-weariness, politicians were chary of risking large expenditure on army reform lest they expose themselves to charges of both militarism and extravagance. And when they turned for guidance to their military advisers, the latter, senior soldiers steeped in nineteenth-century beliefs, found it all too easy to rationalize their fear of and hostility to the mechanized intruders. They simply declined to contemplate the military scene objectively. The social aspect of their situation dominated their consciousness. Tanks and motors, creations of World War I, in their minds were associated only with discomfort, failure, and loss—with protracted national calamity. Swords, horses, and the glorious smell of leather harness, on the other hand, were associated with past success and present social occasions—with traditional glory, sport and pretty women, the nostalgia of youth, and with peacetime soldiering, half play, half exhilarating exercise. So under the very real pressure of a social requirement, they suppressed reality and exalted fantasy; and the less intelligent they were, the easier it was for them to do so. The immediate personal problem of preserving a social system transcended the national one of preserving military security.

No nation completely mechanized its army. But between 1929 and 1939, the U.S.S.R., Italy, and Germany, all acting under dictatorial authority, raised homogeneous armoured forces, using Vickers and Christie-type armoured equipment for combat and for training. Britain, France, and the U.S.A. shrank from this bold step, choosing instead to mechanize their cavalry with a view to forming new types of cavalry divisions. The British General Staff turned its back on its own army's Experimental Armoured Force, appearing to find the Royal Tank Corps' self-developed independent role an embarrassment. It solved the problem by defining independent long-range mobile operations as always contingent upon the outcome of a "main battle", a fleeting possibility which therefore had only marginal importance.

Soldiers who believed in the fundamental importance of long-range operations were to be found mostly in the Royal Tank Corps; to satisfy them, an experimental Tank Brigade was formed in 1930, consisting of at first two and later four battalions of the Royal Tank Corps. Its operations were watched keenly from overseas, but at home it was regarded as outside the main stream of development.

In 1934 the General Staff issued a directive on army reorganization. This said that the army would have two types of division. The first of these was styled Mechanized Infantry Division, and had truck transport, a tracked carrier machine-gun battalion, and a battalion of infantry escort tanks. This project was strongly supported by the new Master General of Ordnance appointed in 1934, General Sir Hugh Elles, who had commanded the tanks in France as "front man" to Fuller's behind-the-scenes planning. He had become unsympathetic to the post-war theories of Fuller and Liddell Hart, and his slogan now was "Back to 1918". In the year of his appointment, limited research was undertaken to discover the required performance of heavily armoured, slow, infantry escort tanks, of the type being developed in France, and from this were later evolved the slow moving infantry tanks Matilda 1 and Matilda 2, which served in the early years of World War II.

The second type of division was designated Mobile Division. It had cavalry, on horses and in trucks or light tanks; some truck or carrier-mounted artillery and engineers; and a brigade of Royal Tank Corps units, which would be replaced by cavalry when the latter became fully mechanized. In this directive we see a wedge to split the Royal Tank Corps between the immediate support of infantry, and on the other hand the support of cavalry. Moreover, we see that while the inevitability of mechanizing the cavalry is accepted, this is only at the expense of the Royal Tank Corps. In both types of division the tanks have become subordinate agents. Coincidental with this "reformation" of divisional organization was much talk of training infantry units to man their own tanks. Obviously, were this to come about, and were cavalry to become tank-mounted, the hierarchical problem would be solved and the army would be firmly back to 1918, for the role of the Mobile Division was limited to skirmishing, flank guarding, and, very vaguely, "pursuit and exploitation".

But before this could happen, the type of organization and military technique advocated by Fuller, Liddell Hart, and their adherents, and demonstrated by the Royal Tank Corps with its Tank Brigade, had to be effectively discredited. This was accomplished in the autumn manoeuvres of 1934.

For the greater part of these manoeuvres, the Tank Brigade was assembled as in previous years to practise its own peculiar brand of mobile war virtually alone, quite apart from the routine drills of the rest of the army. But at the very end of the training season, Sir John Burnett-Stuart, Chief of Southern Command and director of Army Manoeuvres that year, ordered Brigadier Hobart's Tank Brigade to assemble with an infantry brigade and a field brigade of artillery as an improvised mobile force under the overall command of Major-General Lindsay. Openly declaring that he thought it was time the "older kinds of troops" received a "restorative to their morale", he allowed Lindsay no time for the co-operative training so essential to the success of mobile operations but ordered him forthwith to attack a number of objectives which he specified, and which he then made known to the "defenders", who at once disposed their defences accordingly. Further, he required the mobile force to approach its objectives from a starting point seventy miles away, prescribing the hours of its marching and making these known to the defenders.

Had Burnett-Stuart genuinely wished to experiment with a mobile force, one imagines he would have outlined a general military situation, set his two forces to dispose themselves for offence and defence according to the strategic concepts held by their leaders, and watched to see how far the current organization of a mobile force was suited to actions based on secrecy and surprise. As it was, the manoeuvre was channelled into a frontal clash between two forces dissimilarly organized, one of them handicapped by the bizarre requirement of making a public seventy-mile approach march, and closing on its objectives through a defile guarded by a well prepared and waiting enemy. Finally, when the mobile force was fully committed, Burnett-Stuart halted it inside enemy territory, and ordered it to withdraw through an enemy which of course never had been surprised at all, and which now, as if it had received prior intelligence of the withdrawal, was preparing road-blocks and minefields on possible lines of retreat.

The watching British military world was therefore impressed by the apparent facts that:

a) "powerful" mobile force failed to reach its objectives;
b) it was obliged to retreat;
c) it was partly trapped and seriously incommoded by "older kinds of troops".

It was very sad that the older arms had felt it necessary to create such an Orwellian situation.

The outcome of the struggle was that the Royal Tank Corps' long-range experiments were laid aside, as something hyper-theoretical, a by-play of war to be utilized if "fleeting opportunity occurred". "Mobile war" was established as it were on a tactical plane, as an adjunct to the "main battle" of the 1918 type.

The implementation of the General Staff's post-1934 policy was effected by separating the erstwhile tank leaders from the development of armoured warfare, by moving the Royal Tank Corps units around from one job to another, and by reducing the fast tank specification to satisfy cavalry requirements.

The dispersal of the tank leaders was of course the decisive blow to the work of Fuller and Liddell Hart. Lieutenant-General C. Broad, who had pioneered the development of large-scale manoeuvres by fast tank formations, was given an infantry command. Major-General G. M. Lindsay, who had been one of the most persistent advocates of general mechanization, was sent to an administrative post in India. Brigadier, later General, F. Pile, a most dynamic armoured leader, was sent first to infantry and later to anti-aircraft, where he made a great reputation. Hobart was isolated with his "exotic" Tank Brigade, which sometimes, as Royal Tank Corps units were moved around, had no equipment. After the political crisis of 1938 he was appointed to the command of

Britain's second raised Armoured Division, but was not allowed to command it after war broke out. Although an exceptionally able man, intelligent and gifted in improvisation, he was never given a command in the field throughout the entire war period. Fuller said of him that he could have been "a British Guderian"; we shall see later what this could have meant to Britain.

Changes in British tank equipment came with the new policies. By 1939 British tank building had settled in three streams:

a) heavily armoured, slow moving infantry tanks of several sizes;
b) lightly armoured "light" tanks armed only with machine-guns, for cavalry reconnaissance, flank screening, etc., in mobile (cavalry) formations;
c) lightly armoured "cruiser" tanks, armed with a cannon as well as a machine-gun to provide a tank punch for mobile formations.

The development of powerful medium tanks was virtually discontinued. Britain, which from the time of Alexander Forsyth had been the birthplace and centre of machine warfare, had once more rejected its most promising offspring. Priority in tank building was given to the heavy armoured infantry support types, and the building of Mobile Divisions was not pressed. The slogan was "Back to '18".

After 1928, the French army (which had earlier organized infantry "bus columns" with supporting tanks) created a number of mechanized cavalry divisions of three types, with equipment ranging from horses to heavy tanks according to what they were required to reconnoitre, hit, or exploit; it was assumed that the enemy would always present himself in a manner which permitted his engagement with, successively, light, medium, and heavy forces. These mechanical cavalry divisions used engineer, artillery, and supply troops, etc., but training was not integrated; the troops were organized in echelons (as distinct from homogeneous combat groups) and were expected to "unlock" enemy defences step by step, each arm (infantry, artillery, cavalry, tanks) carrying out merely its own allotted part in the preconceived whole. There was no allowance for co-operation against the unprecedented. It was all very academic and unreal. In practice the separation of roles led to disharmony of action, which a general lack of radio communications did nothing to relieve, and which, moreover, encouraged high commanders to split up the divisions into piecemeal groups to satisfy local defence requirements.

At the same time large numbers of new tanks were built: heavily armoured slow machines for the immediate support of infantry; lightly armoured Vickers types for the various cavalry roles, such as the "auto machine-gun for reconnaissance" and "auto machine-gun for combat"; plus larger tanks in three sizes. This range of cavalry equipment existed because the French General Staff had drawn a direct analogy between light, medium, and heavy cavalry and light, medium, and heavy tanks. It was very muddled thinking, for a tank of 20 tons can travel as fast as one of 5 tons, while carrying better armament and armour. As with British armoured development in the thirties, it was a triumph for the cavalry, but it led to disaster for the nation. This possibility passed unobserved, because it was widely considered that the "real" tank role was that of 1918—immediate support of infantry in frontal attack.

The U.S. Army, influenced by the British Armoured Force and the British General Staff decision to mechanize, but also deeply under the influence of French doctrine, was committed to mechanization before 1930; but no clear policy for it emerged until World War II erupted. For example, the cavalry were prohibited by Act of Congress from operating tanks, and had to circumvent the rule by operating machines called "combat cars", which of course were really tanks. The U.S. General Staff appears to have taken little interest in the basic principles of mobile warfare; instead, it tended to favour static situations in which the immense industrial potential of the U.S.A. could make itself felt. This attitude was very marked during World War I, and there can be no doubt that the German government in 1918 was moved to seek peace by, amongst other considerations, an awareness that their war industries could not long compete against America's. But confidence in industrial might is a poor basis for a long-term strategy, as the nuclear stalemate of today shows very clearly.

Is it surprising that the U.S.A. should have such a simple, almost naïve attitude to the conduct of war? Perhaps not. In the first place, a democracy as vast as the U.S.A. must present its policies to the electorate in very simple terms. And conversely, the need to maintain popular goodwill must tend to shape policies according to election requirements rather than objective purposes. The U.S.A. has a very materialistic culture, in which the human features primarily as a "consumer". And in the materialist view, opposition is a material thing to be removed by material means, which in warlike terms means overwhelming it with firepower as straightforwardly as possible, regardless of expense.

Mechanization of the U.S. Army was, therefore, simply a matter of motorizing the nineteenth-century style forces already existing. Where tanks were concerned, the advanced Christie designs[2] were rejected in favour of something simpler and more heavily armoured, that could be crammed with men and have guns pushed out on every side. The Christie airborne tanks and the ideas behind them did not even receive serious attention. In the view of the U.S. General Staff, the primary role of tanks was to support infantry in frontal assaults. As in Britain and France, the slogan was "Back to '18".

In contrast to the U.S. Army, some departments of the Red Army were deeply influenced by the theories of Fuller and Liddell Hart, and serious attempts were made to give them expression. General army mechanization (in the sense of provision of motor vehicles) became part of the Five Year Plan 1929–34.[3] Several tank designs based on Christie and Vickers designs were put into production, and a Christie airborne tank was purchased and studied. Vickers amphibious tanks were built in large numbers. Cavalry divisions received an infusion of tanks and motorized infantry, and in 1929 work began with a "Mechanized Experimental Regiment" under the command of Colonel Kalinowski. The following year, this was enlarged to become "Brigade Kalinowski", and by 1932 it had become "Mechanized Corps Kalinowski", containing 500

[2] The influence of J. W. Christie on the evolution of machine warfare is discussed in Appendix C.

[3] Most of the information given here on Soviet armoured development is from Andronikov and Mostovenko *Die Roten Panzer* and Magnuski *Wozy Bojowe*.

tanks, 200 armoured cars, 60 artillery pieces and other troops, all motorized. In the early thirties this type of organization promised to spread throughout the Red Army, replacing infantry-with-tanks, and cavalry-with-tanks. A typical Mechanized Brigade consisted of three tank battalions of 31 tanks each; two Motor Infantry Battalions, one of them an assault battalion; an Artillery Battalion, plus engineer and reconnaissance units, etc. But the doctrine laid down in 1929 revealed that these developments were not unopposed. Independent long-range (paralysis) action was deemed contingent upon the outcome of a conventional assault and the availability of a large reserve of tanks. And the tactical support of cavalry was considered more important than long-range operations. Nevertheless, in 1934 the "Provisional Instructions for the Distant Wide Ranging Fight" envisaged large-scale surprise operations up to depths of 120 miles. But it was by no means wholly conceded that these encircling and paralysing operations would actually replace, or even rival in importance, conventional assaults by the "older arms".

In the U.S.S.R., the mid and late thirties were marked by a particularly bloody struggle for power within the Communist hierarchy. As the Stalinist party emerged triumphant, there developed a hysteria of mass-killing, whose outward manifestations were treason trials at which the fantasy of the charges was exceeded only by that of the confessions. The Red Army was of course deeply involved in this power struggle. One of its most important aspects was the clash between the protagonists of mobile armoured warfare, and the representatives of the "traditionalist" school—between the followers of the progressives and the reactionaries. The principal supporter of the former was Sergei Mironowicz Kirov, a man powerful enough to be a possible rival to Stalin. To what extent Kirov subscribed to the views of Fuller and Liddell Hart is not known. Possibly he sought only to increase his political strength by supporting Marshal Tukhachevsky and Colonel Kalinowski in their endeavours to modernize the Red Army; possibly his main interest lay in securing the support of the Chief of the Red Army, plus the armoured and mobile forces, and probably the artillery, which were administratively linked with the armour, in a future clash with Stalin. The latter did not wait for this situation to mature. He had Kirov assassinated (by a Komsomol member named Nikolayev) on

December 1, 1934, and his elimination at once exposed Tukhachevsky and the latter's protégé Kalinowski to political attack, as Stalin
prepared to strengthen his own faction in the Red Army and
eliminate those of his political rivals. Thus, we see that in the Red
Army, as in those of Britain and the U.S.A., the development of
armoured forces was shaped by power struggles, but to a degree of
violence unknown in the West, because of the direct involvement
of major political figures.

The actual operational value of these forces was scarcely
examined at all: the alignment of the "progressive" element with
S. M. Kirov quite precluded this. It is possible, however, that the
dismissal of Fuller and Liddell Hart in England in 1934, and the
reaffirmation there of 1918 methods, reinforced Stalin's desire to
eliminate even the least important adherents of Tukhachevsky and
Kalinowski.

After a decent interval, during which Kirov had an (unsuccessful) tank named after him, Stalin "purged" the Red Army, aiming
directly at the elimination of Tukhachevsky.

As the terror and hysteria built up through this barbarous period,
Russian officers who subscribed for purely professional reasons to
the Liddell Hart-Kalinowski theories of mobile war found themselves criticized and denounced not on technical grounds which
could be tested objectively, but on moral and political ones. Mobile
war as advocated by Fuller and Liddell Hart was denounced as
reactionary, bourgeois, and unworthy of a Marxist society, inasmuch
as it put faith in a suspect technocracy instead of the armed proletariat. Fuller and Liddell Hart were denounced as the effete spokes-
men for a decadent capitalism which dared not place its trust in
the masses, and so hid behind mechanical contrivances. The rifle-
carrying proletariat—that is, the "Back to '18" school—would
never be defeated. . .

Such was the mood of the times that this nonsense passed for
reason, and its corroborative evidence, of Communist experiences of
tank warfare in China and Spain, was not objectively examined.
Many supporters of mobile warfare, including Tukhachevsky and
Kalinowski, were put to death. Others, less deeply committed, were
able to recant and save their lives at the price of their professional
judgment.

In 1937 the new leaders of the Red Army, under the nominal headship of Field Marshal Klimenti Voroshilov, announced that as minefields and anti-tank defences were now stepped in depth (as if they had not been since 1918), independent armoured operations were out of the question, and only set-piece offensives on narrow fronts, by infantry with tanks and artillery in support, could be successful.

The word "stepped" conveys some idea of this rigidity of thought, which largely ignored the psychological effects of indirect manoeuvre. Stalin and Voroshilov believed that mines and anti-tank guns could slow down and soak up the fast armoured/mechanical attack, as successive trench lines soaked up infantry attacks in 1918. The Communist leaders were echoing contemporary orthodox Western views; and as in Britain and France, the great fallacy in the "Back to 1918" argument was not recognized. It just was not seen that the stronger a defence, the greater the need to unhinge it by manoeuvre, lest the cost of trying to smash it frontally prove impossibly high.

To implement the "Back to '18" policy, the Red Army decided to centre tank production on two heavily armoured models derived from existing fast tank designs. The designers entrusted with this task were instructed to retain desirable "mobility" features such as low ground pressure, long range, and cruising speeds of around 20 mph. They succeeded in combining these characteristics with stout armour and powerful armament, and the resulting diesel-engined T34 and Klimenti Voroshilov tanks of 1939 were in reality powerful general-purpose tanks, very different from the slow infantry escorts of France and Britain. They were inferior to the best Western tanks only in optical and radio equipment. But their merit as fighting machines could not offset the disadvantages of their piecemeal deployment.   .

German army mechanization took a course altogether different from that of the West and the U.S.S.R. The man responsible for this was Heinz Guderian, light infantry officer from East Prussia, who found himself in 1918, at the age of thirty, highly dissatisfied with both the shape and the difficulties which the German army had acquired; while he was convinced that the latter's future must lie in some form of mechanization, he was in doubt as to the form this must take, and the direction it must lead.

He was certain about one thing: the armoured cross-country vehicle. But beyond thinking in general terms of tanks and motorization and radio signalling—he had specialized in the latter during World War I—he was for some time at a loss to see a clear way ahead with them.

Enlightenment came with German translations of works by Liddell Hart, Fuller, and Martel; the first of these, Liddell Hart's essay describing the ideal constitution of a New Model Army, set an uncompromisingly revolutionary tone. Guderian became, as he later described himself, a disciple of these British prophets. He studied the German translations of their writings, made intelligent acceptance of the substitution of paralysis for killing, and simultaneously sought both to infuse his fellow officers with this new concept of the nature of war and to devise organizations through which the German army could realize it. He gained acceptance as an expert in armoured warfare, and the factor that worked most to his advantage was the non-existence of a German tank force. Unlike the British, French, and American armies, the German one was untroubled by jealousy over the status of the new arm. For Guderian had no desire to build a tank corps as such. He aimed to integrate armoured troops with other motorized troops of all kinds in a homogeneous highly mobile formation, reckoning that only this type of fully integrated unit would possess the flexibility and speed of response essential to long-range mobile operations. This vision was, to say the least, highly advanced.

On the eve of Hitler's accession to power, Guderian was serving on the Motor Transport Instructional Staff, and was experimenting with mobile warfare techniques under the guise of developing a motor supply service. In 1932, largely on his suggestion, light tanks' chassis were purchased from Messrs. Vickers, ostensibly as self-propelled anti-aircraft gun carriages, but actually to form the prototype for a new light tank, Panzerkampfwagen 1, to be used as a training tank. Guderian used Panzer 1 to train his Motor Transport troops in techniques based on the British Royal Tank Corps experiments; thus he created the nucleus of a German Armoured Force within the Supply Service without any need for a tank corps, yet without treading on the toes of the cavalry and other combat arms. Hitler's accession to power and his decision to rebuild German military strength gave Guderian a unique opportunity to develop a co-operative armoured force. In 1933 he demonstrated his tank-motor-infantry technique before Hitler and won whole-hearted approval; the composite armoured force was established, not as a specialist tank arm, but as an all-arms armoured force of the most adaptable and flexible kind. There can be little doubt that this was achieved through Guderian's indirect approach; he did not try to graft other arms on to a tank arm, but unobtrusively put his Motor School on tracks and behind armour.

His thoughts on panzer force organization were still far from settled, and his tour de force before Hitler had aroused no little jealousy among more senior establishments. But the newly-appointed Inspector of Motorized Troops, General Lutz, strongly favoured his ideas, and gave him essential support when he proposed the establishment of panzer divisions, supporting his arguments with detailed lists of the personnel and equipment required, and calculations of the fuel and supplies on which to run it.

He also succeeded in terminating the existing work on tank development, with a view to bringing all tank policy under his own control and shaping it to his "paralysis" ends. This must have appeared quite urgent in 1933, for in that year a large Vickers-type tank was under consideration for quantity production. He had alternative proposals ready, stressing the importance of long range, speed, comfort, and other factors bearing on his concept of armoured warfare. Soon, two new designs were started for medium tanks of about 18 to 20 tons, with the moderately high power-to-weight ratio of 16 to 1, road speed of 20 mph, a high standard of crew comfort, good radio and optical equipment, and a very high standard of mechanical reliability. One was to carry a high-velocity gun, the other a howitzer, and both had wide turret rings giving roominess, and allowance for future increases in the calibre and trunnion pull of armament. Both, significantly, were thinly armoured, and were of little use for frontal assaults on strongly defended positions. They eventually became known respectively as Panzerkampfwagens 3 and 4.

At the same time, a light-medium tank based on the Vickers

chassis was authorized, which would serve as an interim model during the unknown period it would take to develop the medium machines. This became Panzerkampfwagen 2.

Guderian was interested also in the provision of other specialized armoured equipment, such as self-propelled artillery, tracked infantry carriers, armoured command vehicles, and armoured reconnaissance cars, but was unable to secure control of all their development. With Germany now openly re-arming, the policies dictating the shape of machine weapons became matters for departmental rivalry. No self-propelled artillery pieces entered service before 1940; in their absence the Panzer 4, with its short-barrelled howitzer, specialized in the role of assault artillery in a "support" section within the tank regiment. Likewise, the number of cross-country infantry carriers produced was very low, and much use had to be made of commercial lorries with little or no cross-country ability. To summarize: once the idea of an armoured force was accepted, Guderian had to work very hard to keep it heading in the direction he had chosen, and even then he could not retain complete control of tank policy, let alone armoured vehicle policy. For example, in 1938 the firm of Henschel was producing a prototype 65-ton monster for advocates of "immediate support for infantry", and another firm was being induced to build an 18-ton, slow, heavily armoured version of the little Panzer 1 training tank. These were intended to serve as slow break-through and infantry escort tanks, and reflected orthodox German acceptance of the British, French, American, and Soviet "Back to 1918" policies. In consequence of this confusion acting on hurried development programmes, the German army approached 1939 with relatively few tanks actually in service, most of them Panzer 1 training machines.

On the ideological side Guderian made much swifter progress. He was made commander of an armoured division in 1935, and by 1937 was appointed Chief of Mobile Troops—not, be it noted, "Tank" troops. This placed him in a strong position from which to practise a unique co-operative type of training. In France, the Division Léger Mechanique had brought together elements of tank, infantry, artillery, and cavalry to serve vaguely co-operative purposes contingent upon the "main battle", while in Britain, the armoured forces of 1928 and 1934 had briefly done something similar. But the latter never came near to a state of homogeneity, while in the French D.L.M. the various arms remained together only as it were on the line of march. Functionally, they remained separate, for they had no unifying operational purpose. To Guderian, homogeneity based on intelligent movement was the pivot of all training. His tanks did not fight as a "tank force" duelling with enemy tanks in knightly encounters before moving on to destroy the peasant infantry, but as an intelligent instrument co-operating with other intelligent instruments to paralyse enemy resistance. Although their cannons could be used for destroying enemy tanks when necessary, the German medium tanks were not armoured to withstand tank duelling. To cope with enemy tanks encountered in large numbers, tank crew co-operated closely with highly mobile anti-tank gun teams, and on being attacked by enemy tanks, were trained to retire slowly through their own anti-tank screen. While this fire checked and confused the enemy, the German tanks worked round the enemy flank.

The Royal Tank Corps, by contrast, came to specialize in tank-versus-tank fighting to such an extent that new British tanks were fitted with cannon which could fire nothing but anti-tank shot. This was largely due to the British army's failure to develop co-operative techniques, and was an over-specialization destined to cost Britain the lives of many tankmen, and the price of many war machines. For Guderian, tanks were just a part of a divisional organization: an important part, the key part, in fact, but still a component part. Likewise, his motorized infantry had no "infantry attack" function outside the furtherance of the division's "paralysis" manoeuvres. Their vehicles did not simply ferry them to a pitched battle, but were part and parcel of their tactical expertise. The Panzer Grenadiers, as Guderian aptly named them, were foot soldiers who had to think and move at tank speed.

To this end he made the division the most important unit. Troops came straight to the Panzer School Division after receiving their recruit training, and there learned to use their basic skills co-operatively in precise, rapid and intelligent manoeuvre. The structure of panzer divisional training was based on four supports, one psychological, and three technical.

The psychological one was dynamic control on the part of every commander at every level. The idea of bringing troops to a battle-field, lining them up by textbook precept, and then sitting back to watch the outcome, was completely out. The commander was expected to lead his men to success through intelligent manoeuvre, and to obtain a deciding punch by assembling locally superior fire-power quicker than the enemy could react. Guderian recognized that intelligence was a prerequisite to this kind of work, among the troops as well as the officers. He believed that tank crew should possess an I.Q. equivalent to that required of air crew, and there can be no doubt that alert intelligence helped compensate for the German armoured forces' quantitative inferiority.

The technical cornerstones proved to be as Liddell Hart and Fuller had accurately forecast; multi-lateral radio communications, tactical air co-operation, and efficient motorization. None of these can be singled out as predominant; each is essential to the profitable utilization of the others. Radio communications are the means of maintaining flexible command of complex, fast moving formations; air power is essential to secrecy of movement; motorization allows attacking troops to break the deadlock of machine weapon defences, by rapid movement to a vulnerable area beyond the defensive shield.

Guderian's recipe for a truly mobile military organization was quite modest. A panzer division consisted of:

a) H.Q. Divisional Commander and Staff, travelling in armoured command vehicles and in constant two-way touch with all troops by·radio, aircraft, despatch rider, and pigeon;

b) Divisional Reconnaissance Unit;

c) Tank Brigade of four battalions, each of 72 tanks in the propor-tion of three light to one medium (in reality only the first four panzer divisions held this strength—later divisions held only three, or even two, battalions);

d) Motorized Infantry Brigade, four or two rifle battalions in lorries, and one MG battalion on motor cycles;

e) Artillery Regiment of three battalions, each of 12 guns, organized in 4-gun batteries (later many 75mm calibre guns were self-propelled);

f) Anti-Tank Battalion;

g) Engineer Battalion.

These formations were maintained in the field through a complex supply echelon which had to function in the face of great difficulties, the nature of which may be guessed when it is realized that (a) a panzer division consumed up to 10,000 gallons of motor fuel in moving ten miles by road, or 20,000 gallons in moving the same distance across country, and (b) it was designed to operate deep in enemy-held territory, marching distances of hundreds rather than tens of miles. Thus, a 40-mile advance could make a daily demand on the supply echelon for more than 50,000 gallons of fuel, as well as the stores needed for feeding men, refilling ammunition bins, maintaining vehicles, and ferrying casualties and reinforcements.

It is obvious that apart from the acceptance of paralysis as a strategic principle, the prime requisite in the commander was great flexibility of mind, both in acceptance of ideas and in their interpretation and development. No force, no matter how closely it aped the panzer division in its material aspects, could hope to function as Guderian's panzers functioned, unless its commander made mental acceptance of strategic paralysis and had mental agility enough to work it. Of course, we should not imagine that every German officer and man in the panzer division made this acceptance, rationally and consciously. As we know, most people accept their environment as given, provided it is not too bizarre, without much evaluation. Besides, the junior commanders and the fighting men functioned exactly as did their opposite numbers in conventional "killing" armies: through the positioning and operation of weapons, and through destruction of humans and their belongings. All differences in these respects were in terms of scope, intensity and duration, and were therefore related to the mental activity of the overall commander—the panzer leader.

How far did Guderian succeed in building his panzer force to an ideal specification? By no means as far as he had hoped. The whole of the German army was never converted to panzer organization or to paralysis purpose. By 1939, only six panzer divisions had been created, and only fourteen more were raised before Guderian was dismissed in 1941. Nor was Guderian unopposed. In Germany, as in Britain, the cavalry fought against a threatened domination by mechanized forces, and stood apart from the panzers in their own Light (Mobile) Divisions. Likewise, the airt force (Luftwaffe) was as jealous of its independence as was the R.A.F., although a control mechanism was evolved whereby the Luftwaffe stationed within a given area could be brought under the direct control of the army officer conducting operations. And in the specialist field of armoured vehicle design there were many advocates of policies rivalling Guderian's. As already remarked, the task of establishing his requirements for fast medium tanks and self-propelled artillery proved far from easy. It was made even more difficult by insistence in some quarters that the new machines were excessively thin-skinned, and thus unfitted to confront a technologically advanced enemy. This attitude was supported by evidence from the Spanish Civil War, in which some Panzer 1 tanks on loan to General Franco were misused as infantry escorts. Ironically, the same argument was used in the U.S.S.R. against the advocates of what was called there the "Wide Far Ranging Fight".

So we see that the concept of strategic paralysis gained but an insecure grip on the German military consciousness before 1939, and the limited progress it made was largely through the effort of one man who introduced it indirectly through the training of motor troops. In Germany, as in Britain, France, the U.S.A., and the U.S.S.R., the idea of developing manoeuvre at the expense of battle was a minority view, whose ascendancy in Germany came about largely through the conditions imposed by the Treaty of Versailles, which left the German army in an undeveloped form. With the advent of Hitler, Guderian was by chance enabled to implement his concept of modernization. But as with Fuller and Kalinowski, his views were opposed by powerful professional interests which were ready to unseat him as soon as opportunity offered.

Curiously, the German panzer division, which was an improved copy of the British Experimental Force of 1927, was itself copied in Britain and the U.S.A. on the eve of the outbreak of World War II, and by the U.S.S.R. on the eve of the German invasion of Russia in 1941. But as was to be shown during the course of the war, although the outward form of the panzer division was copied, the ideas which animated it were not. The American armoured division, for example, had two commanders, an armoured one and an infantry one, who were to succeed each other as circumstances dictated. That fact summed up the mental limitations of the "main battle" school of thought. It could not create and exploit a situation; it could only follow one that chance, or the resources of a war industry, or a more dynamic opponent, had created.

So far little has been said about air forces. These originated at the outbreak of World War I as adjuncts to the ground forces, particularly to the artillery. Some aircraft reconnoitred enemy territory, and observed enemy movements and the effects of fire. Bombers were able to deepen the zone of artillery fire, until it extended to the enemy's capital. Ground-attack aircraft, as flying gun platforms, carried out harassing fire tasks of machine-guns and light artillery. And, of course, fast and agile "fighters" were developed to prey upon enemy aircraft, and to prevent them from observing and striking home territory. The complexity, specialization, and importance of the air arm ensured a high degree of independence, and in some countries, notably Britain, the air force achieved parity of independence and status with the navy and army. In the U.S.A., on the other hand, air arms remained as important branches of the navy and army for many years. The struggle for status and enlarged establishment that characterized all air forces during the period between the wars brought forth its extreme theorists, who argued that the air arm was destined to usurp more of the functions of surface forces, and possibly to become the prime military instrument, with surface forces acting only in ancillary roles. General "Billy" Mitchell was such a one in the U.S.A. Another was General Giulio Drouhet in Italy, who advocated "strategic" bombing on the grounds that the material and moral destruction it caused would be sufficient to make an enemy capitulate, without the need to employ land forces against him. Drouhet's views, which were widely published, gained considerable acceptance in Britain, France, and the U.S.A., but had far smaller followings in Germany, Russia, and Japan.

On the eve of World War II, the R.A.F. had become independent, with status equivalent to that of the army and navy, and was deeply committed to the Drouhet theory of strategic bombing at the expense of army co-operation. On the other hand, the Royal Naval Air Service was firmly tied to tactical requirements. The French air force was independent and similarly disposed. The German Luftwaffe was administratively independent, but was tied operationally to army co-operation and support at the expense of strategic bombing. Its most highly developed form of ground attack was dive bombing, a form of "instant artillery" that could be effective, but was often inaccurate, and rendered the aircraft vulnerable to counter-attack. At the same time, Luftwaffe leaders were very sensitive to and jealous of this army control, and sought to break it; some of them were would-be Drouhets. The U.S. air forces were split between army, navy and marines, and while the army branch had strong interests in strategic bombing on the largest scale, there was still ample development of other roles, particularly dive bombing and torpedo bombing. The Soviet air forces were under direct army and navy control and were fully committed to support roles, their ground-attack units being the first to develop aircraft specializing in the attack against tanks, using cannon and rockets. Unlike the Germans and Americans, the Russians did not place much emphasis on dive bombing. The Japanese air forces were also under army and navy control; the predominance of the latter led to a development of specialization against maritime targets.

Before 1939 it was possible to consider the evolution of land fighting apart from the evolution of air power, at least in Britain. The effects of air intervention against, and co-operation with, ground operations were still matters for theorization—or perhaps speculation—right up to the commencement of World War II. The author can remember exercises during whose nocturnal periods R.A.F. aircraft carried their navigation lamps lit! They had to— otherwise no one would have known what to do about the unseen aircraft they could hear buzzing around, and the exercise would have become untidy. This, of course, is yet another example of the difficulties experienced by our species in adapting itself to machine warfare, which, by repeatedly making sudden technological leaps ahead into the unknown, causes military societies to experience insecurity, and motivates them towards the acceptance of unreal dogma, leading to stereotyped battle-formulae unrelated to the actual forces engaged.

Chapter Five

Apotheosis of the Tankmen

It is the purpose of the author to give an outline of the main developments in machine warfare, and not a potted history of World War II. But it is impossible to describe the acceptance and use of strategic concepts, without in some measure describing the campaigns which they influenced.

At first sight it seems unlikely that the "strategic paralysis" theories could have influenced the course of World War II at all, for in 1939 it seemed that the Fuller-Liddell Hart-Christie novelties had been dropped at last, and the armies of the major powers would march to the commencement of a new war arrayed as they were when the last one ended. No progressive personalities were to be found among the highest military leaders of the major industrial powers. In the U.S.S.R., the 1937 purges had seen most of them shot. In Britain they were retired or dispersed to uninfluential posts. In France and the U.S.A. they had never attained power. In Germany, Guderian and his followers found both their importance and their autonomy diminishing: the armoured forces which had dominated the miniature German army of 1932 were not enlarged in the same proportion when the German army as a whole was enlarged. As in France and Britain, the greater part of military expenditure went to the elaboration of the older arms in the pattern of 1918. Germany, France, Poland, and Russia went to war relying on horses and railway systems for the greater part of their military transport. Britain was the only European power to have a fully motorized military transport system. Likewise, all the European powers, including Britain, still made use of horsed fighting troops as late as 1939. Britain did not complete the mechanization of yeomanry regiments until 1941, and horsed cavalry units were used by both Germany and Russia almost until the end of the war.

The transportation of infantry remained at World War I level in all major powers, including the U.S.A., until after 1945, in that it was mostly wheeled and roadbound, and organized largely in "pools" operating ferrying services. Infantry units holding their own cross-country combat transport were very rare in 1939, being found only in armoured or special mobile divisions. The "tankette", evolved by Martel in the twenties as the means of providing fast infantry movement across country, now survived only as the tracked weapon carrier, humping the infantry battalion's mortars and heavy machine-guns.

It would appear also that this outward backwardness was matched by the strategic concepts of the General Staffs concerned. We have already seen how responsible soldiers reacted with hostility to suggestions for experiment leading to change in the constitution and equipment and the roles of their troops. It could hardly be supposed that generals who resisted change in the outward aspects of their charges would envisage positive, clearly reasoned strategies based on a contemporary war technology. Their concepts of the initial manoeuvre for position, the first clash, the wearing-out fights of varying duration, and the final decisive blow and subsequent pursuit, were essentially of the nineteenth century. For while they saw military decision as taking place only through the physical destruction of an army, the wars of the twentieth century had all shown that this wearing-out process was no longer a matter of generalship, but was dependent primarily on the organization of industry. If machine warfare was to restore the art of generalship, it could do so only through conferring a new power of cross-country movement, by which situations could be kept fluid and thereby subject to the direct influence of a dynamic mind. But World War II was set squarely and deeply in the mould of World War I, and there can be little doubt that most people recognized this and accepted it. From this point of view, the Polish government was justified in expecting to delay the Germans long enough to allow France and Britain to pull them off, and the British and French governments were justified in expecting sufficient time for intervention before Poland could be smashed. Germany, with 35 divisions against the Polish 30, did not possess the superiority of 3 or 4 to 1 in men and guns essential to success in the conventional offensive, and it was known that France could field more divisions, and

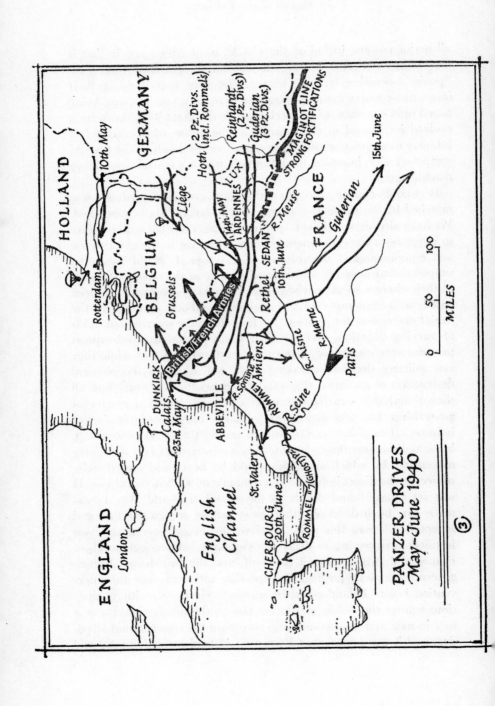

ENGLAND

London

English Channel

HOLLAND

Rotterdam

10th May

GERMANY

BELGIUM

Brussels

Liége

Hoth (2 Pz. Divs. incl. Rommel's)

14th May

ARDENNES

Reinhardt (2 Pz. Divs)

Guderian (3 Pz. Divs)

MAGINOT LINE STRONG FORTIFICATIONS

15th June

FRANCE

SEDAN

10th June

Rethel

R. Meuse

Guderian

DUNKIRK

Calais

23rd May

British/French Armies

ABBEVILLE

R. Somme

ROMMEL

Amiens

R. Seine

R. Aisne

R. Marne

Paris

St. Valery

20th June

ROMMEL ("GHOST")

CHERBOURG

PANZER DRIVES
May–June 1940

0   50   100
MILES

③

more tanks and artillery, than could Germany. Thus, even though the Polish front was enveloped by East Prussia and Czechoslovakia, the Polish government was justified in estimating that their armies could contain the German onslaught for six or seven weeks; their reserve forces were ready for mobilization, while France had promised intervention within fifteen days of mobilization, and British sea power would begin to make itself felt at once. These considerations must have appeared especially valid when the great political crises developed in the second half of 1939. With the arrival of September, the best campaigning weather was past. Another two months, and any normal offensive would slow and stabilize, first in the mud, then in frost. By Christmas, the German government would repent its aggressiveness.

But in 1939 the armies of Europe were not altogether "Back to '18"; they were actually in a curious state of unbalance, such as had not occurred since the barbarian invasions. Europe had often seen little armies defeat big ones, or competent ones smash incompetent ones; but big or little, competent or otherwise, they had all used similar organizational methods, and had fought according to common strategic concepts. Their differences were primarily tactical— line against column, for example—or in the quality of weapons and training. But in 1939, the common ground was partly broken, because in the armies of all the major powers there existed some form of mobile armoured and mechanized formation. The most highly developed of these were the German panzer divisions, of which there existed six, several of them still incompletely equipped, in 1939. They represented only a very minor part of the German army's 35 divisions, which were mostly infantry and which used horse transport. The status of the panzer forces was minor; their roles were ill-defined. But they had enormous potential, which lay not in simple firepower, but in the combination of firepower with surprise power, through superior forms of command and flexible organization. Thus, their potential effect could not be measured by their size alone; it was their relationship to the older type of forces that mattered. To an army consisting of infantry and mechanized cavalry, with artillery and tank support, they were as the Roman legion was to the Greek phalanx. The legion defeated the phalanx not because it was "stronger" but because it was better organized, in flexible groups, and so by moving its hitting power around in unexpected ways and concentrating it in unexpected places, it could create situations with which the phalanx could not cope. This led at once to the latter's disorganization, and thus to its destruction. Organized societies function according to learned patterns of behaviour. If the pattern is changed suddenly, the society is made suddenly ineffectual, for its responses are inapt. That is how the legion dealt with the phalanx, by making its responses inapt, and that is what the armoured divisions were potentially capable of doing to armies still moving at horse and foot speeds. The speed and range of operations of a homogeneous armoured force acting upon the range of its weapons enabled it to make its presence felt in several places, several miles apart, in one day; its moral effect was thus enlarged to an absolutely unprecedented degree—a degree which could precipitate not merely the immediate collapse of a field force, but also political and social crises of the severest kind.

Three panzer forces were incorporated with the forces leading the attack on Poland, and played a primary part in collapsing that country's effective military and political resistance in seventeen days. The Polish defence forces occupied their frontier zone, which formed a huge salient outflanked on the north by East Prussia, and on the south by German-occupied Czechoslovakia. They were neither smashed nor pulverized. They were by-passed. The German armoured divisions—a mere sixth part of the forces actually sent against Poland—entered Poland from north and south, instead of the west, which was the natural invasion path from Germany. It would have been impossible for "conventional" forces to do this on an adequate scale, first because it would have been impossible to supply them, as they would not have followed the main rail and road routes; and second, because they would have been checked and caught between the Polish frontier and the reserve armies, before they could have been deployed. This particularly applied to the south, where the German advance came through mountain passes. In the north, successive river crossings would have slowed them fatally. As it was, the panzer divisions succeeded in effecting indirect penetrations by these difficult routes within three days, and virtually decided the issue of the campaign within that time. Being entirely motorized, with an advanced system of forward-control radio communications and their own remarkable supply system, the panzer divisions were able to move far more quickly as organized combat units than the Polish forces sent to check them. They literally ran rings around the latter, and destroyed them before they could become organized. At the same time, the German air force concentrated on the destruction of Polish communications, especially military airfields. As a result of this combined operation, Poland was divided in two: the German frontier region, containing a large intact army facing the wrong way, and the rest of the country, which never became fully mobilized against the invader because the latter was several jumps ahead of all counter-moves. Eight days after the invasion began, the Polish frontier army was trapped between Germany and the German invasion; it tried to break out, and within ten days had destroyed itself, just as the Germans would have destroyed themselves had they attacked it frontally in 1918 fashion. This set the seal on Poland's defeat, for on September 17, two days before the break-out attempt finally collapsed, the Polish government sought refuge in Rumania, and Soviet forces invaded the eastern frontier: the campaign was thus really over inside seventeen days. The fact that Warsaw and other cities were defended by isolated Polish forces, causing minor siege operations to continue until October 4, was essentially irrelevant. Practically speaking, Poland was defeated in three days, having been fatally disrupted internally by the highly mobile offensive force.

The dramatic collapse of Polish resistance did not bring about a general revaluation of the Fuller-Liddell Hart theories of mobile warfare. In Germany itself there were many officers who saw more glory and professional advancement in bowing to the Nazis, attributing their armies' success to the moral impact of the Master Race or to the innate superiority of German war weapons. In Britain and France, evaluation of the brief campaign was generally based on the Germans' apparent ability to physically destroy an enemy on the field of battle, and was discussed in terms of 1918-type killing power. Thus, it was generally considered that the Germans had succeeded partly through brute strength, and partly through Polish inefficiency and lack of modern armaments. The futile charges of Polish cavalry against German tanks and field positions were cited as evidence of the latter, and it was widely believed that the German armour was "immensely powerful" and present in "overwhelming strength". This view was put forward very strongly by Winston Churchill. It was also argued that the attacks succeeded so rapidly because they were on the flank, against relatively unprepared defences.

On the whole, evaluation was not methodical, being based on preconception and dogma rather than the objective assessment of experience. In Britain and France, and in Germany too, the panzer divisions' unique ability to move about in unexpected ways, and the effect of this on an enemy command system, received little or no attention.

In consequence, the British General Staff still gave priority to the production of slow, heavily armoured infantry tanks, and made but little effort to complete their armoured division then being raised for service in France. The French General Staff made no efforts to re-combine their numerous armoured and mechanized divisions, elements of which were diffusely located and in some instances miscast as support units for infantry divisions. In Germany, much alarm was expressed concerning the flimsiness of the tanks then in service. The German tank which had been the prime agent in collapsing Poland was a little 5-ton training machine, based on a commercial Vickers design of the period 1928-30. It was not even proof against heavy machine-gun fire. Much war effort was accordingly spent in designing and producing prototypes for heavily armoured infantry support tanks in various size categories. In the U.S.A., the only fully mechanized force was the Experimental Armoured Brigade. It continued as an unwanted experiment ten years after the British Armoured Force, and nearly a year after the German invasion of Poland. Its commander and chief protagonist, Colonel Adna Chaffee, died shortly before it was raised to divisional status. Only in the U.S.S.R. was the significance of mobility better appreciated, and serious efforts made to re-establish large mobile armoured formations. But this was not easy, owing to the effects of the 1937 purges and the "infantry support" dogma which had conditioned tankmen's thinking in the immediate pre-war period. A radical change in national military policy could not be effected in a few months. The Red Army as a whole certainly did not grasp the psychological possibilities in what they termed "deep operations", which they had been trained to discount. Thus, we see that even the first full-scale demonstration of strategic paralysis in real hostilities against a prepared enemy was not enough to persuade orthodox soldiers of its value. Instead, the campaign was explained in purely physical terms that involved misrepresentation of the actual strengths of the armies concerned.

The Nazi government decided to prosecute an offensive against France before the winter of 1939 closed down, but the German General Staff could not countenance the idea, and urged instead that Germany should prepare for a defensive campaign. France could be reached only through the Low Countries, beyond the extremity of the Maginot Line defences, and the German General Staff believed that a repetition of the German advance of 1914 would again result in stalemate and attrition war, to Germany's disadvantage. They argued that were the Nazi government to insist on fighting such a campaign, the army would have to be re-organized, especially the armoured forces; although the latter had proved useful in mass against "backward" Poland, it would be necessary to allocate most of the armour to the direct support of infantry for a campaign against technologically advanced France and Britain. This train of thought shows quite clearly that the effects of strategic paralysis had not been evaluated at all by the greater part of the German General Staff.

It must have appeared to them that German armoured strength was not great enough to warrant putting all of it into one "gamble" against France. In 1940 the total monthly production of armoured fighting vehicles was only 83, and most of these vehicles were armoured cars, weapon and personnel carriers, armoured command vehicles, etc. Medium tanks were still relatively scarce, fully equipped tank battalions holding no more than 18 of them as against 54 light tanks. The German General Staff knew that their armoured forces were grossly outnumbered by those of the U.S.S.R., and by those of Britain and France combined. The shortage of motor fuel and armoured fighting vehicles must have reinforced their disregard of Guderian's "paralysis" theories.

Hitler, however, was insistent that Germany assume the offensive, and plans were made for a repetition of that of 1914. Had they been implemented, it is probable that World War II would have developed very differently, to the advantage of Britain and France. Most of the German generals accepted the situation, however they may have deplored it; an exception was General von Manstein, a great military theorist, whose reserved character, however, prevented him from gaining popular support for his ideas in open conference.

In December 1939 he had private discussions with Guderian on the time-and-space conditions governing the movements of homogeneous armoured forces; these discussions led him to advocate a surprise tank assault through the hills and forests of the Ardennes (Luxembourg), where ordinary troops could not easily be deployed, and where in consequence the Allied defences were weak. But this proposal was received with great hostility by the German General Staff. Strange as it may seem, the German generals who feared a repetition of the disasters of 1914 were even more afraid of what seemed to them a novel operation, in which unusual formations were to be moved at unusual speeds over unfamiliar terrain. They resolved their fears in classic psychology textbook style, by rejecting the man who proposed the novelty. Von Manstein was sent away to command a third-line infantry corps. Nevertheless, the German General Staff was obliged to study the Manstein plan seriously, first because their own "Schlieffen" plan became accidentally compromised, and second, because Hitler after a private interview with von Manstein accepted the latter's arguments.

In its original form, the Manstein plan required a feint attack through the Dutch and Belgian coastal plain, which would draw the Allied forces to confront it. The Allied commanders would feel quite safe in turning their forces away from Germany, because their flank and rear would be protected from north and south, first by the difficult country of the Ardennes, and thereafter by the Maginot Line chain of fortifications. It followed that if the real German thrust could travel through the Ardennes, it would enter France behind the right shoulder of the Allied armies facing the feint attack, and would thus be in a position to throw the enemy off-balance, and possibly trap him, crushing him from the rear against the forces attacking on the coastal plain.

Curiously, the German General Staff did not develop the psychological possibilities of this plan; for example, they did not envisage retiring their feint attack after the first clash, in order to draw the Allies on and so reinforce the effect of the projected Ardennes flank-rear attack. In fact, they seriously doubted whether the Ardennes route was feasible. This was understandable. At a conference with Hitler in March 1940, Guderian proposed to move an armoured corps past two frontier defence systems, a river, and 70 miles of difficult country in five days, and to be then in a position to advance rapidly westward. Having silenced the conference with this astounding proposal, he calmly announced, "The supreme leadership must decide whether my objective is to be Amiens or Paris. In my opinion, the correct course is to drive past Amiens to the English Channel." General Halder, who was Chief of the German General Staff, had already denounced Guderian's projected move as "senseless". Now, as Guderian openly declared himself before Hitler and the assembled generals, there came a buzz of doubt and derision. One of the army commanders, General Busch, could not contain his indignation. "I don't think you'll cross the river in the first place!"[1] he exclaimed. Hitler made no comment at all. And no instructions whatever were given as to the future movements of the attack once it had passed through the Ardennes! But it was not really surprising that the German General Staff did not anticipate the outcome of their own offensive, since they had not studied the manipulation of fast armoured forces.

When the feint towards Holland with its spectacular and wantonly destructive air support drew the British and French armies north-eastward to face it, and when the German reconnaissance revealed them moving ponderously on their way, the five panzer divisions concentrated to the south burst through the Ardennes, as Manstein and Guderian had said they would. And then Guderian set off for the channel ports, as he had said he would, spreading a storm of confusion, dismay, panic—in fact, paralysis—through the Allied armies as the panzers operated on their lines of communication, now here, now there, now, it seemed, everywhere, in a strength that imagination soon inflated to invincibility. But the German General Staff had not sent all ten panzer divisions through this

[1] See Heinz Guderian, *Panzer leader*, Ch. 5.

backdoor route. One was retained for the feint in Holland; two (Panzer Corps Hoppner) were sent head-on against the Allies in the area of Waterloo, south of Brussels; and two more (Panzer Corps Hoth) were sent against the southern shoulder of the Allied front. These had greater difficulty in effecting a frontal penetration, and might not have succeeded had not one of the divisional commanders, Erwin Rommel, proved a man of exceptional flexibility and resource. He led his corps through the southernmost positions of the French and British forces moving into Belgium, hurrying his troops, reversing and diverting them, keeping them moving all the time, and preventing them from settling down to a static exchange of missiles whenever they bumped solid opposition.

The consequences were disastrous for the Allies. Even while the British and French commanders were convening at all levels to draw up conclusions and judgments which could be formulated by the office staffs (with all necessary emendations) into a sensible plan of action, the thin-skinned, under-gunned little German tanks, working in concert with the specially trained mobile infantry and artillery, and supported by air force units, swiftly and adeptly stabbed their enemy's nervous system and soft vitals, and soon the case-hardened Allied fighting front fell backwards in confusion upon nothingness.

The campaign had opened on May 10, 1940. The panzer forces paralysed the French command in the first few days, and the end came five weeks later, on June 17. And the chances are that less time would have been required if all the panzer forces had been fed through the gap created by Guderian's and Reinhardt's panzer corps, to fan out on a pre-arranged paralysis tour from Sedan to Mezières. The shock to Britain and France of such multifarious disruption might have ended Germany's western campaign in a fortnight or less. As it was, the main British and French forces were encircled and virtually collapsed in seventeen days. Another thirty-one days, and the French armies of the south were similarly by-passed and encircled. On June 16, the French government began to negotiate for an armistice, which was agreed and signed on the 22nd. The campaign was over.

The German successes against Poland and France gave rise to the term "blitzkrieg", or "lightning war". It was an apt name, for blitzkrieg was forged in electricity and fire—radio communications and the internal combustion engine. In its efficient working, low cost, and high profitability, blitzkrieg amply vindicated the theories of Fuller, Liddell Hart, and Christie, all of whom had advocated the use of industrial technology to transcend the ancient limitations of battle. By midsummer 1940, the lesson was clear enough; but how was it interpreted?

Such were the times that calm assessment of military exercises was almost impossible. War hysteria on a massive scale has characterized our century, and the German successes of 1939 and 1940, so dramatically swift, seemed to intensify it, precipitating a world-wide spate of nationalistic fervour and aggression. Japan promptly invaded French possessions in the Far East; Britain and the U.S.A. swiftly responded with an oil embargo that threatened to wreck Japan's economy, whereupon Japan equally swiftly prepared for all-out expansion over the whole of South-East Asia. Italy invaded Greece and menaced Egypt, and the German government, apparently intoxicated by their armies' successes, prepared to invade the U.S.S.R., whose strength they well knew to be vastly greater than their own. The U.S.S.R. meanwhile fell upon the small Baltic states and annexed them.

One consequence of this world-wide outburst of violence was that interpretations of the panzer successes were markedly affected by national fears and propaganda requirements, in Germany as well as in other countries. In Germany, the propaganda service equated military success with the supposed superiority of the types of human to be found in Germany and with the invigorating effects of national socialism. From this point of view, Poland collapsed largely because the Poles were a decadent lot of Slavs—"unter-mensch"; and France collapsed because the people had become effete, and the government corrupt, owing to the machinations of international Jewry. That this was unadulterated rubbish is immaterial: from subsequent acts and utterances of the Nazi government, we may infer that Hitler, who appointed himself commander-in-chief of the German armed forces, to a considerable extent believed in his own propaganda. He certainly appreciated that the panzer divisions were the prime military agents responsible for the 1939 and 1940 successes, but it is by no means certain that he understood the way in which they gained their effects. On being told by Guderian that the casualties of four divisions after breaking through the Polish corridor amounted to only 850 dead, wounded, and missing, he was amazed, and tried to equate the figures with World War I casualties. His own regiment (equivalent to three battalions brigaded), he said, had suffered 2000 casualties in one day, disputing a few hundred yards on the Western front. How, therefore, did four panzer and motor divisions overrun hundreds of square miles, capturing thousands of prisoners, for fewer than 150 dead? But the important thing is that, having marvelled at the panzers' profitability, he made no attempt to investigate their profit-and-loss working in detail; this failure was destined to cause his own and Germany's downfall.

In evaluating the blitzkrieg successes, the Allied war leaders divided the credit between the German air force and the panzers, crediting both with tremendous massiveness, vast numbers, and colossal powers of destruction. The collapse of France and the rapid exit of the British force were thus attributed to an overwhelming shower of blows beyond their power to withstand. Winston Churchill spoke, and later wrote, of "cannon-proof panzers" and "heavy armour", and from 1940 to the present day, politicians, generals, and the writers of popular histories have perpetuated the myth that the German successes derived from "overwhelming superiority of heavy armour".

The following table is intended to place the matter in a more realistic perspective.

German and Allied Tank Strengths in the Field: May 1940.
1. Heavy Assault Tanks, approx. 60 tons
   Allied 10 (Char 2C bis)
   German none
2. Heavily Armoured Infantry Tanks, approx. 30 tons
   Allied approx. 320 (Char B1 and Matilda 2)
   German none
3. Heavily Armoured Infantry Tanks, approx. 11 tons
   Allied 54 (Matilda 1)
   German none

4. Fast Medium Tanks, approx. 17 tons
     Allied 856 (Somua 35, Renault D1 & D2 [200] Vickers
       A9/10, Nuffield Christie)
     German 666 (Panzers 3 and 4)
5. Light Medium Tanks, approx. 11 tons
     Allied 2510 (Renault 35, Hotchkiss 35, FCM,
       Hotchkiss 39)
     German 1399 (Panzer 2, Czech TNHP)
6. Light Tanks, approx. 6 tons, armed with MG only
     Allied 277 (Vickers Light, Renault AMR 35)
     German 619 (Panzer 1)

It can be seen that Germany held superior strength in only the lightest and least formidable class, the one least useful for making assaults on well defended positions.

The tank gun calibres then in use were 93.5mm (short-barrelled mortar); 75mm (short-barrelled howitzer); 47mm (dual-purpose shot or shell cannon); 40mm (armour-piercing cannon); 37mm (dual-purpose cannon); and 20mm (dual-purpose cannon). The Germans were heavily outnumbered in gun barrels, because the Panzer 1 was armed only with a machine-gun, while their most numerous tank, the Panzer 2, carried a gun of only 20mm calibre. Of their remaining tanks, the Czech TNHP and the Panzer 3 carried a 37mm cannon, and the Panzer 4 a 75mm howitzer. The Allies had 277 tanks armed only with a machine-gun; all the rest carried a gun of 40mm calibre or larger. The Char B1 carried two guns, a 75mm howitzer and a 47mm cannon.

All the Allied tanks except the A9 and A13 Cruisers wore armour thicker than their opposite class in the panzer forces. The British Matildas 1 and 2 and the French Char B were virtually impenetrable to all German tank cannon, while the maximum thickness of the German plating (30 mm on the frontal plates) was penetrable by every Allied armour-piercing cannon.

The only real advantages enjoyed by the German panzer troops were a relatively high cruising speed of about 15 to 20 mph on roads, long-range reliability, and superior radio communications, and these obtained against only some of the Allied machines. But it is obvious that these are not advantages which pay great dividends in pitched battles, for no tank can out-run or dodge the shot fired at it. The important conclusion to be drawn from the above comparisons is that the Germans were quite unable to mount "massive armoured blows" against the bodies of two modern European armies arrayed against them, because the panzers were materially unfitted, insufficiently numerous, and their replacements were being built far too slowly (the total production of all classes of armour in 1940, for example, being only 1664) to give them any success in conventional battles of attrition.

But it would appear that the Allied war leaders did not perceive this. In their view, the German successes derived from German air and tank power as a spectacular combination of overwhelming strength, acting upon French national decay, and the "unprepared" and "ill-armed" condition of the Allied armies. That is to say, they saw the paralysis of the Allied forces as deriving from a bodily sickness and weakness—not as what it really was, the result of an attack upon the nervous system. Had we been strong enough, they argued (forgetting that the Allied forces in France were in fact stronger), the collapse could not have taken place. And so they set to work to raise armoured formations, and to develop ground-attack aircraft, on the German pattern.

In 1940 there were only two British Armoured Divisions, intended to function in cavalry roles; soon there were a dozen intended to play key parts in future campaigns. In 1939, the heavy, slow infantry tank had production priority over the fast medium tank, 55% to 45%. After Dunkirk, the General Staff changed the proportion to 78% for mediums, 22% for slow infantry tanks.

At the same time, increasing attention was paid to development of ground-attack aircraft, both British and American fighters and light bombers being adapted to this role. The German dive bomber was not copied, the Russian technique of mounting cannon in aircraft being adopted instead. Rockets were developed as a means of destroying tanks and strong-points from the air, and low-level bombing was cultivated, with both high-explosive and oil-fire bombs.

By the end of 1941, the British and U.S. armies were very well equipped with the type of armoured formations used by Guderian in 1939 and 1940, and had ample close air support. In North Africa, the R.A.F. eventually won air supremacy over the Luftwaffe during 1941 (thanks largely to the Royal Navy's stranglehold on the German-Italian supply lines across the Mediterranean), and was then able to develop ground-attack techniques to a level the Germans never reached.

But with all this, the psychology of blitzkrieg was scarcely studied at all, and all the newly raised armoured mobility and air power was trained and directed to operate against the enemy's body on the battlefield, and to consider his rout and collapse only as the outcome of his defeat there. Until the very end of the war, the idea persisted that mobile forces were intended to "exploit" situations which had been brought about by other means. First fight your battle—then exploit the result. This was true not only of the Allies, but also of the supreme German command. Guderian remarked, apropos preparations for the invasion of Russia, "Despite the very plain lessons of the Western campaign (1940), the Supreme German Command did not hold uniform views about the employment of armoured forces. This became evident during the various war games that were held in preparation for the operation and for the purpose of training the commanders for their missions. The generals who came from arms of the Service other than the panzer troops were inclined to the opinion that the initial assault should be made by infantry divisions after heavy artillery preparations and that the tanks should only be sent in to complete the break-through after a penetration to a specified depth had been made."[2]

Guderian and the panzer generals "wanted the panzer divisions to be in the forefront... they expected the armour would thus achieve a deep and rapid break-through..."[3] In turn, everything depended on the object of the attack. Guderian made it plain that he did not expect tanks to lead assaults on strongly fortified areas: "Tanks could only have captured a citadel by means of a surprise attack..."

A similar absence of uniform views about armour obtained in Britain. Lieutenant-General Martel, one of the earliest protagonists of tanks, became commander of the Royal Armoured Corps in 1940. He later recalled that on asking for a charter defining the

[2] See Heinz Guderian, *Panzer leader,* Ch. 6.
[3] Op. cit.

Corps' duties, he was told, "Do you mind if you don't have one, because we've tried to write it, but found it very difficult to do so?"[4] Controversy over the use of tanks lasted a long time, and eventually led to Martel's displacement, the post of "Commander R.A.C." being later abolished and replaced by "Adviser R.A.C.", one peg lower in rank. However, through the intrigue and confusion there emerged a theory, if such it could be called, that "armoured divisions should be reserved for use when conditions are favourable"; "if a commander can succeed in destroying the greater part of the enemy armoured divisions while retaining his own fit for action, he will be able to operate freely and boldly ..." and "the value of superiority in divisional strength is therefore very great ... the clash between the armoured divisions of the two sides seems a likely prelude to many operations."[5] Aphorisms which no doubt allow a general to take credit for every successful fluke, and give him cover from all hostile criticism. The actual techniques evolved by German, British, American, and Soviet armoured formations differed little, except in the Germans' forward offensive use of anti-tank guns. The essential differences lay in purpose and speed of reaction —in the sphere of command, rather than execution.

It is obvious that even the most oblique strategic moves entail a physical clash between armed forces, and that to be successful, this must be carried out energetically and efficiently by troops who are confident and aggressive, and who see the war as a local, personalized affair. It does not follow that the higher aim of a campaign should be merely an aggregation of platoon-size objectives. Yet that is most certainly how World War II developed after 1941. There was an increasing and hardening tendency to "frontalism", and to a view of success as the outcome of successful piecemeal physical destruction of the enemy. This was accompanied, on both sides, by increasing devotion to the fetish of holding ground; success or failure was directly associated with moving forwards, or backwards, over disputed ground, regardless of its military usefulness. No general ever dreamed of moving backwards deliberately—probably he would not have been permitted to do so by his government, which would have considered any military gain from such a move

---

[4] See G. le Q. Martel, *Our Armoured Forces.*
[5] Op. cit.

to be outweighed by propaganda losses. This was particularly true of the German and Soviet governments. And to this tendency was closely related the propaganda importance of killing. In the popular view, the sole purpose of military operations was to kill enemy personnel. Success was measured by the enemy's casualty list, and as the popular object of military operations was the physical annihilation of the enemy, so the natural direction towards it was the straightest and shortest.

Consideration of these reactions to Guderian's first demonstration of the paralysis technique in armoured warfare has taken us too far ahead. Strategic paralysis was used again, in 1941, first by Rommel against the British in the North African desert, and then by Guderian and other panzer leaders against the U.S.S.R.

The desert campaign was regarded somewhat as a sideshow by Hitler and his entourage; but it was of the first significance to Britain and Italy, and was recognized by Rommel as being, in addition, potentially the key to successful operations against the U.S.S.R.

Although Rommel's demonstration of panzer technique commenced in May 1941, the desert campaign had opened several months earlier. In the autumn of 1940, a large Italian army consisting mostly of unmotorized infantry was amassed upon the frontier between Cyrenaica and Egypt. In December, the British Army of the Nile under the overall command of General Wavell, and commanded in the field by General O'Connor, attacked and defeated the Italians in four set-piece engagements at Sidi Barrani (including the Nibeiwa camps), Fort Capuzzo, Bardia, and Tobruk, and in an ambush and encirclement at Beda Fomm which the more mobile part of O'Connor's force carried out after making a daring desert drive to outdistance the road-bound retreating Italians.

At all these battles except the last two, the deciding factor was the local invincibility of the Mark 2 (Matilda) infantry tanks. Matilda was quite impenetrable to nearly all Italian artillery, and the Italian infantry appeared unable to improvize means of stopping her. At Sidi Barrani and at Beda Fomm, the psychological element of surprise was of very great importance in deciding the issue rapidly; at Tobruk the absence of heavy tanks was compensated by a sudden sandstorm; and at all times the British force's considerable numerical superiority in light and light-medium tanks, and in motor transport, allowed it to seal off the Italian positions from their sources of supply while attacks were mounted against them. The configuration of the desert at Beda Fomm trapped the Italians at the British road-blocks. They had to assume the offensive, but were unable to break out. The survivors surrendered when water and ammunition were exhausted.

Italian tanks were not only poor in quality, they were also in short supply. There were only 200 of them, and many of these were actually light weapon carriers (CV/3/35) and light tanks (L/6/40). They were opposed by 230 British cruisers, 160 light tanks (the Vickers Mark VI Light), and 45 Matildas. It is interesting to note that most British tank losses in this campaign were due to mechanical failure. By the halfway mark (Tobruk), 29 Matildas (Vulcan foundries), 120 Cruisers (Vickers and Nuffield), and 110 Lights (Vickers) had fallen by the wayside. There were few battle casualties. The machines were all less than ten years old and had never seen battle before. Their performance is worth comparing with that of the German equivalents, which campaigned first in Poland in 1939, then in France in 1940, and finally in Russia or in the desert in 1941. And without breakdown! When panzers became out of date, their chassis were modified as self-propelled gun carriages.

The campaign lasted two months, almost to a day. On February 8, 1941, the way to Tripoli appeared open, for after its five defeats the Italian army seemed to have no fight left in it.

This British triumph appeared to the German government as a threat to German-Italian security meriting prompt intervention, and the Italian government was persuaded to accept a German mechanized force to supplement the efforts of the Italian troops, most of whom were unmechanized infantry. Elements of the 15th Panzer Division, the 21st Light Division, and other units were sent to Tripoli. Their task: to restore the eastern frontier of Italian North Africa to its recent position *vis-à-vis* Egypt. Their commander: Erwin Rommel.

In the spring of 1940, Rommel had driven through France in command of the 7th "Ghost" Panzer Division on the right flank of Hoth's corps, which in turn was on the right flank of the whole armoured push; his enterprise and success showed that apart from Guderian himself, he was the most dynamic of all the panzer leaders.

He was very efficient and, in the early days of the break-through, very ruthless. To increase enemy confusion he drove his tanks through French villages by night, firing left and right into the houses without regard for the helpless civilians inside. To help navigate his division in circumstances of difficulty on May 17, he ordered a captured French colonel to mount a German tank, and when the Frenchman properly refused to aid his enemy in this way, Rommel had him shot in cold blood on the spot. He excused this casual killing by describing his victim as "glowing with hate and fury . . . a thoroughly fanatical type".

Rommel was a light infantryman, like Fuller, Liddell Hart, and Guderian. He was a late convert to the concept of strategic paralysis, but a whole-hearted one, finding it well suited to his own dynamic approach to tactics. In 1939 he commanded Hitler's personal bodyguard, and his boyish enthusiasm for military operations must have appealed to Hitler's own sense of the romantic, for when Rommel begged for the command of a panzer division, Hitler granted the wish at once, possibly seeing himself as a latter-day Nordic chieftain, great sword-bestower and ring-giver, arming a fiery bare-sark. Rommel's earlier writings are very jingoistic and infused with a sense of glory, showing him exhilarated by the proximity of shells and bullets, while burned farms, destroyed crops, and wrecked railways were just part of a great adventure. As for Hitler, "The Fuhrer's visit was wonderful" (he wrote to his wife in June 1940).[6] "His whole face was radiant . . . and I was the only Divisional Commander selected to accompany him." However, Rommel matured and grew in compassion as the war progressed. Perhaps the new concept of war based on psychological forces which he had adopted opened his mind to a new evaluation of poor struggling humanity.

This appraisal of Field Marshal Rommel is important to help us understand the pattern of the desert fighting. Rommel was a dynamic tank leader who subscribed to the theories of Fuller, Liddell Hart, and Guderian (as he acknowledged in his writings). He ran a "sideshow" which he firmly believed should assume major

[6] See B. Liddell Hart (Editor), *The Rommel Papers,* p. 43.

proportions, with a view to indirect operations against the Soviet Union and to securing unlimited oil fuel.

Rommel flew to Tripoli, hastened the disembarkation of his tiny mobile force—60 Panzers 1 and 2, 60 Panzers 3 and 4—and set to work. He decided to take the offensive while his stores were still unloading, calculating that the British would not expect him to fight until he had everything "in position". So on March 31, he began a "reconnaissance in force". For nineteen days the panzer leader rode forward in a captured British armoured vehicle, or flew over his projected line of advance in a light aircraft, taking photographs and making notes to ensure the correctness of his decisions. For nineteen days the tankmen and motorized infantry, and their escorting aircraft, moved and fought swiftly to his on-the-spot instructions, and by April 18, the British were back in Egypt. As in the French campaign of 1940, relatively few were killed, but many were captured, among them the whole staff of the British force—two full generals and a host of smaller fry.

By directing their main efforts to beating their enemy's body, the Army of the Nile had required two months, 230 Cruiser tanks, 160

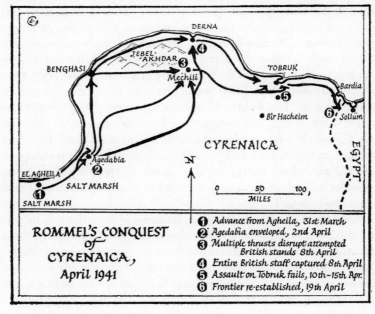

ROMMEL'S CONQUEST
of
CYRENAICA,
April 1941

① Advance from Agheila, 31st March
② Agedabia enveloped, 2nd April
③ Multiple thrusts disrupt attempted
     British stands 8th April
④ Entire British staff captured 8th April
⑤ Assault on Tobruk fails, 10th-15th Apr.
⑥ Frontier re-established, 19th April

Light tanks, and a regiment of Matildas with 3-inch armour to advance 350 miles against an enemy badly led and possessing poor equipment. Had that enemy possessed more powerful anti-tank artillery, it is very probable that several months more would have been needed to see the job completed; it might even have proved impossible. The blood-letting, in fact, would have favoured the bigger infantry battalions, those of the Italians.

By using the principle of strategic paralysis, and with only one under-strength panzer regiment, a reconnaissance regiment, and some anti-tank and motorized infantry units, Rommel collapsed a first-class enemy superior in numbers, equal in quality of equipment, and enjoying an efficient supply organization and a vast fleet of motor vehicles (which the Germans did not), in only nineteen days.

It has been argued that the British soldiers encountered by Rommel (not all of them original members of the Army of the Nile) were raw to the desert, while their commander, General Neame, was quite unused to the conditions prevailing there. But neither Rommel or his troops had ever seen a desert before, and went into action without any preparatory training in "desert fighting". Yet it was General Neame who was surprised—hunted and captured by a troop of German motorcyclists; and at the very moment of his capture he had the veteran desert general O'Connor with him to advise him. They were the nerve centre of their army and they went in the bag together. Rommel believed it more important to demoralize and, if possible, to capture a general than to kill a few private soldiers.

It has also been said that the British army in the western desert in the spring of 1941 was numerically weak, owing to new dispositions in the Middle East ordered by the commander-in-chief. This argument has less force than is commonly supposed. Field Marshal Wavell had made his dispositions only after completing a comparative analysis of British and German-Italian armoured strength—on the basis of conventional war. He was perfectly justified in his belief that Rommel dared not attack until he had amassed the necessary 3-to-1 superiority in tanks, guns, and aircraft to allow for normal wastage in the attack. Unfortunately for Britain, Rommel was not contemplating a conventional killing-war attack; he proposed

using not the "armoured might" of his panzers, but their speed and
mobility, in order to get at the enemy commander's mind and
paralyse it. And, of course, he succeeded. Had he attempted a solid
frontal assault on the British positions, he would probably have failed,
as he was to fail against the prepared defences of Tobruk in 1941 and
those of Alamein in 1942. As he said himself, the panzers split open
far too easily under concentrated British anti-tank gunfire.

This lightning conquest of April 1941 was the high-tide mark of
the German overflow into North Africa. This does not mean that
we have forgotten either the famous "Rommel's raid" of the winter
of 1941, which after the battle on Sidi Rezegh airfield penetrated
eastward as far as the Egyptian frontier and, it is said, precipitated
a panic of document-burning among the more timid of the distant
Cairo staffs; or the outcome of the Cauldron tank battles of the
summer of 1942, when the British retreated as far as El Alamein.
This, the last panzer advance culminating in the battle of Alam
Halfa, is popularly represented as Rommel's farthest fling. But the
nineteen-day panzer drive from Agedabia to Halfaya in April 1941
was the most unqualified success that Rommel gained in Africa
through strategic paralysis. From that month on, the war in the
desert began to assume the characteristics of what Rommel called
"position war", with results gained by attrition.

After his panzers reached Halfaya, Rommel relieved them with
an army of Italian infantry. He had no difficulty in finding this
garrison; Italy has never experienced under-population. He also
tried the taste of position war by ordering a German assault upon
the besieged Australian garrison in Tobruk, and found his fast but
thin-skinned panzers all too ready to brew when subjected to a
concentrated anti-tank fire in the confines of a pitched battle.
Likewise, his motorized infantry, familiar only with paralysis work,
suffered disillusionment when asked the price in blood of the yard-
by-yard acquisition of a plot of land. Though he did not know it,
this first abortive attack on one little fortified harbour was a very
real foretaste of the war fate in store for Germany. More than 1000
Germans fell or were captured at this onset, and the figure is worth
comparing with the total number of casualties suffered by Rommel's
"Ghost" Division during the whole six weeks of its campaign in
France—2624, of whom only 682 were actually killed.

But in 1941 position war was not yet an overriding compulsion, and Rommel was able to call most of his Germans out of the mill at Tobruk, and set the inexhaustible hordes of Italian soldiery in concentric rings around the besieged Australians to do the man-costly work. For his Germans, he preferred the petrol-costly detour around the Australian positions, which bestrode the solitary metalled road. In 1942, Rommel's grim verdict on the Tobruk peri-meter was that it was literally soaked in the blood of infantrymen—Italian mostly.

The successes of the panzers in France, followed by Rommel's spectacular drive across the North African desert, no doubt en-couraged Hitler to mount an all-out attack against the U.S.S.R., a power for which he held a pathological and un-statesmanlike hatred. But Hitler's failure to understand the workings of mobile armoured forces acted upon his distrust of the upper levels of the German army's officer corps, causing him to form entirely erroneous notions of what in fact these panzer forces could and could not do.

It might have been expected that Hitler would have taken Guderian further into his confidence, and sought his advice in properly equipping the panzer forces for the contemplated invasion of the U.S.S.R. This could have made the panzers an even surer means of realizing expansionist policies. But Hitler did nothing of the kind. Secretive and distrustful, he made no provision for expert, objective evaluation of panzer requirements for the coming offen-sive. On the contrary, on being warned by Guderian that the existing panzer strength was inadequate for the great task, he simply ordered the number of panzer divisions to be doubled; and as there were insufficient tanks and cross-country vehicles to accom-plish this, he arbitrarily halved the number of tanks in each division, and ordered the vehicle strengths to be made up with captured lorries and the incoming personnel to be drawn from the infantry. As the tanks constituted the main element in a panzer division, and as the French and British lorries were not cross-country vehicles, and, most importantly, as the incoming personnel could not be retrained overnight to think at "motor speed" instead of "infantry speed", this expansion was effected at the expense of the panzer divisions' most important characteristic—high-speed flexibility.

This consideration carried no weight with Hitler or his close advisers. Instead of seeing manoeuvre as a means of obviating battle, they saw it only as the prelude to battle.

For Hitler and most conventional generals, battle was an end in itself. For Guderian it was a means, to be used sparingly. Here it is worth remarking that some of the most spectacular panzer drives resulted from off-the-cuff and somewhat insubordinate decisions, by Guderian, Hoth, Rommel, von Mellenthen, and other panzer leaders. For example, the rapid collapse of Poland was due largely to decisions by von Rundstedt, Manstein, and Guderian to drive away from, instead of towards, the main Polish armies. Also, in 1940, the panzer leaders entered France well ahead of the main infantry forces, and bolted deep into the enemy territory without waiting to achieve the "consolidation" and deliberate advance which the majority of German generals thought essential. And it is noteworthy that the rapid panzer drive across the rear of the Anglo-French armies caused almost as much consternation in the German Supreme Command as it did in Paris and London. Guderian maintained that the collapse of France could have been greatly accelerated had not four orders to halt being given by the Supreme Command between May 15th and 24th.

The German invasion of the U.S.S.R. in July 1941 was essentially a speculative affair based on an aura of past but unanalysed success, and was very much lacking in essential supplies, clearly envisaged aims, and general understanding of technique.

In the first place, the German armies were considerably inferior to the Russian ones quantitatively in tanks, artillery, and, most obviously, in manpower. The German army held 3200 tanks and self-propelled guns, all of pre-1936 design and most of them light medium. The Red Army fielded 4000 large, 8000 medium, and 12,000 light machines.[7] Of the large machines 1475 were the new Klimenti Voroshilov and T34 designs, far superior in hitting power and protection to the best German tanks. The Russians later alleged, after losing many of their tanks to the Germans, that the panzers all enjoyed qualitative superiority, but this was certainly not so. The panzer divisions enjoyed superiority only in organiza-

[7] Stalin to Harry Hopkins (U.S. President's personal representative, July 1941).

tion, communications, and initiative, the latter reflecting a training that stressed flexibility and forward control. Most of the Russian tanks were captured after running out of ammunition and fuel, subsequent to their formation's being outmanoeuvred and cut off from supplies.

The Germans had insufficient cross-country supply vehicles and thus were over-dependent on the Russian railways and roads, a factor which told seriously against them as their penetration deepened, when the weather deteriorated and guerilla activities commenced.

The German air force barely held parity with the Soviet one, and later became overmatched. And there was absolutely no provision for a continuation of the campaign under Russian winter conditions. There were not even any winter-weight uniforms for the troops, many of whom began their first winter in Russia in cotton clothes, augmented only by what they could loot. Lack of tow ropes when the autumn rains set in caused forward supply difficulties, and an unexpected but serious trouble was a lack of salve to smear over optical gunsights, which consequently tended to mist over as soon as the gunner put his face near them. In the depths of winter, the German and captured French tanks and transport frequently could not start up, because the petrol would not vaporize. The Russians did not experience this difficulty because since the late thirties they had adopted diesel engines for military transport. Considering these material disadvantages in relation to the vast spaces and industrial resources of the U.S.S.R., one is forced to the conclusion that Hitler had fully intended to overthrow the Soviet government in the same way as the Polish and French ones, in a campaign of a few weeks, but had quite failed to make a proper study of his proposed methods. The method he actually employed precluded the possibility of a rapid complete success, for his objectives were mutually contradictory. He prosecuted major offensives, not feints, in three directions simultaneously.

And these divergent efforts were each given multifarious aims to be accomplished simultaneously: to collapse military resistance by paralysis; to encircle enemy armies and defeat them in siege actions; and to capture territory economically important to Germany, such as the Baltic regions with their industries and timber, the Ukraine

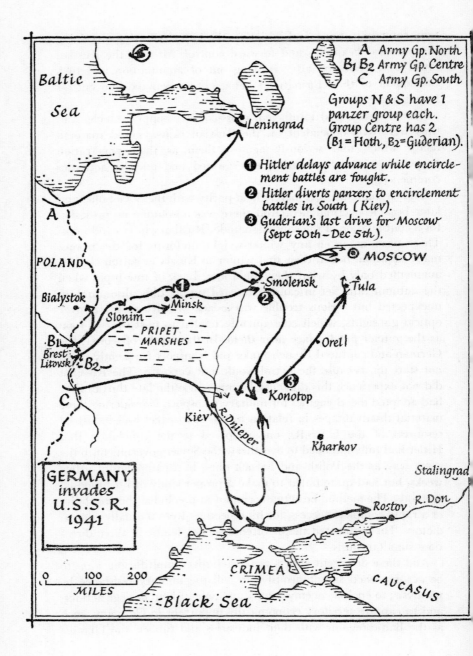

Baltic Sea

Leningrad

A Army Gp. North
B₁ B₂ Army Gp. Centre
C Army Gp. South

Groups N & S have 1
panzer group each.
Group Centre has 2
(B₁ = Hoth, B₂= Guderian).

① Hitler delays advance while encirclement battles are fought.
② Hitler diverts panzers to encirclement
battles in South (Kiev).
③ Guderian's last drive for Moscow
(Sept 30th – Dec 5th).

POLAND

MOSCOW

Bialystok

Smolensk

Tula

Slonim

Minsk

PRIPET
MARSHES

Orel

B₁

Brest
Litovsk

B₂

Konotop

C

Kiev

R. Dnieper

Kharkov

Stalingrad

GERMANY
invades
U.S.S.R.
1941

Rostov   R. Don

0   100   200
MILES

CRIMEA

CAUCASUS

Black Sea

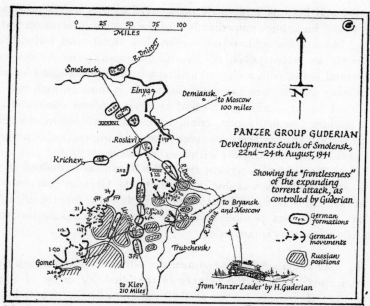

PANZER GROUP GUDERIAN
Developments South of Smolensk,
22nd–24th August, 1941

Showing the "frontlessness"
of the expanding
torrent attack, as
controlled by Guderian.

German formations
German movements
Russian positions

from 'Panzer Leader' by H. Guderian

with its grain, and the Caucasus with its oil. At the same time,
Hitler withheld the 1941 output of tanks from the German forces
allotted to this stupendous task, reserving them for unspecified
future campaigns. The panzer divisions certainly enjoyed some
remarkable successes, in view of their reduced strength and the
odds against them, but these were primarily tactical; and in the
business of seizing territory and fighting siege actions against encircled Russian armies, they eventually found themselves much
depleted through the recurring need to fight pitched battles on an
increasingly large scale. For a time their growing weakness was not
fatal, since it was counter-balanced by Russian confusion—it is
instructive to study German operational maps of the period, which
show amazing mixtures of units and, at the height of the blitzkrieg
rush, no "fronts" at all. But the Germans' sole advantage was in
tactical manoeuvre, and this was lost when first the autumnal rains,
and then the winter snows set in, and the two sides really got to
grips on well defined fronts.

Having lost his advantage in mobility, Hitler did nothing to
recover it. Because he regarded manoeuvre only as the prelude to

battle, and because large-scale manoeuvre was no longer possible, he swung his armies immediately into the routine of attrition warfare, bidding his soldiers die where they stood, and forbidding generals to retreat even one yard. Guderian retreated several thousand yards, with a view to finding advantageous ground for his defensive line; he was promptly sacked. It is most curious that a national leader, and one who had assumed supreme command of his country's armed forces, could have held such emotional and unrealistic attitudes, veering so widely between impractical extremes of mobile and static warfare within so brief a time.

Thus the campaign against the U.S.S.R. was not resolved in a few weeks, and this was due primarily to the German government and General Staff's inability to see how mobile war functioned, and what in fact was possible and what was not possible, given the mobile forces they commanded.

In 1942 and 1943 Hitler resumed the offensive, but although the initial moves were in the manner of the blitzkrieg drives of 1939 and 1940, their successes, for all their apparent size, were only local in relation to the size of the enemy, and were quickly followed by canalization of direction, heavy attrition fighting, and stalemate, which at Stalingrad in 1942 and Kursk in 1943 proved disastrously costly to Germany. Subsequently, the main use of panzer mobility was defensive. Outmatched in men and machines by the Red Army, the German armies, which still relied heavily on rail and horse transport, would have been seriously cracked whenever the Russians switched the direction of their relentless pressure, but for the fully motorized panzer divisions. The latter were called upon to stem the gaps which appeared, using their superior mobility to weigh in with a counter to flank or rear and delaying the Soviet advance until the breach could be filled.

During the later years of the war this became their principal and final role: mobile stops and counters to enemy offensives.

Chapter Six

A Process of Attrition

Time, it is said, is money, productivity being measured against time units. Time is also a matter of life and death. And as life is also wholly dependent on productivity, and as machine war at its most costly can waste productivity more quickly than industry can produce, we should be able to measure the efficiency of machine age armies largely by the time they require to attain their objectives.

Curiously, the time required to complete the subjection of Germany by American, British, and Russian forces between 1941 and 1945 was approximately five times that required by Guderian, Rommel, and company to promote Germany's territorial expansion between 1939 and 1941. The panzers completed the collapse of Poland in twenty-two days; France in thirty-eight (with the rest of mainland Europe collapsing like a pack of cards in sequence from the shock wave); and the rich western areas of the U.S.S.R., including the Ukraine and the Kharkov district, in ninety-five days between July 22 and October 24, 1941. Rommel effected the reconquest of Italy's western desert coastline from Tripoli to the Egyptian frontier in nineteen days. Total campaigning time—174 days in three years, and on only one front at a time.

There are good grounds for believing that the turn of the tide came really at the end of 1941, with the mere possibility of a second tide in 1942. The winter of 1941 saw the onset of attrition war, and stalemate setting into German disadvantage. The fighting then became much more continuous, and there was no question of a campaign being decided in one summer season. This process of attrition, on first two and later three fronts, and with a non-stop day and night air bombardment to boot, continued day and night, week in, week out, the four seasons round, until May 1945: more than a thousand days of it, eight times as many as were required to steal the territory in the first place by the panzer technique. What is more, the speed of reconquest was not markedly accelerated by the superiority over the German war industries gained by the Allied industries.

In 1942 the population of Germany was approximately 70 million. That of the U.S.S.R. alone was approximately 195 million. By 1942 the German air force, despite accelerated production, had but moderate offensive power relative to Allied air power, and by 1945 it had almost ceased to exist, except for nocturnal bomber interception. In contrast, the air forces of Britain and the U.S.A. had gone from strength to strength in all specializations: night and day bombing at all ranges, ground attack, and home defence. The failure of the German Luftwaffe released many thousands of Allied fighter aircraft from defensive duties, and they were then used offensively in ground-attack roles.

The armoured odds against Germany became equally spectacular. Between 1934 and 1945, Germany was able to produce no more than 42,478 tanks and armoured assault guns, whereas the Allies were able to build at least 231,240 tanks alone, plus many assault guns, giving them a superiority of more than 5 to 1.

Germany's output of armoured vehicles increased steadily until 1944 (despite ceaseless American and British air bombardment), but still fell farther and farther behind Allied production. Total German production of tanks between 1943 and 1945 was 14,324, of which 6872, or 40.2%, were of pre-1937 design. The remaining 7452 up-to-date models should be compared with 12,000 British, 49,000 American, and 60,000 Soviet machines built to successful wartime designs. Thus, the overall adverse odds of 5.4 to 1 give a false picture on the conservative side, for as in 1940 they were 1.5 to 1, towards 1944 and 1945 they must have been somewhere in the region of 8 to 1. It should be clearly understood that all the major German blitzkrieg offensives were undertaken without superiority in armoured strength. The significance of this is plain when we appreciate that for a conventional limited offensive, a superiority of 3 or 4 to 1 is considered essential.

It is sometimes alleged that the German tanks designed and built on the basis of war experience were so superior to Allied machines as to outweigh any quantitative inferiority. A study of the comparative specification table will reveal that this was not so. In fact, they were actually outclassed in several important considerations, especially by the Russian tanks. The big German tanks were notable chiefly for their powerful cannon, but the effect of these was diminished at the tactical level by the intervention of Allied ground-attack aircraft, and by reduced vehicular mobility owing to mechanical unreliability; while at the strategic level, the difficulty of transporting bulky, indivisible 56- and 67-ton units by rail and road proved a tremendous complication. And when they attacked, they were as vulnerable as the Allied tanks to concealed anti-tank guns. The all-round armour protection of the Tiger 1 was no better than that worn by the British Churchill, which was never considered impenetrable. When first used against the Red Army at Leningrad in 1942, and against the British in Tunisia in 1943, the Tiger was stopped at once by standard anti-tank cannon (in the latter case, of only 57mm calibre) which easily penetrated both hull and turret in the flank, "normal" impact being readily obtained against its vertical plating. We should remember that while the British and American tankmen complained frequently of the inferiority of their equipment, their German counterparts were making similar complaints, especially in Russia, and with very good cause.

From this we may deduce that it is the way in which a tank is used that determines its degree of invincibility and its longevity—which amount almost to the same thing. We may also conclude that the legend of the German tanks' qualitative superiority was created during the years of German expansion, when the operational techniques of the Expanding Torrent preserved them from the disasters of attrition fighting.

The legend was perpetuated by the head-on battering practised by the Allied commanders. The shattering losses and constant checks experienced by the Allied tank forces in their frontal assaults, which invariably discovered the enemy by the crude expedient of killing the leading crews on his anti-tank screen, so contrasted with the successful long-distance, high-speed running of the early panzer divisions, that there built up a general feeling of qualitative inferiority among Allied tankmen. How else could it have been? The average life of a tank in attrition warfare is only 500 miles. And that does not mean 500 miles of advance into enemy territory.

Just a few days of motoring here and there, and then destruction.

We are now in a better position to work out some sort of profit-and-loss account for the campaigns fought on a basis of attrition, and can look around for some battles on which to begin. The desert fighting provides a suitable choice. The campaigns fought there were of the greatest importance to Britain, and the commander of the German armoured forces employed there recognized that their outcome could likewise be vital to Germany. But the German Supreme Command appeared to regard the desert war as a sideshow, useful for propaganda purposes but from a grand strategic point of view concerned only with the Italian African empire and the convenient tying-up of British forces. Viewed upon the world stage, perhaps the desert fighting was not the most important. Far greater forces were engaged in Russia, Europe, and the Far East. But the desert saw the highest development of mobile war—the peak of refinement in high-speed co-operation between air and mechanized land forces. It also contrasted more clearly than any other campaign the startling differences in cost and profit between "position" and "paralysis" attitudes to warfare, for the commander of the German forces, Field Marshal Erwin Rommel, subscribed to the paralysis theory but had little material with which to implement it. He therefore switched from one type of war to the other as circumstances dictated, and attempted to fight "battles of material attrition",[1] as he called them, against adverse odds. The desert was a great proving ground of military theory. For this reason, and because the desert was so important to Britain, I have dealt with it here in relatively greater detail than the Russian campaign, the conquest of Italy, and the reconquest of Europe.

Because of their machine power, the Germans were identified as the major enemy in North Africa, despite their numerical inferiority to the Italians, and during 1941 two attempts were made to destroy their power through tank warfare. Both were inconclusive in their immediate outcome, but between them they succeeded in depriving Rommel of the power to exploit strategic paralysis, and so in the long term pinned his forces down until they could be finally

[1] See B. Liddell Hart (Editor), *The Rommel Papers*, p. 197.

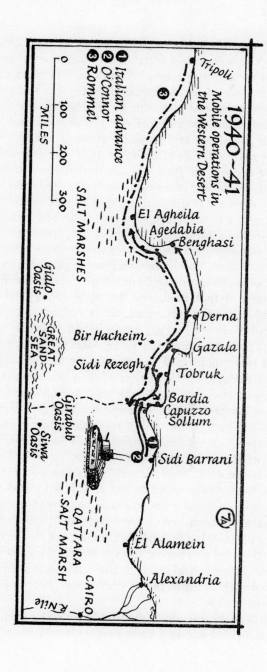

1940~41
Mobile operations in
the Western Desert

① Italian advance
② O'Connor
③ Rommel

MILES
0
100
200
300

Tripoli
El Agheila
Agedabia
Benghasi
Derna
Bir Hacheim
Gazala
Sidi Rezegh
Tobruk
Bardia
Capuzzo
Sollum
Gialo
Oasis
SALT MARSHES
GREAT SAND SEA
Girabub
Oasis
Siwa
Oasis
Sidi Barrani
El Alamein
Alexandria
QATTARA SALT MARSH
CAIRO
R. Nile

defeated by overwhelming front-line forces in 1942 and 1943. Of course, the German mobile forces were not pinned down in static positions in the ordinary sense. We must hold in mind the peculiar geographic nature of the desert campaigning ground, and think of it as a highway between desirable goals. The panzers could run to and fro along some 800 miles of this highway, yet still be pinned down so far as gaining any profitable strategic end was concerned.

The first major British offensive of 1941 was Operation Battle-axe, which opened on June 15, and lasted three days. Its first purpose was to destroy the enemy in battle. This was rather un-realistic, as the estimated British superiority was as low as 3 to 2 in tanks, and 2 to 1 in men. Actually, tank superiority was 4 to 1, but Field Marshal Wavell was not aware of this, Rommel's springtime victory having prompted him to over-estimate the German strength. Battleaxe was based on the mistaken assumption that this victory was a sort of accident arising from the off-balance condition of the British armies at that time, and the equally mistaken conclusion that orthodox position war with parity obtaining between com-batants could succeed in 1941 when it had failed in 1914, 1915, 1916, 1917, 1918, 1939, and 1940. The Battleaxe assault forces were arrayed in two groups made up of infantry led by Matilda tanks, each group working in the manner of Cambrai against important objectives near the coast road, with their left or desert flanks pro-tected by a fast tank force. After the infantry had captured their objectives, the fast tanks, with motorized infantry and artillery, were to make "an exploiting drive" to Tobruk. Here we see a perversion of Plan 1919 and the Expanding Torrent. The paralysis drive has become an "exploitation" of a situation that has been created earlier by some other means. And it is to be directed from the rear, thus precluding any rapid implementation of change of plan. That a strategic deep penetration could have obviated the need for a primary battle, and that the fact of the primary battle would destroy the surprise of the subsequent long-distance move-ment, were not seen. And worse, it was not seen that in view of the relative material strengths of the combatants, the set-piece frontal assault could not succeed.

For the Matilda infantry tanks, Battleaxe was a tragic massacre. They were divided into two main striking forces, one of which was to attack the important positions held by the Germans and Italians on the coast road at Halfaya, and the other to attack Fort Capuzzo, which constituted the back door to the Sollum-Halfaya group of positions.

The Matildas were sent to attack the key positions at Halfaya in broad daylight, after the defences had been thoroughly alerted by a brief and purposeless artillery bombardment. They advanced slowly, like the dismounted French chivalry of Poitiers, not on ill-armed Italians but on resolute German anti-tank gunners in concealed emplacements. In those days, British infantry tanks could fire no shells; their cannon fired only solid shot for duelling with other tanks, and they were helpless as the ambushing gunners at Halfaya raked them from every angle. Eight of Rommel's twelve eighty-eights were sited there; they sent their massive shot through hull and turret fronts. The smaller fifties let the Matildas pass slowly across their muzzles before planting their shot home in the flank; or they waited until the slow machines reared up to clamber over stony obstacles, then sent their four pounds of tungsten steel crashing through the thinner belly plates. At first in ones and twos, then in great numbers, Matildas rocked to a standstill on their front suspensions while smoke and flame belched from cupola, hatch, and visor, and the scorched survivors clawed their way out of the inferno to seek comparative safety in the lee of their stricken hulls, which staggered on their bogies in the throes of their sudden brew. The distant eighty-eights they could not range; the flanking dug-in fifties they could not strike with their solid shot; the enemy infantry they were advancing to attack, they never saw; and so the main attack on Halfaya died with them in a holocaust of oil fires and exploding ammunition.

The Matildas and infantry attacking Fort Capuzzo were more successful: the Matildas penetrated Italian positions without suffering excessive losses. This was because Rommel had sited all his infantry support anti-tank guns at Halfaya. But the success at Fort Capuzzo could not become an overall one, unless the whole of the British reserve strength were fed into it to turn all the German and Italian positions inside out. And this was not possible, partly because the British control system was too sluggish, and partly because garbled ideas about tank-fleet fighting had got the British fast tanks on the flank disastrously entangled in the German mobile anti-tank net, where they soon lost nearly half their strength. So at the end of the first day's battle, the situation was that the main British attack on the right had failed; the fast tanks guarding the left had failed, through attacking on "speculation"; and the centre had succeeded. But the Germans had lost scarcely any tanks, and consequently Wavell's initial superiority in material strength was now entirely dissipated. It was Rommel who now held the stronger army. And now he used its power of forward mobility. He divided his tank force in two, and sent one part to counter-attack the British centre and the other to menace the British rear. The counter-attack proved to cost more than Rommel was prepared to pay, so he plucked this force swiftly out of the clinch and sent it to join the force menacing the British rear. Threatening to cut the British supply system, they set about the now outnumbered British fast tanks which constituted its protective screen. The situation became confused and Wavell ordered a general withdrawal.

The British had lost the more heavily in tanks—91 against 12 panzers. Actually, the Germans had between 30 to 50 knocked out in battle, but being left in possession of the field were able to salvage all but 12. It was a model lesson in the relationship of mobility to force and mass, and technically it was a victory for Rommel. But such was the disparity between the two sides' rates of reinforcement that the Germans, for all practical purposes, had suffered a severe check.

The failure of Battleaxe cost Wavell his post as Commander-in-Chief Middle East, and he was succeeded by Sir Claude Auchinleck, who deferred a renewal of the offensive until he was satisfied that his forces held adequate material superiority over the enemy. By November 1941 he had amassed a considerable armada of tanks, guns, and vehicles, and all things needful for their supply. There were 1236 tanks held on strength in Egypt, and 96 more were in shipment. Auchinleck deployed 756 of them for immediate battle, and held 480 in reserve, ready to be sent forward at the rate of 40 a day.

Against these the Germans and Italians could muster only 414— 170 Panzers 3 and 4, 90 Panzers 1 and 2, and 154 assorted Italian tanks—and they had no large reserve from which 40 replacements could be sent each day.

The air was neutral. Neither side held overwhelming superiority, with the result that while the rival commanders experienced difficulty in determining each other's courses, their troops enjoyed some freedom from air interference. Under these circumstances, forward control would pay handsomely, and rearward control would be handicapped.

Auchinleck recognized that the key to success in gaining his objectives must lie in the manipulation of fast, long-range armoured formations. He therefore divided his total force into two main corps, one predominantly infantry on foot, with infantry tanks, artillery, etc., in support, and one predominantly fast tanks with motorized infantry, artillery, etc., co-operating with them. The "slow" corps was to grip the enemy positions on the frontier, while the fast one, consisting of three independent columns in line abreast, circled around them on the desert flank on a line of march leading to an area south of Tobruk, about 80 miles away, where they were to join the besieged garrison of that port in completely severing the Germans and Italians from their main bases to the west. Of course, such a threat could be met by Rommel only with his armoured divisions, because these were his only considerable mobile forces. On November 18, Auchinleck launched his armada towards the enemy under the operational code name Crusader. The primary objective was apparently quite straightforward, being the trapping and destruction of the enemy in battle. The secondary one was the occupation of the North African coast up to Tripoli.

Thus, Auchinleck's plan was to force the German tank forces into a mêlée which would finish them off, after which the British would be free to surround the German-Italian infantry positions and either attack them, starve them, or force them to fight another Beda Fomm.

Across the cool winter desert the three brigade-strength mobile columns advanced, wheeling around the fixed infantry positions where the Matildas and Valentines waited to play a now secondary role, and headed north-west towards Tobruk—and towards a tomb. A landmark on a gravel plain partly surrounded by escarpments, the white tomb of the saintly Rezegh gleamed in the winter sun, marking upon an ancient camel route a rendezvous for tanks and aircraft—the desert landing ground and fighting place of Sidi

Rezegh. The three columns rumbled towards their battle ground, the embodiment of modern war industry, yet absolutely medieval in their panoply. Ahead, the armoured cars skirmishing across the plain, lightly armoured fast gallopers, nimble and alert. Then the main force of tanks, pitching and nodding in chivalric progression, each one flying its proud tail of sand and fluttering its gonfalons from lance-like wireless aerials. The orange blurs that were the faces of armoured men gleamed half-seen from behind open visors, while some commanders, lounging with deceptive knightly relaxation upon the turret top, savoured the new security of a raid-proof umbrella of fighter planes. For like any armoured medieval army, this one was free from air attack. Behind the warriors, long columns of servant lorries laboured their loads across the sand, lines of humped shapes and dust clouds stretching across the visible world, horizon to horizon.

The massed motor force of Britain is all round; the generals are in their caravans, far to the rear. The tomb is still turret down ahead, below the horizon which seems in this clear air of early morning so infinitely far away, in time as well as space. What lies in store there, tankman? Who can tell? Enjoy your winter sunshine in the security of your air umbrella, conform your movements to the squadron navigator, listen to the steady roar of your engine, and the squeal and clatter of your track suspension; check over your latest orders in your mind and on your map, and marvel at the strangeness of this desert war.

Battleaxe had lasted only three days; Crusader was destined to go on for thirty-eight, a veritable whirlwind of land-fleet fighting, like a tropical cyclone which rages around a clearly defined zone, devastating some places in it more than once.

The first phase opened with the march of the three brigade-strength columns out of Egypt, and ended on the airfield at Sidi Rezegh six days later, when the British were reduced to 70 tanks in consequence of their generals' inability to co-ordinate the efforts of their forces. During this phase the initiative passed almost at once to Rommel, whose use of the technique of forward control and the sword-and-shield tactic saved his tanks from destructive embroilment with the unarticulated British forces and allowed them to destroy stray detachments of the latter, which were all too numer-

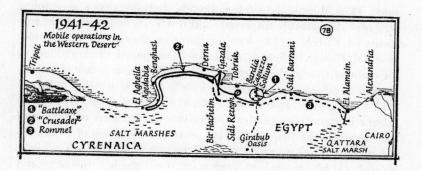

ous, by engaging them with overwhelming strength and a mobile anti-tank screen. Such was Rommel's moral ascendancy that he was free to send first one half of his tank force, and then the other, away to the coastal area to collect supplies and enjoy a brief rest! On the evening of the 23rd, the British had not only failed to defeat their enemy in not-so-simple battle, but had forfeited all chance of doing so at the existing balance of forces. Rommel accordingly ordered his anti-tank guns and other unarmoured mobile units to grip the British forces frontally on the airfield, while his massed panzers moved secretly around them to attack them from the rear, destroying their supply echelons and headquarters. It was his intention, when this move was accomplished and the British fast tank forces were neutralized, to make a paralysis drive towards Egypt.

The battle's second phase began at 11 a.m. on the 24th, when Rommel launched his drive. It was a very shaky effort, owing to the Germans' shortage of air power (especially air reconnaissance), tank reinforcement, and motor fuel. In the first place, after two accidental and unnecessary fights with the 3rd Royal Tank Regiment and the 5th South African Brigade, the panzers were depleted to the tune of 70 tanks, and delayed in starting. Secondly, these unnecessary fights had prevented the panzers from completing their move against the rear of the British mobile forces. Rommel did not know this; anxious to start his paralysis drive, he had set off leading part of his force, with orders to the remainder to follow at once. Thus, the paralysis force, already short of tanks and supplies, was now dangerously dispersed, and unknown to Rommel, detachments of British tanks were reorganizing themselves to his rear, near Sidi Rezegh airfield. The inevitable happened. Owing to lack of air reconnaissance, the Germans failed to locate any British supply dumps, although passing within a mile and a half of them. A British tank force which came to life again at Sidi Rezegh moved out and caught Rommel's supply train, depriving the panzers of the petrol they urgently needed. Finally, the scattered condition of Rommel's command caused its radio network to break, and he lost positive control of his troops' movements. After passing through and paralysing the Headquarters of 30th Corps, 7th Armoured Division, 1st South African Brigade, 7th Supply Group, and 7th Armoured Brigade, and stampeding thousands of British lorries, cars, and motorcycles, the strategic thrust came to a halt on the Egyptian frontier, a mile or two away from 8th Army Headquarters. The British 8th Army Commander wished to order a general retreat, which would have had the effect of allowing Rommel to pull his forces together again and press on; he was forbidden to do so by the British Commander-in-Chief, Sir Claude Auchinleck. So the British armoured body was not completely paralysed, for Rommel's thrust had not reached deep enough. Nor was it battered to death in spite of its suicidal behaviour. The issue of the battle was still wide open, and Auchinleck rose to the occasion. Personally intervening in the conduct of the action, he issued a "fight to the last tank" order, and began an infantry push along the coast.

It was the German command that was paralysed now. To obtain petrol, the panzers had to detour northward. Rommel's radio network having broken down, the panzer leader was roaming the area in his armoured command vehicle, trying to keep his disintegrating force under control and losing the struggle hour by hour. He had lost touch with his headquarters, his tank strength was reduced to 40, and the officer left in charge of the Panzer Group Headquarters ordered a German retreat on his own initiative. For once a British commander-in-chief had assumed "forward control" in a moving fight, and success had followed immediately.

The third phase now began, and considering the disparity between the British and German armoured forces—the German tank strength soon sank to 40, while that of the British soared to 200—it was extraordinarily protracted; it lasted a whole month, and was clear evidence of the superiority of the defence in machine warfare where the latter possessed sufficient mobility to bring its effective firepower to bear at critical positions, particularly when the generals directing the offensive allowed their forces to engage the enemy defences in "penny packets", as the troops put it at the time.

But Rommel's mobile force was almost destroyed by internal weakness. It had received no tank reinforcement since the battle opened, thanks to the efforts of the Royal Navy and the R.A.F. On December 8, Rommel started to withdraw it westward, playing sword-and-shield all the way, and he had it safe behind the salt marshes and anti-tank guns at El Agheila by the 26th. This cleared the area for a general British outflanking move round the non-motorized German-Italian coastal garrison. Some of the weaker ones were assaulted by tank-and-infantry combinations, others were deprived of water and food until they surrendered. It was a triumph for attrition warfare; but at what a cost! The wreckage of hundreds of vehicles and the bodies of thousands of men were strewn across the desert between Agheila and Tobruk, both armies were exhausted and motionless, and no final decision had been achieved. Moreover, after all this tremendous exertion, after the butchering of thousands of men and the wholesale destruction of millions and millions of pounds worth of military stores, Rommel came back in less than a month to give another demonstration of strategic paralysis.

Early in January a small convoy of Italian ships arrived in Tripoli, bringing, as well as food, petrol, and ammunition, 55 replacement tanks. These, added to the number repaired by the German fitters, gave Rommel the enormous strength of 111 assorted tanks between his two panzer "divisions". On January 21, 1942, he launched them at the British rear areas. The sword-and-shield held off the British tanks, which again were committed, and were destroyed piecemeal. Within four days, the panzers were 100 miles forward, were behind the British front, travelling under tight control within the retreating British forces and simultaneously menacing a bewildering variety of alternative objectives.

Auchinleck again ordered "no retreat", but this time to no avail. The subordinate British commanders were unable to match their speed of control to Rommel's, and so were unable to unite their forces to cut off the Germans. The traffic continued to flow eastward faster and faster, and did not stop until the Tobruk area was reached again. Then both sides settled down, temporarily unable to move. The British built a line of fieldworks and minefields southward from the coast, and both sides began to lay in stocks of men, vehicles, ammunition, and fuel, in readiness for the next round.

As the summer of 1942 approached, the opposing armies reached their final states of preparation. The large Italian and British infantry masses, approximately equal in number, faced each other astride the coast road at the tiny harbour of Gazala. From this main area, their dispositions extended southward as a line of minefields and a chain of fortified encampments, the Italian line for 20 miles, and the British for 40 to the Roman site of Bir Hacheim, where a fortress or "box" was constructed and garrisoned by French troops.

The British army possessed about 900 tanks, 620 of these being deployed for action and 280 held in reserve. The Germans had 330 tanks, of which the most formidable were the Panzer 4 Model F2, with long-barrelled 75mm cannon, and the Panzer 3J Special with long-barrelled 50mm cannon. There were only 4 of the former at Gazala, and 19 of the latter, and as ammunition for the long-barrelled 75mm had not arrived with the Panzer 4F2's, these were unable to participate in the battle anyway. Seventy-eight per cent of Rommel's Panzer 3's were Model H, with short-barrelled 50mm cannon. The Italians had 240 tanks, all of them out of date and seriously outclassed.

Field Marshal Auchinleck was well aware of Rommel's supply difficulties, especially in the matter of petrol, and anticipated a conventional infantry attack by Italian forces near the coast. His subordinate commander in the field, General Ritchie, shared this view, but recognizing the possibility that Rommel might nevertheless make the outflanking move around Bir Hacheim, he divided up his tank force and disposed the parts in a way which he thought would meet all contingencies. The Matildas and Valentines were locked up in the infantry boxes, and the Crusaders, Honeys, and the new American Grant medium tanks were dispersed in smallish groups, as self-propelled knobkerries to be banged on any heads which might appear from any direction, whether poked around the corner from Bir Hacheim or thrust through the minefields and boxes. Apart from the fact that the best anti-tank weapon is not a tank, but a mobile and easily concealed anti-tank gun, we may reflect upon Ritchie's dispersal of the fast tanks from a time-and-space angle. As the front was only 40 miles long, they could have been concentrated in one force, capable of motoring in two hours to any part of the line from a point some 35 miles behind its centre. The dispersal would have been justified had some form of supreme forward control existed for drawing the threads together. But the British formations were rear-commanded. Dispersal merely condemned them to belated and unco-ordinated moves.

Rommel mounted his attack in three closely timed aspects, the first diversionary, and the other two following it closely and simultaneously elsewhere, one as a mobile battle of attrition, and the other as a paralysis strike. The diversion was to be made by infantry forces near Gazala under the command of General Cruewell, who normally commanded the highly mobile Afrika Korps. Rommel detailed one German and one Italian tank regiment to support attacks on the British outposts while other armoured forces marched in their support, permitting British aircraft to observe them. Rommel anticipated that this move would draw the British command network taut, and set the British armour facing what they imagined to be the threatened break-through area.

After darkness fell, all the German and Italian armoured formations were to turn away from the feint attack and assemble in column of march, then drive southward to the limit of the Gazala Line. Rounding Bir Hacheim, they were to turn north again and drive up behind the British line in a compact mass—the Trieste Armoured, Ariete Armoured, 21st Panzer and 15th Panzer in line abreast—catching the dispersed British armoured formations one by one, and overwhelming them instantly with complete local superiority and the sword-and-shield tactic.

The armoured formations were accompanied in this turning

movement by a force of unarmoured combat teams, designated
90th Light Division, cobbled together from various German units
and equipped largely with captured British transport. After rounding the Bir Hacheim positions, this unarmoured force was to travel
north-east, its course diverging from the panzers' route, towards the
British rear areas. There it was to operate against selected command and supply objectives, and seal off the main fighting area.
The resulting confusion, Rommel anticipated, would guarantee him
three vital factors: first, that his panzers would find the British tank
units in a dispersed and bewildered condition; second, that the
paralysis of the British command would allow his troops to refit and
refuel in British cachement areas; and finally, that the combined
effect of these successes would allow him to enter quickly the
Tobruk defences, which of course were not then manned, thus
securing that important port to his army.

This was his programme for the first three days of battle
manoeuvre. And after that? Possibly Cairo, the Nile, and the Suez
Canal. It would depend upon the fuel situation; on May 26, when
he launched his attack, Rommel could not plan ahead for more
than three days without taking undue risks, because he had exactly
three days' supply of petrol for the whole of his army.

After their moonlight drive around the French "box" at Bir
Hacheim, the German and Italian mobile forces saw the sun stride
up into the sky from the direction of Cairo to light their enemy's
territory, all open and inviting, spread before them. The 90th Light
plunged headlong north-eastward to the British command and supply
areas, guided personally by Rommel. The 15th and 21st Panzer
Divisions, some 200 assorted tanks motoring together in a compact
mass with their transport columns streaming out astern of them,
drove on a similar compass bearing but between the 90th Light and
the Gazala Line. The Italian armoured formations made little progress: the Trieste had strayed into minefields during the night, and
the Ariete could not keep up with the panzers.

The panzers did not have long to wait before they bumped the
first British tank positions. The sun was still low, casting vast
shadows westward across the plain and making the sunward side of
the tanks gleam despite their camouflage, when they overran a
British hussar regiment in leaguer and annihilated it. And then they

met another British tank regiment at Bir Harmat—but this one was not in leaguer. It was deployed ready for action, and moreover it was equipped with a formidable new tank the Germans had not met before. At Bir Harmat lay the Third Royal Tanks, a regiment, we recall, which had dealt the panzers a particularly unwelcome blow in Crusader. Since then they had been blessed, through the bargaining of Britain and America, with a new American tank, a big medium of 28 tons known as the "General Grant". It was a roomy tank, an odd-looking machine with an ungraceful octagonal hull boxed up above a simple robust chassis; its glacis and driving compartment were pushed high by a bulky front drive and differential, and its main cannon, a long-barrelled seventy-five throwing a hefty 14-pound missile, was in a barbette set in the frontal plate to the right hand of the driver, where it was limited to but a few degrees traverse left and right of the tank's centre line. So far, the Grant resembled rather a self-propelled gun than a tank; but above its high boxy hull there was a turret, offset to the left of the centre line, and in it a 37mm cannon, which threw high velocity 2-pound shot or shell at a deadly 2600 feet per second. The Grant's armour, 76mm on the frontal plate, was much stouter than that on the Panzers 3 and 4, and the engine, transmission, and tracks were all tried and proved by more than five years of service in the American army; the complete reliability of their type had already been demonstrated by the little American "Honey" light medium in 1941. It was a very good general-purpose machine, robust enough to withstand more knocks than most of its German opponents, and having the unique advantage of being able to deal two severe blows simultaneously.

It was breakfast time in the leaguer of the Third Royal Tanks when the news came crackling over the wireless net to make each man forget his food. The regiment was alone, entirely alone, with not a friend to share the weight of the coming blow, in the path of a German panzer division advancing up into the British rear areas. There is an old Saxon saying: "Bare is his back who has no brother." The Third Royal Tanks had brothers—somewhere. Also in their brigade were 5th Royal Tank Regiment and 8th Hussars, besides a battery of artillery and other troops. But where were they? The organization was so loose and chaotic that no one knew.

Two squadrons of Grants and a third of Honeys scramble to action stations in the rumbling path of 100 assorted panzers—36 tanks facing up to 100. Heavy odds. The rest of the 4th Armoured Brigade are somewhere near, but where? In the absence of an over-all positive plan, in the absence of forward control by a tank leader, each regiment is fighting on its own. Breakfast fires kicked out with sand; mugs of tea half gulped, half thrown away; the shambling run of the man who has just emptied his bowel and is still pulling up his trousers as he heads for his tank. Up on the high hulls of the Grants, hatches and visors clanging, engines roaring into life, gun barrels elevating and traversing, headphones adjusted, binoculars wiped tenderly clean and map-cases sorted out everywhere, a last bite on a corned beef sandwich and a last delicate adjustment to the radio's vernier tuner. On net, A set . . . On net, B set . . . Regiment to Squadrons . . . Squadron to Troops . . . Troop leader to Tanks. The last fight of the Revenge and the Spartans at Thermopylae all tumbled together, then spread on the Libyan sand with cannon and petrol engine. One commander, one driver, two gunners, two leaders (one of these the radio operator) in each Grant, and the oil, ammunition, petrol, and everything else checked while the tank engine suddenly roars louder: "Driver, Advance." The clutch comes in, and everyone braces himself as she begins to pitch and lurch her way forward. Forward . . . Command over the radio . . . Colonel to Squadron Leaders . . . Squadron Leaders to Troop Leaders . . . Advance . . . line abreast . . . select a fighting place in the lee of the next low ridge ahead . . . Tank Commanders to Gun-ners . . . Load AP. The engine roars steadily; the sand plumes stream back from the top runs of the track. The humming of the radio, and the quiet scrape of a round of armour-piercing shot drawn out of its bin. Ahead the desert is alive with tanks, blackened by columns of motor vehicles—a head-on meeting with a whole panzer division.

The opposed tanks drove right on, until the range between gun muzzles was about half a mile, and then they stopped moving. For a minute or two, the only sound to be heard was the deep throbbing of tank engines; then suddenly a Panzer 2 fired its cannon, and the battle commenced. Perhaps the panzers had expected to overrun the British regiment in leaguer. Perhaps they had expected to meet

Honeys or Crusaders. They had never seen Grants before; they did not even know of their existence, and the first they learned of them was when each Grant roared into life with not one cannon but two, the bigger one a seventy-five hurling 14 pounds of solid shot.

It was an epic fight. The two panzer divisions were in close formations, the tank columns massed in the lead, their attendant lorry columns blackening the desert for miles to the south-west behind them. The Grants snugged down as close as possible to the partial shelter of their low ridge, although even the kindest of hollows and shot-proof crests could never shield them from much, because with their main cannon mounted in the hull-front, they were obliged to remain hull-up from cover in order to shoot—exposed from the chassis upwards to every passing missile.

And how the shot flew—what an incredible volume there was of it. The small stuff from the 40 little Panzer 2's whizzed and cracked amongst the heavier missiles from the massed ranks of Panzer 3's, while the shells from the 4's, marshalled as these were towards the rear, droned over the heads of intervening contestants to fall bursting among the Grants, sending stones and splinters sizzling between the bogies, chipping and cracking at wheels and suspension units, seeking out the lives of baled-out crews of stricken tanks who might be sheltering there.

Each Grant wore 76mm of frontal armour—proof, one might imagine, against most tank gun strikes of mid-1942. The German shot, 20, 37, and 50mm, cracked and clanged upon them everywhere, but it did not penetrate them easily. For a long time, for minutes that stretched into hours, the line of Grants held back the weight of the German advance. But so great was the volume of shot that struck them, weakening and wearing them down, that at last they began to go. Here, a shell plunged down an open turret hatch to send tank and crew up like a ball of fire. There, a turret ring jammed, or a seventy-five was struck and wedged immovable in its embrasure. Trunnion beds on turret faces were sheared away, visors stove in, periscopes blinded, hull flanks penetrated; and every Grant bursting into flames or stricken silent with a dead crew inside it meant an increase in the volume of fire poured on the survivors.

Yet the line of them stood fast, each tank still in the gun duel rocking back on its rear suspension every other minute to the

trunnion pull, first of its seventy-five, and then of its turret gun;
the crash of the big gun echoed by the lighter note of the 2-pounder
meant always that two more shots were hurtling on a flat trajectory
towards the panzers, where more and more smoke columns were
climbing skywards from the massed division.

Soon British reinforcements, tanks and guns, came motoring
across the desert, summoned by radio but soon steering by the air-
concussion of gunfire and the sight of distant oily smoke columns.
As they reached the battlefield they were committed piecemeal to
the fight; there was no manoeuvre at anything above regimental
level. The fighting machines just drove in and began to shoot,
like armoured warriors in a medieval mêlée, each one banging on
the enemy's plating with no thought for any purpose beyond the
immediate orgy of destruction. There was no overall plan. The
British Headquarters—Army, Corps, Divisional—were too upset
that morning; they had been paralysed by the deep thrust of
Rommel's unarmoured motorized troops of the 90th Light.

The fury of the battle swelled and spread hour by hour as the
panzers strove to force a way forward to the coast road, regardless
of the fact that every hour increased their opponent's strength and
decreased their own. The German tankmen were as blindly bull-
like as the British. It was not an organized battle; it was a tank
fight.

Rommel exclaimed bitterly afterwards that his tankmen should
never have allowed themselves to be drawn into this sort of mutually
destructive combat, which could favour only the materially richer
British; they should have let the anti-tank guns come up to clear
the way defensively. But ordinary soldiers see no more than the
ground before them, and in this case the German tankmen lacked
the guidance to manoeuvre as a division, because their divisional
commander, General Cruewell, had been shot down in his light aircraft and captured.

The fighting went on all the long summer day, until the sun went
down and the survivors went into leaguer by moonlight. The British
losses were serious enough, for the Germans had eventually brought
up their anti-tank guns, setting the eighty-eights to pick off the
Grants at maximum range. But the German situation, proportionate
to strength, resource, and supply line, was even more serious; they

had lost one-third of their tank strength in this stand-up tank fight, and more serious still, they had lost the original secrecy and surprise of their purpose. Most serious of all, they had come at last light disastrously to a stand, marooned with no hope of relief on the wrong side of the Gazala Line. Thanks to the Grants at Bir Harmat, Rommel's plans were completely checked.

Both panzer divisions had become embroiled. They succeeded in advancing a mere 15 miles from the first contact with 4th Armoured Brigade, to a point 8 miles south-west of Acroma and 18 miles from the coast road and Tobruk. The British system of fortifications was intact; and although the British tank forces were somewhat thinned, their losses would soon be made good. It seemed as though the very last demonstration of strategic paralysis had been made, and that the stage was now clear again for the triumph of position war. But strategic paralysis was due to win one more success—a slow-motion, payment-deferred, bizarre sort of consequence to the 90th Light's fast movements in the early hours of that May morning.

The 90th Light had captured 7th Armoured Division Head-quarters, and had caused the mobile 30th Corps Headquarters to flee for its life. While the battered panzers clustered on what to them was the lee shore of the Gazala Line, desperately short of water, petrol, and ammunition, General Ritchie, lacking accurate reports on the fighting, could think of nothing but threats to his own headquarters and rear areas; leaving the real German force in unlooked-for peace, he sent his subordinate tank leaders scouring far into the desert in search of more deep-thrusting German paralysis strikes. The British tank crews had suffered much when their command had sent them in penny packets against the panzers, but still they had battered them to a standstill. Yet now, although they knew it was possible to finish off the job, because the line was intact and the French garrison at the southern end of it (the box at Bir Hacheim) was busy severing the thin German "Cape Horn" supply line, they saw their war change, distort, and dissolve, as if they were held helpless in an evil dream. For while they cruised the desert upon nervous errands, the Afrika Korps, helpless and at a stand, was left free to practise its own private, desperate version of attrition war upon the backside of the Gazala Line. And with success! First a "box" in the centre of the line, manned by

Northumbrians, was hit from the rear and broken open, making a
path through the Gazala Line by which the Afrika Korps could be
watered, refuelled, and fed. Then the same method was applied to
the Frenchmen at Bir Hacheim, with a view to freeing the southern
supply route. As a Northumbrian infantryman said to me, "Why
aye man, it was like this. They brought us to Gazala, and they put
us in a bloody box. Then Rommel came along and put the bloody
lid on it. And that was all we ever knew about it, man."

That the boxes were shut up so quickly, or broken open, depending on your point of view, may indeed seem odd. Tobruk had withstood its siege in 1941 and Rommel was very chary of committing
his tanks and men to a stand-up fight against prepared defences.
Indeed, General Ritchie expected his Gazala boxes to stand up to
all the kicking and hammering the Germans could give them; but
unhappily, he had made no provision for the maintenance of their
supplies under siege conditions. *The Rommel Papers* make it plain
that the German assault teams could at first make no progress
against the close-woven Northumbrian defences; they stormed
their way into them only when the defenders had fired off all
their ammunition, and, equally important, consumed all their
water.

General Ritchie's failure to relieve the Northumbrians' boxes was
only further evidence of the paralysis of his mind by Rommel's
personal direction of the 90th Light on the first morning of the
battle, when so many headquarters were overrun before any conventional fighting had taken place. It all agrees with Ritchie's
general condition of unease, his mixture of confidence and fear. He
knew that every material advantage was his: aircraft, tanks, motor
transport, fuel, well equipped infantry. Yet he was afraid to move.
Strategic paralysis had struck his system of command, and the
numbing effect of it lamed all British actions throughout the
remainder of that unhappy battle.

After the breaking of the boxes, the Gazala Line splintered to
pieces. First, the British command trembled into life again, rallied
their tankmen, and set them all, whether in cruiser or infantry
tanks, to attack the Germans, still closely grouped in the hole in the
line. But the Germans were no longer besieged; the opportunity for

attacking them when their water and ammunition were nearly gone no longer existed. Now, they had all the weapons, petrol, and water needful for repelling head-on attack. And so there followed the last and most tragic of all those tank-fleet battles, the Cauldron and Bir Lefa.

The gravel plain on which the Germans were still concentrated at the gap in the line was called the "Cauldron", and it was the British command's intention to encircle it and "boil it dry". But the movements were so clumsily timed that Rommel countered them with ease, and shot them to pieces. Many a British tankman died in the Cauldron. After the battle petered out, an uneasy quiet pervaded the British positions for six days, until the French at Bir Hacheim were forced to give up their fight through shortage of water and ammunition. After the Germans had secured their supply route through Bir Hacheim, they commenced a new move eastward. The British command belatedly ordered their destruction at Bir Lefa, a few miles east of the Cauldron, but failed to take cognisance of the fact that the Germans had secured the ridges flanking the line of their advance. The British armoured forces therefore attacked through a defile—in other words, entered a trap—and after maintaining a piecemeal tank expenditure for three days, were again destroyed. Except that the climate and terrain were some-what different, and except that men now rode in armoured vehicles and petrol was the largest item on the requisition lists, it was the Somme and Third Ypres all over again: ill-timed, head-on attacks against machine weapon defences. And with the same consequences: depressing failure.

The Cauldron and Bir Lefa! tragic names, marking the last great tank battles in the long-disputed Sidi Rezegh area. And heroic, too. Who can doubt the heroism of the Royal Armoured Corps, which returned again and again to struggle against not only a brave and resolute enemy, but an inefficient system of command? Rommel drove his crews until they nearly fell asleep in battle—but he drove himself even harder, thinking and planning to give them every advantage, and they knew it. The British crews fought just as hard, but were gnawed by an inner sense of insecurity; no one, it seemed, thought for them. Their successes and their lives depended entirely on their own high standard of tactical skill, and what could this avail if the overall situation pre-doomed them? They were aware of this, yet did not crack, and that is the measure of their heroism.

After Bir Lefa the British armour was really weak. Yet one must remember that it never vanished absolutely and entirely in one action, like a square of infantry overrun by Dervishes, partly because tanks are essentially man-savers, and partly because of the lavish scale of British war material. As regiments were depleted, the baled-out survivors joined with reinforcements to crew scores of repaired and replacement machines sent up regularly from Cairo. A regiment might be wiped out in battle in the Cauldron one day— the British tank strength was reduced from 400 to 170 there in two days—yet muster again in two or three days' time to the tune of, say, one and a half squadrons. But this process also brought disorganization; it stiffened the fingers of an organization that was already partly paralysed. And so when Rommel's mobile troops threatened to move up to the coast road to cut off the rest of the Gazala Line garrison from their supplies, there ensued a general British retreat and the fall of Tobruk. The latter disaster was a consequence of "delayed paralysis". After confusion about whether or not the place was to be defended, the British command allowed the German attackers and the South African defenders to enter it almost simultaneously. The Germans, having the advantage of knowing what they were supposed to do with the place, captured it in a matter of hours. There followed a general retreat eastward beyond the Egyptian frontier, the surviving British tanks guarding the flank and rear in a waking nightmare that flickered sleeplessly between incessant tank and gun duels and endless desert drives.

Yet it would be difficult to say just what the British command was retreating from. Most certainly, it was not from "overwhelming enemy strength", for by June 23, the Germans and Italians had only 60 tanks left between them, and were riding for the most part in captured British transport powered by British petrol. Claude Auchinleck, the British supreme commander, was well aware of this, and ordered several successive schemes of defence which he was sure must check the eastward flow of warring vehicles. But the situation was not only material; it was also psychological. It centred on the inability of a large, unwieldy, and thoroughly upset organism to get to grips with an elusive assailant. And the inability centred on a disorder of the intermediate nervous system, which no amount of "get well" instructions could possibly cure. The psychologically disturbed need rest, security, stability—and Rommel made sure they didn't get them.

And so the intermingled armies, British, German, and Italian, passed the Egyptian frontier and streamed nearer to the very nerve-centres of command. And they might well have reached it, had not a combination of material factors given the British command network the security it craved. On July 1, the panzer force, now mustering only 50-odd tanks, moved almost blindly forward against the defences within the "pass" of El Alamein. It was almost devoid of air reconnaissance. The R.A.F. ruled the skies. Hampered by deep soft sand and heavy air attacks, the Germans bumped the defence positions head-on instead of "pinning" them and passing through. Within the confines of sea, soft sand, and salt marsh was little room for manoeuvre: stability was re-introduced. The labouring semi-mobility halted and weltered down into position war.

The days of the tank-fleet battles were over. Through all the summer, as the contending armies strove in futility to break each other's lines, tanks and infantry and gunners moved inconclusively and briefly to and fro across their little wilderness, groping in disharmony to re-learn the battles of 1918: short journey, escorting and escorted, ending in brief battle-flurry, burning tanks, smashed guns, dead infantrymen. In manpower the armies were of approximately equal strength, and each found it impossible to burst frontally through a close, confined flankless system of infantry fortifications: earthworks, wire, and minefields defended by machine-guns, anti-tank guns, field artillery, aircraft, and tanks serving as mobile blocks. From time to time each side made a temporary advance measured in yards, and inevitably this was followed quickly by a return to the old fixed positions.

The situation was strongly reminiscent of the Western Front 1917–18, but with sand instead of mud, and rather more flies.

The battle of El Alamein, fought in the western desert some 40 miles west of Alexandria between October 23 and November 4, 1942, inaugurated the Western Allies' advance against Germany by land. It has been reckoned a great victory and a decisive battle.

And most important for our present purposes, it was a straight-forward frontal clash between modern armies of which the defenders, who were heavily outmatched in machine weapons, were also fixed in their positions like the medieval occupants of a besieged castle and received no supplies, while the attackers enjoyed free communications and unlimited supplies. This enables us to measure the cost of the battle relatively easily.

We must remember that this was the second battle of El Alamein. During July and August 1942 the British and German forces had fiercely contested the narrow front within the Alamein bottleneck, neither side winning success, and this deadlock was called the first battle of El Alamein. In consequence of this battle, the Alamein front became a sort of dry, sandy version of the 1914–18 Western Front. Early in August the British Commander-in-Chief, Claude Auchinleck, was removed from his post, and replaced by General (later Field Marshal) Harold Alexander, with General (later Field Marshal) Bernard Montgomery as a new subordinate general to order the battlefield. An August 31, the last push by the German-Italian forces petered out rapidly as, unable to deploy because of Montgomery's menace to their flank, they felt the effects of non-stop air bombardment and a chronic shortage of motor fuel. This last spasm of the first battle of El Alamein was dignified with its own title: the battle of Alam Halfa. After this action the German forces were largely isolated from their European sources of supply, thanks to the combined efforts of the Royal Navy and the R.A.F., and had passively to await Montgomery's offensive; this was launched at last on October 23, when he was confident that his amassed superiority in armour, aircraft, guns, and motor fuel was enough to overwhelm the German defences.

Let us compare the strengths of the combatants. Out of respect for our species, I suppose we must start with human numbers, although it would appear that since Maxim took out his patent, the human as a fighting animal is the last consideration in calculating army strength. The British put some 150,000 men in the field, the Germans and Italians together some 100,000, and this is sometimes quoted as evidence of superior British generalship—that victory was attained with the meagre numerical advantage of 1.5 to 1. However, this was a machine age battlefield, in firepower if not in manoeuvre, and we should not fall into the error of reckoning fighting manpower apart from air power, armour, and mechanical mobility.

In the air the British had very much the stronger side, being able to fly on any one day 800 bomber sorties, including some heavy bombers, and 2500 fighter, including ground-attack sorties. The Germans on the other hand were never able to fly more than 114 bomber sorties, mostly by out-of-date JU87 dive bombers which fell easy prey to hordes of British fighters and dense anti-aircraft fire, and 128 fighter sorties. As the battle wore on the numbers fell almost to zero. It can be seen that most of the British flying operations were free from enemy fighter interference, while the rapid decline of enemy air power freed more British fighters every day for the harassing of ground targets. The effect of this air superiority on the power of Allied movement in battle will be discussed later. An equally important aspect of it was that British air power extended far beyond the battlefield and was co-ordinated with naval power to diminish German-Italian supply traffic across the Mediterranean and along the desert coast road. The Germans received no fuel supplies at all for two weeks before the battle and during the early battle period, and very little ammunition.

In artillery strength the British again held considerable advantages. Not only was Montgomery able to amass more cannon, he was free to dispose them as he wished: to change their sites, to disperse them to mislead the enemy, and finally to line them up almost wheel to wheel to demolish chosen sectors of the enemy's front. He was able to do this under the R.A.F. umbrella because his artillery units received unlimited supplies of petrol with which to move the guns. And when the guns were in position, they were free to bombard the enemy with as much ammunition as they could throw. The Germans may not have been so vastly inferior in numbers of gun barrels (although the British certainly enjoyed a numerical superiority), but their absolute lack of petrol and their extremely meagre ammunition supply combined to prevent them from interfering with the British troop movements or from hindering the British artillery with counter-battery fire, even when the latter lined up in the open in preparation for an exercise in demolition. When Rommel returned to Alamein during the battle he wanted to know why General Stumme, in charge during his absence, and who died of heart failure early in it, had not directed artillery fire onto the British arraying themselves in the open for the assault. He was told that Stumme had held his fire because there was insufficient ammunition available to shell the British thoroughly both while they were preparing the assault, and while actually delivering it. Stumme had opted to save his shells in order to destroy specific targets at critical moments of the battle.

Of tanks, the British in Egypt in October 1942 possessed a grand total of 2670, of which 1440 were immediately available for battle. The remaining 1230 were in every kind of pre-battle condition. Some had just been unloaded from cargo ships and required only fuel, lubrication, ammunition, and a check by fitter and armourer. Others were under repair for battle damage or mechanical failure. Among the latter, some tanks would remain unserviceable throughout the battle period, as the spare parts they required proved unobtainable. Others, Crusaders for example, would be receiving additional layers of appliqué armour or more powerful cannon. Some machines, such as the Vickers Light, the earlier Vickers and Nuffield Cruisers, and the Matilda infantry tanks, were regarded as obsolete and unfit for participation in battle by comparison with the new American vehicles being unloaded at Suez.

The Germans and Italians had many equally old-fashioned tanks, but were obliged to keep them in active service. They also had tanks in need of overhaul and modification, but could not spare them for it. It can be seen, then, that of the 1230 British tanks held in reserve, only those few detained through lack of some essential part should be regarded as entirely out of service for the battle period. After scraping the rear area depots for anything on tracks that could run, no matter how old, the Germans and Italians could raise only 558 tanks, giving overall odds against them of 4.8 to 1.

The figures for both sides then break down like this:

British ready for battle
Churchill Heavy Infantry Tank with 3″ Howitzer,
    40mm gun and 100mm armour   4
Sherman M4 with 75mm gun and 76mm armour   400
Grant M3 with 75mm gun; 37mm gun and 60mm armour   100

Crusader 3 with 57mm gun and 52mm armour	468
Stuart (Honey) with 37mm gun and 40mm armour	468
	1440

in reserve

Shermans, Grants, Crusaders, Matildas, early Honeys, assorted Cruisers and Lights	1230
Grand Total	2670

German–Italian ready for battle

Panzer 4 with long 75mm gun and 60mm armour	35
Panzer 3J Special with long 50mm gun and 60mm armour	80
Panzer 3 with short 50mm gun and 30mm armour	80
M/13 with short 47mm gun and 40/50mm armour	318
Panzer 2 with short 20mm gun and 30mm armour	15
L/6/40 with short 20mm gun and 20mm armour	21
	549

in reserve

Panzer 3 in workshop at Derna	9
Grand Total	558

Beyond all this overweighting of the enemy with men, aircraft, artillery fire, and tanks, Montgomery ordered the unfolding of a complicated plan to deceive the enemy: the construction of false camps, vehicle parks, and tank leaguers, the noisy despatch of lorries disguised as tanks to the southern part of the desert, and the secret nocturnal despatch of real tanks to the northern part of it. It was a splendid plan to persuade the Germans that everyone was where everyone appeared to be, and to dissuade them from thinking otherwise, but its value is difficult to estimate in view of the shortage of fuel which inhibited not only German and Italian reconnaissance, whether by air or land, but also their tactical mobility. The shortage was so severe that Rommel had to divide his panzer force in two—it hadn't enough petrol to move to a threatened part of the front and back again, if the alarm proved false. The masses of Italian infantry were virtually fixed in their positions, and suffered

badly from water shortage, as well as from the attentions of the
R.A.F. and the Royal Artillery.

In launching his offensive frontally against the enemy's field
fortifications at the northern end of the Alamein front, Montgomery
did more than set the clock back to '18. He set it back further even
than Cambrai, to the first French tank attack of 1917 at the Chemin
des Dames, when the French commanders, aware that their tanks
would not cope with the difficulties of the terrain, optimistically
sent workmen ahead of the tanks to prepare paths for them.
Montgomery's tanks were faced not by impassable trenches but by
minefields, and so he sent workmen ahead to lift the mines; the
poor fellows, like the Frenchmen at Chemin des Dames, were shot
down as they worked. The tanks were then left sitting out in a
half-cleared minefield. The remaining ten days of battle were
occupied by tank, infantry, and tank-cum-infantry attempts to
batter through the minefields and enemy positions, and this was
eventually done at a price of . . . what?

Of men, the British lost 12,000 killed and wounded, the Germans
4900, and the Italians 2200. The Germans and Italians also lost
27,900 men taken prisoner, but this fact is essentially related to
their air-and-naval created state of siege, not to the form of the
battle. Rommel lacked petrol and vehicles to ferry all his troops
westward, but he neatly withdrew, without exposing his front to
sudden penetration, all the men for whom vehicles and fuel were
available, despite not only Montgomery's frontal pressure but
pressure from Germany in the shape of directives not to retreat a
single yard.

Of tanks Britain lost 840, both "destroyed" and "knocked out
but later salvaged". The Germans lost 207, and the Italians 339.
However, we must remember that not all the German and Italian
tanks later found on the battlefield were, in the first place,
immobilized by British battle-action. If a British tank ran out of
petrol or ammunition, it was refilled and sent back to the fight. If it
broke a track or its gearbox selector spring, it was repaired and
sent back. A German or Italian tank suffering any one of these
minor misfortunes, especially the apparently trivial one of fuel
exhaustion, could not be refuelled or salvaged owing to overall fuel
and transport difficulties; it would remain on the battlefield until

the British advance slowly high-tided past it. Obviously such a machine when captured might appear to have been destroyed in combat, for while it sat helpless and idle on the battlefield it would have been a sitting duck to all the artillery and tank cannon in the neighbourhood, and moreover its crew might have damaged it extensively before abandoning it. This seems to indicate that the disparity between the numbers of British and German-Italian tanks destroyed at Alamein is greater than is indicated in some published casualty lists, with the British suffering considerably the more.

This was now the pattern of land war movement. The tanks rolled cautiously forward towards the unseen enemy until the leading squadron bumped their screen of anti-tank guns, and poor Bill and Tom and Harry were brewed. The survivors took cover, and the squadron leader held a radio conference at which the total observed and map-read knowledge of each troop was pooled. Then, when the pattern of likely enemy lurking places was compiled, the squadron carried out a systematic bombardment of them one by one. Unable to prevail against dug-in anti-tank guns which could not be seen or outflanked, which were too densely patterned to be rushed, which were alert and waiting in pitched battle, not taken by surprise by intelligent unanticipated movement, the tank gunners came to rely heavily upon the power to shoot indirectly, like artillery gunners. This power was made available to them by the Azimuth Indicator M19, fitted to the M4 Sherman tank's 75mm cannon. This device could have been of inestimable value in a paralysis drive, greatly increasing the tanks' scope of activity and thus their essential mobility. As it was, the Azimuth Indicator was used merely to turn tanks into unnecessarily heavy and expensive field-guns. There was no shortage of ammunition; armoured carriers fed refills for the emptied bins along swept paths in the minefields, through the infantry (still winkling the last German and Italian survivors out of the newly cleared combat areas), up to the sheltering tanks. A stupendous volume of fire poured out at maximum range, and when it was judged the work was done, the Shermans moved on to see what they could see ... and to resume their work of clearing the machine-guns out of the way of the infantry. But, of course, the tankmen's bombardment had not eliminated their personal enemies. Just as indirect shell-fire on the pre-tank battlefield could not clear away all the machine-guns, so now indirect shell-fire could not clear away all the anti-tank guns. Soon the anti-tank gun screen was bumped again, and Jack and Sam and Pete went up in flames—a brief flurry of duelling with the half-guessed-at concealed enemy, perhaps one or two anti-tank guns destroyed, but then some more tanks erupt in smoke and flames, a whole troop goes west in seconds—and then the inevitable retirement to the lee of a crest to recommence the plotted bombardment. A costly wearing-down process, where regiments entire at first light creep into sundown leaguer only six tanks strong. It can be seen that the tank was no longer functioning in its prime attrition-war capacity of machine-gun destroyer. It was fighting for its own life with the expedients of an artillery-type sighting device and limitless supplies of ammunition discharged at maximum range.

As the infantryman of World War I was made helpless by machine-gun fire and required a tank to clear the way for him, so now the tank was helpless before the anti-tank gun screen and required a friend to help it through; for British and American tanks, that friend was, in fact, the air arm, which sent fighter or bomber aircraft to destroy the ambushing weapons with cannon, rockets, or bombs which bathed them in liquid oil-fire. This, it will be recalled, was a procedure initiated with simpler equipment, but under similar circumstances, by 8th Squadron R.A.F. late in 1918. When all was stalemate and hopeless, the leading tanks still shrouded in sullen oily smoke and the survivors from the ambush reversed into cover, their commanders chin down in the hatchway and scanning the way ahead through binoculars with an intensity derived from the knowledge that life itself depended upon vigilance, then came the radio call for air assistance, the rocket fighter or the oil bomber.

We can see that this was a battle of attrition. The two fronts engaged through their missiles, and while both suffered grievous loss, one was virtually worn away. While in the process of being worn away under continual massive air, tank, artillery, and infantry assault, the Germans and Italians, although totally unable to modify the course of events through air intervention, still contrived to inflict on their attackers casualties far more severe than those suffered by themselves: 1.5 to 1 in men killed and wounded; 1.5 to 1 in tanks destroyed.

And when all this monumental effort had been expended, when fleets of aircraft and tanks had at last subdued all resistance within the confines of the battle area, "pursuit" of the traditional, Napoleonic, final-annihilation type was still far from attainable. Despite the massiveness of the attacks and the attackers' unchallenged supremacy in the air, the defending general was able to disengage those of his troops for whom motor transport remained available, and conduct an orderly retreat with them, his rearguard, meagre as it was, ever sufficient to ward off the fiercest blows its enemy could rain upon it. In the "defeated" army, neither the general nor his troops lost their grip on the situation. They were not outmanoeuvred, and therefore they were neither panicked, nor paralysed, nor yet annihilated. And as men, they were not worn away very much, except when sheer lack of motor transport condemned them to capture. Their fate was decided solely by the prevailing odds in machine weapons, and of these primarily by aircraft and tanks. In turn, this meant that the ultimate "decision" was made not by generalship, or by courage in the field—though these were by no means lacking—but simply by the relative outputs of national war industries. And in turn, these were governed by the location of mineral deposits—geographical accidents of epochs that passed long, long before man emerged from the mammalian stock.

One must ask, then, if these results obtained when the combatants were so unevenly matched that one of them was virtually unable to move by daylight; was deprived of supplies, including food and water as well as petrol and ammunition; and was quite unable to reply to continuous air attack: what would have been the result, let alone the cost of the battle, had the Germans and Italians been able to match the R.A.F. with aircraft, the Royal Armoured Corps with tanks, and the Middle Eastern refineries with motor fuel?

What would have happened, indeed, had the German High Command sent to the Alamein front a mere half of what they rushed to Tunisia in 1943? Is it conceivable that the British would have succeeded in breaking it? Could the cost have been long supported? Or would movement have ceased until the Americans established themselves on the North African seaboard and began to ferry their inexhaustible supplies of war stores against the German rear?

This scrutiny of the tactics employed at Alamein shows clearly that had the Germans and Italians been able to match British air power, the R.A.F. would have been hardly capable of intervening in the ground fighting; in that case, the 1000-odd British tanks would have been obliged first to defeat in pitched battle a large number of concealed anti-tank guns, the destruction of which could not be left to the air arm. On the completion of this terrible task, the survivors would have been confronted with a force of enemy tanks which now seriously outnumbered them. And only when this second hurdle was overcome would they have been free to carry out the prime attrition-war tank function of clearing away the defenders' machine-guns. But why continue with such speculation? At Alamein, vast fleets of first-class armoured vehicles were unable to crack open a relatively small kernel of opposition, and came gradually to rely first on indirect fire from their guns, and finally on direct air intervention, to grant them power to move against their enemy.

The cost and the dreadfully small achievement of these tactics became typical of attrition warfare wherever it was fought.

In the U.S.S.R., North Africa, Italy, and north-west Europe, a dreary programme of "decisive" battles unfolded month by month, each one dignified by a code name, each one progressively more massive than the last: every one more massive in sheer missile power than the early efforts of the panzer forces, but none of them capable of paralysing the enemy's will to resist. Directed solely against the enemy's body, they could never achieve more than local success, any more than could the great artillery battles of World War I. The enemy command retained its grip until the very end of the war. The enemy armies were never irrevocably broken; they were just worn away, because primarily the conflict was between not men, but industrial powers.

To fight in front-line terms was to attack a vacuum cleaner factory by catching its travelling salesmen one by one. It was a war of all too easily replaceable pawns. The real targets were the mine, the railway, the factory, and above these, the minds that co-ordinated their activities. The machine age attacker could attempt either the general destruction of a nation's industrial organization or the strategic paralysis of its leaders' will, and it is apparent that the latter method is by far the swifter and cheaper.

Unhappily, the idea of unseating the enemy by manoeuvre, of surprising him and paralysing his opposition, was not held vital by the Western war leaders. As General Marshall, American Chief of Staff, most powerful counsellor of that vast nation, said, "Such psychological and political advantages as would result from the possible capture of Berlin ahead of the Russians should not override the imperative military consideration, which in my opinion is the destruction and dismemberment of the German armed forces." Smashing up as an end in itself—the unhinging of the enemy command as a mere irrelevancy. In this light, it is interesting to note the reaction elicited when an American armoured force tore away from the clinch in Normandy in 1944 to start a deep penetration of German-held territory.

It was Major-General John S. Wood, commanding the U.S. 4th Armoured Division, who broke through the shattered left wing of

German Fronts
U.S. Armoured Drives
German Retirement
U.S. 4th Armoured Div.
AUGUST 1944

Major-General Wood disputes General Bradley's order to split the armoured forces and invade Brittany—on a course 180° away from the main enemy. Bradley insists, and Wood's drive is fatally weakened and delayed, and insurmountable supply difficulties created.

the German defensive line in Normandy on July 31, 1944, and proceeded to "paralyse" the German command and communications zone on his own initiative. General George S. Patton assumed overall command of the movement later, and confirmed Wood's policy of developing the movement as a deep penetration, rather than a pursuit of the German front-line elements. The first move covered 40 miles in four hours, but this was quickly speeded up, and the U.S. 4th Armoured ran 210 miles from Lorient to St. Calais in thirty-six hours. They by-passed centres of resistance, the Germans (whose air force was already defeated) "lost touch", and the front collapsed. General Wood wrote to Captain Liddell Hart from his forward headquarters on August 23, ". . . shows what can be done by using following principles—all of them old for thousands of years;

1. De l'audace.
2. Indirect approach.
3. Direct oral orders—no details, only missions.
4. Movement in depth always—allows flexibility and security of flanks.
5. Disregard old ideas of flank security, i.e., by other units on left and right.
6. Organization of supply (taking rations, gas and ammunition in rolling reserve).
7. Personal communication with commanders (only possible by plane now).
8. Never taking counsel of fears.
9. Never fearing what 'they' will say or do (they being the same old bogie—higher officialdom or general opinion).
10. Trusting other people in the rear to do their part (a trust sometimes misplaced, but not generally).

There are others, but these will do. Best regards. Would be glad to see you if I ever stop long enough. You'll have to catch up with us."

General Wood was soon only 80 miles from the German frontier; the by-passed German garrisons in French towns had started to stream back in confusion; the French resistance movement had erupted; the Normandy Front had collapsed and the British were moving into Belgium. Unfortunately, his tenth precept let him down, and his own commanding generals did, in fact, frustrate him as Guderian had been frustrated in Russia. Generals Eisenhower and Bradley, who were the superiors of Patton and Wood, considered the deep pentration to be a chancy and largely irrelevant movement, and Bradley ordered Patton to split up his force in order to round up the Germans in Normandy and to carry out siege operations against German town garrisons. It would appear that neither Eisenhower nor Bradley was capable of mental adjustment to the purposes and pace of a fast deep penetration aimed at the psychological collapse of the enemy. They could not envisage his defeat except in purely physical terms.

As General Wood said later (1948) in another letter to Liddell Hart, "There was no conception of far-reaching directions for armour in the minds of our people—Eisenhower or Bradley—nor of supplying such thrusts. Patton did not come along until after I had taken Rennes. My movements to that time had not been on Army orders, but simply by consultation with Middleton, the Corps Commander, and a fine soldier, as to where I would go next. 1st Army[2] could not react fast enough. When it did react, its orders consisted of sending the two flank armoured divisions back 180 degrees away from the main enemy, to engage in siege operations against Lorient and Brest [author's note—the effects of this were to weaken the main thrust, over-complicate the supply situation, and worst of all, by imposing time-checks, to give the Germans time to collect themselves and re-form a defensive front]. August 4th was that black day. I protested loud and violently, and pushed my tank columns into Chateaubriant, without orders, and my cavalry [author's note—these were mechanized and armoured, of course] to the outskirts of Angers and along the Loise, ready to advance on Chartres. I still believe I could have been in the German vitals in two days... Patton agreed with me, but was forced to adhere to the (1st Army) plan—with the only armour available and ready... One of the colossally stupid decisions of the war—and most costly in results..."

The great drive of Patton and Woods petered out. Split up and spread over a vast area, and with diverse aims, the American mobile force encountered insuperable supply problems. Patton and his subordinate tank leaders made *ad hoc* reorganizations of their

[2] General Omar Bradley.

supply echelons to maintain rolling reserves of fuel, ammunition, food, and essential replacements, but the conflict of purposes proved fatally disruptive. The non-fighting and organizational elements of an army trained for position warfare and "cavalry pursuit" could not adapt themselves in a few days to a novel tempo of war.

The abandonment of mobile war and the re-establishment of position warfare with limited provision for "cavalry" pursuit had its effect upon the structure, as well as the employment, of armoured formations. The American and British armies raised no additional armoured divisions after 1942, and in 1943 began to disband some of those which had been raised during the period of the panzer successes. By 1945 the British army retained only five out of its 1942 maximum of eleven. In both American and British armies the armoured units of the redundant armoured divisions were re-trained in infantry support techniques and allocated to existing, or, more frequently, newly-raised formations of the type known in the British army as the Army Tank Brigade.

In Germany, Hitler's obsession with massiveness, which in armoured policy took the form of increasingly heavy (and slow and unreliable) tanks, led to a similar change of emphasis on the purpose of panzer mobility: from strategic to tactical. The panzer units retained the organization perfected by Guderian, but their influence upon the German army fighting a defensive war was wholly local, compared to the effect of their operations during 1939–41. And there was an increasing tendency to use the panzer divisions as ordinary infantry divisions with tank support, their motor equipment serving merely to transport them to the scene of action.

In the Red Army, on the other hand, the number of formations of armoured division type was increased throughout the war period, and although the doctrine of deep strategic penetration was not applied systematically as part of a general offensive aimed at the total collapse of German resistance, there can be no doubt that the Soviet armoured formations were prepared to undertake this role, and did so in a number of local offensives, particularly towards the end of the war. In these, they were helped by the flexibility of Soviet formation allotment, which permitted the rapid make-up of forces particularly suited to given conditions; but at the same time they were hindered by the Soviet command system, which was rigidly centralized and riveted to the political organization under the supreme command of the dictator Stalin.

In general, it would appear that during the later war years, the high commands of the warring European nations saw the highly mobile operations of the 1939–41 period as strange phenomena already receding into history, and could find no use for them as models for the campaigns undertaken by the Allied nations to achieve the reconquest of German-occupied territory. It was as though the colossal magnitude of the possibilities of success and disaster inherent in machine age mobile warfare, so clearly demonstrated first by the swift overrunning of Europe by German forces and then by the inability of these forces to hold their territory, quite deterred the Allied war leaders from conducting rational investigations into the essential qualities of this type of operation, and encouraged them instead to eschew theories of generalship, and to place their entire reliance upon the power of the combined war industries of America, Britain, and Russia to wear down those of German-occupied Europe—as in 1918.

During the "mobile war" period, air intervention at the tactical level had been important, but not decisive. The panzer advances, and the Allied counters to them, had made use of air reconnaissance and the harassing of ground targets, the Germans in particular using dive bombers functioning as light field artillery in support of the most advanced units. But time and again it was shown that in a war of manoeuvre and counter-manoeuvre, it was not imperative to rely upon air power to blast open a path of advance. The failure of the Germans first to capture the British Expeditionary Force at Dunkirk in 1940, and later to extricate their own army encircled before Stalingrad in 1942, could be attributed largely to Hermann Goering's claims that the Luftwaffe could deal with these situations unaided. On the other hand, Rommel's bewildering desert operations in late 1941 and the summer of 1942 were made at first with a bare parity, and later with inferior air strength.

On the Russian fronts the process of attrition took place primarily through the effect of ground weapons. Both the German and Russian air forces were organized largely for co-operation with ground forces, and functioned in the roles of reconnaissance at all depths, and flying artillery, both "medium" and "field", besides anti-tank work and interception of enemy sorties. Independent air force operations in the form of long-range strategic bombing was little practised, and when the Luftwaffe attempted to intervene on the grand scale, as at Stalingrad, it was with disastrous effect. It would be very difficult indeed to analyse the relative importance of tactical air power to the fighting in the U.S.S.R. As was shown in Italy and north-west Europe in 1944–45, and as was to be shown during the next decade in Korea, it is possible for an army on the defensive in a war of attrition to delay and sometimes prevent the advance of a much better supplied enemy, even when the skies are filled with his marauding aircraft and when every observed movement brings a hail of bombs, rockets, and artillery fire. In the Russian fighting, aircraft did not come to rival artillery as the means of delivering fire, and their greatest contribution, as in the 1914–18 war, was probably in reconnaissance and the interception of reconnaissance.

By contrast, in the West, the relative importance of direct intervention by air power in land battles increased enormously, to the point where the delivery of preliminary bombardments, both prolonged and immediate, was shared by aircraft and artillery, with aircraft taking possibly the larger share. After 1942 the R.A.F. together with the United States Air Force undertook the destruction of the German war industries and the demoralization of the German proletariat by "round the clock" bombing. They attempted this vindication of Drouhet's theories despite the manifest failure of the Luftwaffe's attempts at a similar programme against British industries and urban populations.

Although the wearing effects of any prolonged air bombardment must be considerable, their net effects are highly debatable, partly because they constitute an enormous drain on the strength of the attacker and partly because one of their results is to teach adaptability and flexibility of organization to the society under bombardment. To illustrate the former point we should recall that among R.A.F. Bomber Command aircrew undertaking a 32-trip tour of duty, only one man out of five could expect to escape death, wounds, capture, or nervous breakdown. This is a truly dreadful rate of loss. To illustrate the second point, we should recall that despite the ceaseless "strategic" bombardment undertaken by the British and American air forces, the production of both aircraft and tanks by the German war industries rose steadily until late 1944, when the physical overrunning of German-held European territory decisively reversed the position.

In 1939 the German production of armoured vehicles totalled 249, of all types. In 1944–45 it was 19,087. British tank production could not show a comparable increase despite relative immunity from "saturation" bombing, the figures for 1939 and 1944–45 being 314 and approximately 8000 respectively. Likewise, German production of aircraft rose from 8295 in 1939 to 39,275 in 1944–45. British aircraft production for the same years was 7940 and 26,461. Actually, British aircraft production surpassed that of Germany in 1940, '41, '42, and '43; Germany overtook Britain only during 1944–45, when saturation bombing was at its peak, and German industrial power reputedly crumbling.

The moral effect of air bombardment is equally debatable. Far from collapsing civilian resistance, it appears to stimulate hatred and determination to resist. The civilian under fire experiences a feeling of solidarity with his comrades in the armed services. Yet after the German bombardment of London and provincial cities utterly failed to terrorize the British, the British Prime Minister and the Chiefs of Air Staff deliberately undertook the terrorization of the German industrial population—with similar success. The Germans were not demoralized by air bombardment, although they suffered far more than the British did. The fact is, of course, that humans can adapt themselves to the most uncomfortable environmental conditions provided they are given time in which to do so. Not for nothing are we descended from a million years of Palaeolithic savagery. We are tough.

A prolonged siege intensifies resistance, and the besieged garrison fails only when exhausted. Moral collapse, on the other hand, comes from a sudden and unexpected blow against which no time for recovery and adaptation is allowed. Strategic bombing is comparable in many ways to the prolonged artillery bombardments of World War I—much destruction and stupendous cost, accompanied by no rapid physical overrunning of disputed territory, and achieving no rapid decision. As well as attempting to knock out the

German war industries by prolonged strategic air bombardment, the British and Americans used their large numerical superiority over the Luftwaffe to develop tactical air forces for use against centres of resistance in the field, with the aims of reducing casualties among ground forces and accelerating rates of advance.

During the earlier years of the war the tank was thought to be the best means of overcoming local ground opposition. During the later years, as anti-tank weapons proliferated and the scope for indirect manoeuvre diminished, the tank became exceedingly short-lived, and there developed a tendency to use aircraft as the primary assaulting weapon, with tanks following and in turn leading the infantry—who were also expected to protect the tank against lurking enemy infantry armed with portable anti-tank weapons. In view of the tank's cost in metal, man-hours, money (a Comet of 1944 cost over £20,000), and organizational complexity, its life was very short; its utility in position war was restricted and tending to diminish; and its retention as an essential agent of mobile war was a speculation.

We recall that the original function of the tank in battles of attrition, as conceived in 1916, was to kill enemy machine-gunners and riflemen. For that work, machine-guns and short-barrelled cannon firing 6-pound shell or canister at point-blank range sufficed. By 1918, the tank's primary task had become a fight for its own life, and its original *raison d'être* had become secondary. The resumption of the 1918-type assault in 1942 merely continued this development on an enlarged and exorbitantly expensive scale.

In its early and truly progressive state of evolution, the tank was able to maintain a rapid fire from a well stocked magazine that needed re-charging only once daily. By 1945 its missiles were so heavy that they could not be loaded into the breech as "quick-firing rounds", with the missile and propellant in one cartridge; they had to be loaded separately, like the heavy artillery missiles they were. And they were so bulky that the vehicle could carry very few of them. The 45-ton Soviet JS 3 held only 25 rounds for its main armament! After 25 shots fired at a scarcely visible enemy more than two miles away, this huge gun, to which this massive vehicle was servant, was out of action. Its battle endurance had become less than that of the foot soldiers it was supposed to escort.

The day of the tank that came into being in 1916 and fought at Cambrai and in France, and in the desert and the steppe, was over.

And so the ground-attack aircraft, less easily destroyed by an enemy overmatched in air strength and far more adaptable to a wide range of tasks, came to dominate the Western battlefield. Ground-attack aircraft were on call from what was known as a "cab rank", their crews waiting in turn for a summons to destroy specific objects holding up the Allied infantry and tanks: a fortified house, a concealed anti-tank gun, a dug-in panzer. At Monte Cassino in Italy, 3000 Allied aircraft worked on the cab rank service. At Caen in Normandy, late in June 1944, no fewer than 13,000 Allied aircraft of all sizes up to four-engined bombers operated in this way. The destruction caused by this use of air striking power was immense. At Monte Cassino, as is well known, some exceedingly valuable architecture was entirely devastated. At Caen, the Allied troops moved forward over what they described as a bomb carpet: it seemed that every living thing in the area marked out for bombardment, from grass to tree, from mouse to man, had been exterminated. But at Cassino, caves and tunnels in the mountain enabled adequate numbers of the enemy to survive for an astonishing length of time, inflicting disproportionate casualties on the Allied tanks and on infantry moving to the attack over the devastated zone. In this sense, the Cassino battlefield was a re-creation of the costly and indecisive artillery battles of World War I. At Caen, the elaborate preparations for the Allied attack prompted the German commander, Rommel, to thin out his front outposts and deepen his defences beyond what he calculated would be the maximum depth of the British artillery and air bombardment. His calculations were accurate. The air bombardment fell upon ground which was largely unoccupied, with the result that when the British armoured units began to advance across it, they developed a false sense of security which contributed to their discomfiture when eventually they bumped the main anti-tank screen. The massive preparations, the obliterating bombardment, and the final check upon a deepened defence all echoed the third battle of Ypres, 1917.

There can be little doubt that the massive use of tactical air forces, carefully laid on for the immediate support of tanks and infantry, can save many casualties. On the other hand, it does not seem to have the unilateral power of converting a slow process of attrition to a rapid campaign of paralysis and occupation. Most probably, an overwhelming superiority in ground-attack air power (as held by the Allies against Germany, 1943–45, and the United Nations Forces against North Korea, 1950–53) serves merely to convert utter deadlock into slow progress.

This should not be astonishing. A ground-attack aircraft is merely an elaborate artillery weapon. And the role of artillery has always been to wear away the enemy by firepower until his ranks can be broken by manpower. The ground-attack aircraft is a very high-speed, instant-availability, personal-service kind of flying gun, perhaps better suited than wheeled artillery to the role of bringing concentrated and prolonged fire to bear on individual units of a widely dispersed enemy. The ground-attack aircraft as used by Britain and America is but another artillery-type attempt to break the stalemate of machine war by a simple intensification of firepower, and it is interesting to compare its various specializations with those developed by ground artillery forces. Moreover, aircraft, like artillery, cannot "occupy" ground; their effect is always at a distance, and they cannot move their organization forward until elaborate preparations are made to receive them. Thus the onus of achieving territorial possession is thrust once more upon the infantryman.

And so far as mobility is concerned, the infantryman of 1943–45 was just like his predecessor of World War I; in the forward zone he moved and fought on his feet, and he needed a fantastically slow and complex supply train to keep him alive. The concealed machine-gun surviving the bombardment was still enough to keep him in his place; and the concealed anti-tank weapon with it was enough to knock out his tank support. So, back to square one, and a call to the cab rank for air support—concealed machine-guns and anti-tank guns suspected at edge of wood, map reference 123456.

Although tactical air forces did not take the power of field artillery very far beyond the 1918 level of development, except in the important matters of timing and availability, the strategic air forces of Britain, Germany, and the U.S.A. were destined to enlarge the power of siege artillery to what may be considered, for all practical purposes of mass destruction, the ultimate degree.

Perhaps fortunately for mankind, the opposing forces concentrated upon different aspects of the game. In Germany, research was directed towards improving the vehicle for the agent of destruction until it quite lost all affinities with the conventional bomber aircraft. In Britain and the U.S.A. the vehicle remained quite undeveloped beyond levels attained during the thirties (the Lancaster and Flying Fortress bombers were immediately derived from pre-war prototypes), but the agent of destruction was strengthened out of all recognition, until it acquired a power for annihilation that appalled the more thoughtful of its inventors.

We may well thank whatever gods we worship that the new destructor and the new vehicles for it were not united before 1945. For the German government hesitated not one moment before launching pilotless jet aircraft and long-range rockets to effect the haphazard bombardment of English cities; and the American and British governments did not refrain from exploding their first nuclear bombs over the heads of the Japanese, although the latter were already beaten and anxious to give up the struggle.

And that, of course, was when we reached the end of the cul-de-sac of machine warfare. In the field, all was stalemate; but the perfection of nuclear-cum-rocket long-range siege artillery appeared to render field operations unnecessary. The devotees of war based on attrition—on simple killing and the destruction of war gear—had been given the ideal tools for their clumsy strategy: an explosion that required no selective finesse, and a vehicle that rendered manoeuvre unnecessary.

Chapter Seven

Military Theory and Practice since 1945

THEORY

After the disasters of World War I, there came a wave of military self-examination and professional overhaul which, although allowed to run to waste in a desert of public ignorance and neglect, nevertheless showed that war, as one of our most important activities, was subject to evolutionary influences. But nothing of the kind has followed World War II. After it dragged to its weary conclusion, we in the West were so numbed that we accepted the atomic big stick with a measure of relief; we were sick of war's nastiness. By imagining that its conduct could be locked up in a laboratory with a physicist and a push-button, our minds were freed from the duty of criticizing the squalid process. We could even tell each other that a Western monopoly of atomic weapons ushered in the era of perfect peace. It was easy to escape that way so long as we did not try to work out exactly how the atomic big stick would work if someone bucked against it. Or what would happen if someone else made one, and threatened us with it.

In this escapist mental climate, the conduct of World War II was never overhauled objectively. Although a major part of the industrial way of life, it escaped the time-and-motion studies that have been used to examine efficiency in so many other trades and businesses; as a result, non-nuclear military thought and method continued virtually unchanged into the nuclear age, until, in the sixties, it has become dangerously muddled with so-called nuclear strategies. Our fears of political and military misconduct in war are founded on the nuclear weapon and the strategies hinging on its possible use. And by force of contrast this fear causes us to see any kind of non-nuclear warfare as relatively benign and cheap, almost innocuous. We have largely lost sight of the fantastic cost and destructive power of non-nuclear military forces of the 1945 type. Furthermore, we are in danger of accepting nuclear warfare (total or tactical) as inescapable in the event of a major conflict between major powers, and in consequence, of relegating non-nuclear warfare to the secondary role of policing foreign possessions. As things stand, we accept the army stereotype of 1945 as *the* non-nuclear army, regardless of its actual degree of efficiency (which we have seen to be very low); and we give it police tasks at which it may be even less efficient.

Before we can mentally overhaul the form of non-nuclear armies, we must reconsider the meaning of "conventional" warfare. First, we should recognize that nuclear warfare is entirely conventional. It is not unconventional in any way at all, except that the mechanism of nuclear weapons is not easily understood by people untrained in nuclear physics, and the almost inconceivable destruction they can cause, both immediate and long-term, is not easily grasped. On the other hand, the actual role of nuclear warfare is by no means abstruse, nor is it different in any way from the warfare practised in 1944, 1916, or the Stone Age. Its role is that of siege artillery. Its duty is simply to destroy physically the armed forces of the enemy, which in this age must of course include the sources of industrial power and co-ordination, because modern armies are machine armies. The nuclear weapon is merely an efficient means of achieving this simple object: a logical development of the missile weapon to cope with a vastly enlarged field of opposition. It is the cannon power of Warwick, reducing medieval castles to rubble, the massed artillery bombardments of Ypres, and the massed aerial bombardments of World War II, compressed into four seconds. But this startling performance must not obscure from us its proper classification. It must be defined by its role, not by its spectacular properties. However refined its technology, however superabundant its achievement, nuclear war is still just conventional war that happens to be dangerously good at being itself. The late Professor V. Gordon Childe remarked of conventional war in the Neolithic and early Iron Ages that it was "an activity essentially opposed to productivity". Nuclear warfare merely extends this unproductive conventionality to a point at which it becomes entirely dysgenic.

And as Albert Einstein remarked of it, "If the next war is fought with nuclear weapons, the one after it will be fought with rocks." Which takes us back to Neolithic times—conventional war, still in square one, still with us and full of kicks: an obsolete idea, irrational but compulsive.

Another consequence of our sojourn under the nuclear umbrella has been the preservation of wartime propaganda unchanged, deep in the layers of national consciousness, until its fossilization as accepted history; this is largely because, as already remarked, by comparison with nuclear warfare, even the most costly and barbarous non-nuclear fighting gives the illusion of being both harmless and old-fashioned. This illusion has resulted in a blind spot in the study of military history. The later campaigns of World War II have received relatively little detailed analysis. The shell of fossil propaganda is unchipped. In turn this has enabled Western armies, including those of the U.S.S.R., to remain virtually unchanged during a quarter of a century which has seen rapid and far-reaching change in every other aspect of human life. At first sight this may appear too sweeping a criticism, for Western and Soviet armies have adopted local nuclear missiles and the means of delivering them, and in recent years have reshaped most of their division-size formations on the pattern of the armoured division. But the tactical nuclear weapon, while up-to-date technologically, we have seen to be primitive and unsatisfactory from a social point of view, and if war is to remain a means and not become an end in itself, then it is about as useful to us on the social plane as the wooden spear is on the technological one. As for the classic armoured division, this is a structure devised in the early thirties and used briefly in the early forties for the role of strategic paralysis against a relatively immobile enemy. It cannot under any circumstances be called modern. Captain Liddell Hart, who originally projected its formation and utility, also propounded a logical counter to it in the late thirties.

Strategic thinking by Western governments and service chiefs appears to have passed through three phases since 1945. The first phase, 1945–50, was based upon unilateral possession of nuclear weapons by the West (for practical purposes, the U.S.A.); and it was assumed that any warlike activities on the part of a potential enemy would be of such a nature as to merit instant atomic threat or action. Looked at objectively, it was a crude and naïve idea. The second phase came with the awareness that the U.S.S.R. also possessed nuclear weapons; it was a more insane version of phase one, being described by one of its chief advocates, Sir Winston Churchill, as "broken-backed war". Churchill, and the widespread school of thought he represented, imagined that a potential enemy's warlike activities would take the form of a nuclear onslaught, meriting instant reprisal, whereupon the conflict would take the form of a primitive struggle in and for the ruins of civilization. This phase, 1950–60, was characterized by mutual threats of annihilation from Moscow and Washington, and a competition of nuclear explosions which scattered radio-active poisons around the world and ultimately aroused world-wide fear and disgust.

During phases one and two, non-nuclear or 1945-type forces took time off from the evolutionary scene. All the major powers concentrated upon first the annihilation weapon, and then the means of delivering it, Britain dropping from the latter competition when the U.S.S.R. and the U.S.A. moved on to solid rocket fuels at a cost prohibitive to our economy. Had our government and service chiefs anticipated that the competition between the U.S.A. and the U.S.S.R. would reach a pitch which poor little Britain simply could not attain, and had they then set quietly to work on alternative non-nuclear lines emphasizing mobility as an alternative to mass, we could have gone well ahead of the rest of the world. As it was, the twin hysterias of total deterrence and broken-backed warfare precluded such hard-headed realism. Nuclear warfare was classed as a thing apart, and conventional forces remained vintage conventional, with vintage organization, vintage communications, and vintage armour and other weapons. No doubt the British army really liked it that way. During this fifteen-year period, armoured forces were somewhat run down in strength, and their equipment remained basically unchanged from 1945. Some voices were raised to condemn the tank as completely obsolete in the face of modern tank-destroying weapons; but no attempts were made to produce alternatives to the 56-ton Centurion of 1944 and the 65-ton Conqueror of 1948, which were based on the Russian T34/85 of 1943 and the Stalin 3 of 1945 respectively. In particular, no attempts were made to provide the British army with armoured forces especially adapted to "brush fire" disturbances in the Commonwealth, with equipment suitable for air portage at short notice.

Phase three came in with the sixties and saw broken-backed warfare move to the back of the world stage, being changed into a permanent and sombre backdrop to the long-running tragedy of checkmate. With this change came re-awakened interest in armoured forces. It had been learned by the U.S. Army during the fifties that the U.S.S.R. was integrating a non-nuclear force with a nuclear weapons system. In the sixties, this integration assumed a new dimension. Nuclear physicists engaged in military research had reduced the nuclear weapon's power of devastation to the point where its use might be described as "local" rather than "general". Such a definition is, of course, a purely military one. People dwelling within a zone scheduled for local devastation, and people concerned with the post-war reconstruction of civilization, might have other views. But the fact remains that "low-yield" nuclear weapons are being made in successively smaller sizes, and for several years now they have been made small enough to be used by tactical air forces and by large-calibre artillery. This has led to a new concept of nuclear warfare far removed from that of total, all-out, world-wide devastation. The local nuclear weapon makes nuclear warfare into just another aspect of every modern army's day to day activities.

In the late fifties the smallest nuclear shell, American or Russian, was of about 250mm calibre, suitable only for the heaviest artillery piece, or for a short-range rocket. By the mid-sixties this calibre is reduced to about 150mm, a much more generally useful size. The next step will be availability in about 100mm calibre and this will enable medium tanks to fire them.

The tactical nuclearization of field armies was initiated by the U.S.S.R. with the introduction in the mid-fifties of armoured cross-country short-range rocket carriers, which have since been augmented and in some cases replaced by self-propelled guns with nuclear potential. Theoretical consideration of their striking power has led towards a complete revaluation of the tank, and a tremendous renaissance of mobile armoured forces. The armoured vehicle is seen to offer the best protection, in attack or defence, against nuclear flash, blast, and fallout, and to provide the best means of crossing burnt and contaminated zones. In the U.S.S.R. this quickly led to a reorganization of many infantry divisions as armoured or mechanized divisions, at a time when the U.S.A. and Britain were making no attempts to build up either the strength or the scope of action of their armoured forces, or to provide them with up-to-date equipment. The Soviet reorganization did not introduce any new concepts regarding the organization of armoured divisions; the pattern of World War II was closely followed, but with a marked increase in the provision of hard-skinned personnel and stores carriers.

During the sixties armoured forces in America, Britain, France, and Germany have followed this lead. Their tanks, armoured personnel carriers, and certain other vehicles are modified to give protection against flash and fallout, and are designed for living, as well as fighting in, so that crews need not dismount when they operate across the scorched and contaminated ruins of the bombardment zones. It is known that a modern tank or personnel carrier will give full protection to its crew from all nuclear hazards at a distance of $2\frac{1}{2}$ miles from the centre of a "minor" explosion, although it is not certain what constitutes a minor nuclear blast. This means that in the local nuclear offensive, the tank will itself be able to deliver the nuclear bombardment and then lead the invasion from the very edge of the devastated zone. In a defensive battle, the tank will be well forward to check similar moves by the enemy. Check. It sounds rather like the battle of Bir Harmat, with geiger counters instead of desert compasses on the tanks.

This extension of attrition warfare has obliged all technologically advanced nations to spruce up their armoured forces and radio communications and to intellectualize their officer corps. Today's junior formation leader must be a fighting graduate, his degree preferably taken in technological studies. The resulting compound of brains, armour, motors, and radio quite represents the fulfilment of the Liddell Hart–Guderian ideal of thirty years ago. It is ironic that this late flowering should be so directly opposed to the best and most intelligent aims of mobile warfare. And it is doubly ironic that the complexity and weight of its equipment provide no answer to the politico-military guerilla warfare which our potential enemies are still developing.

From this brief survey we see that two major strategic concepts have dominated Western minds over a period of a quarter of a century: first, the unilateral nuclear "deterrent" accompanied by a run-down of conventional mobile forces; second, the "reciprocal deterrent", giving rise to the miniaturization of nuclear weapons and leading to a renaissance of armoured forces of a heavy and massive kind. The question must be asked: how well adapted have these concepts been to the actual military requirements of armed Europe and America? Have they kept the peace? If not, have they brought outbreaks of war to swift conclusion?

It would seem that they have neither deterred war-makers nor stopped them quickly. Instead, they have brought ceaseless tension and threat of annihilatory war, and have seen the rationalization of guerilla techniques. We have had major conflicts in Korea, India and Pakistan, Malaya and Vietnam, and abortive attempts by Britain and France to invade Egypt, and by the U.S.A. to invade Cuba. The Marxist integration of political with military activity has been facilitated. And when the nuclear showdown was evaded, as in Korea, and conventional non-nuclear forces had to take the strain, the protracted nature of the ensuing conflict showed how unproductive and costly their 1918-type employment can be.

PRACTICE

The Korean war opened as mobile war, and remained mobile for four months. For its remaining thirty-five months, it was a crude frontal shoving match, unbelievably destructive of life, industrial products, and civilization. It began at a time when the U.S. monopoly of nuclear weapons was ending, but the American army had not reorganized itself to deal with alternatives to the "all-out deterrent".

On June 25, 1950, 50,000 North Korean troops, headed by armoured and motorized units equipped with obsolete Russian tanks, crossed the border into South Korea and filtered southward in a manner reminiscent of the French campaign of 1940; they systematically outflanked the South Korean forces which, being trained and equipped by the U.S. army of the "nuclear deterrent" phase, were predominantly infantry and were dispersed and static, lacking overall mobility and dynamic cohesion. Communist police units accompanied the leading North Korean troops, rooting out and killing all right-wing leader elements in the overrun territory. This was done very thoroughly: far more civilians than soldiers died in the swift advance, which, by eliminating political opposition and facilitating the establishment of Communist government, showed an exemplary if barbaric integration of political aims with military means. The United Nations were quick to intervene at the instigation of President Truman of the U.S.A.; and the American commander in Japan, General Douglas MacArthur, was given command of all the United Nations forces that were to be raised. Meanwhile, one battalion of the 24th U.S. Infantry Division, together with units of a cavalry and another infantry division, were sent to check the Communists. The battalion of the 24th was committed piecemeal on the Communist lines of advance, and was overrun or by-passed. The other units were sent to reinforce a defensive perimeter being hastily constructed around the port of Pusan, in the far south-east of the Korean Peninsula. Under the energetic command of Lieutenant-General Walton Walker, this perimeter rapidly became a formidable and impenetrable ring of field fortifications, resembling Tobruk in the North African campaign of 1941. When the North Korean forces reached it, their commanders behaved exactly as Hitler did when confronted by the resistance of Stalingrad. Profitable manoeuvre was abandoned forthwith, and headlong battle of attrition was attempted. The Americans were very good at this sort of thing, and time was on their side, for as the attrition was primarily of material, the North Koreans were likely to come first, and quickly, to the bottom of the barrel. By the end of August their Russian T34/85 tanks were gone, their force had lost half its strength, and their supply lines were long and subject to intensive U.N. air and naval interference. By September 8, their last offensive failed. Stalemate had set in, and the initiative was now with the U.N.—that is, with the Americans. The question was, how should the North Koreans be evicted?

Curiously, in spite of the evidence of the original successful infiltration by the North Koreans contrasted with the ruinous cost of recent
attrition fighting, all the U.N. commanders except one wished to
push the Communists back frontally, yard by yard. The only dis-
senting voice was that of Douglas MacArthur, who quite reasonably
suggested that the U.N. forces should exploit their unique and

CHINA

Pyongyang

N. Korea

Dairen
(U.S.S.R.)

—38°N

Seoul
Inchon

WAR in KOREA,
August-Sept 1950

S. Korea

MacArthur's seaborne
counter-stroke 15th Sept.
1950, collapsing the N.
Korean invading army.

PUSAN
Besieged by
Pusan N. Korean forces
Aug-Sept. 1950

0   50   100   150
MILES

tremendous advantage in sea power, carrying an army northward
by sea to a point at which it would be convenient to land, and from
which it could decisively sever the Communist forces from their
place of origin. The farther from Pusan this landing was made, said
MacArthur, the more prompt and far-reaching its effect would be.
Many American and other commanders thought this idea a fool-
hardy speculation, but MacArthur carried the day; his staff worked
out a meticulous time-table for amphibious operations against
Inchon, close to the original South-North Korean border, where
tides were exceptionally difficult, but where a single landing should
be sufficient to end the campaign decisively. Everything went as
MacArthur and his staff had planned. The landing was effected on
September 15, and as the U.N. forces penetrated inland, the North

Korean invaders streamed back in disorder, thousands of them ending up in the prisoner-of-war cages. The general political situation in Korea was thus restored virtually to its condition of June 25, after less than 100 days of campaigning over a range of 400 miles.

MacArthur's forces pursued the enemy into North Korea, an army operating on the north-west, and a corps (roughly half the size of an army) on the north-east. On October 25, lack of distant reconnaissance allowed these forces while still in column formation to bump a massive Chinese army group with Russian jet aircraft moving southward to restore North Korean fortunes. There followed a fighting U.N. retreat to a port in north-east Korea where the Chinese were unable to prevent sea evacuation. A number of North Korean coastal towns were devastated by warships of the U.S. Navy, while the Chinese advanced down Korea until they were stopped on a hastily formed line of U.N. defensive works 25 miles south of Seoul.

This third swing of the mobile war pendulum reinforced the U.N. generals' hearty dislike of it. No doubt some of them saw it as the due reward for MacArthur's unconventional generalship. For MacArthur was an unconventional soldier and an imaginative one, who saw the military world only as part of a political one. Now, this vision cost him his appointment as he differed with the U.S. President over the future conduct of the war. He was replaced by a man whose strategic view extended no further than the nearest enemy trench parapet: General Matthew Bunker Ridgeway. The latter's scheme for pushing the Chinese back to the 1950 frontier was a straightforward linear advance, a "clean sweep", as he called it, right across the peninsula. The clean sweep worked as a continuous infantry assault, preceded and supported by intense air and ground artillery fire and local armoured strength. Helicopters were to be used to land infantry directly on objectives, saving casualties during the approach. No rapid long-range moves, or seaborne outflanking moves, were contemplated.

Essentially, this was 1918 stuff—and it met with complete approval. While the U.N. sea power was used only for coastal patrol and bombardment, the U.N. land forces inched their way forward, devastating the ground and all that lived thereon as they passed over it, and leaving a wake of impoverished and homeless refugees.

At no time did their Russian jet fighters give to the Chinese forces a control of the air, over their own supply areas or over the fighting front. Their sea communications were exceedingly feeble. Their defences were pounded from the air, and by tanks and artillery of every conceivable calibre. Their concentrations of personnel were drenched with liquid fire; it was customary to drop napalm on a Chinese-occupied hill until the whole feature went up like an ant-hill soaked in paraffin. The Chinese supply system was dominated by U.N. air power to such an extent that their entire forward zone was supplied only by head-loading porters after dark. The Chinese had only one superiority over the U.N. forces: an inexhaustible supply of young cannon fodder to be fed, battalion after battalion, into what the Western troops called the American Meatgrinder. The Meatgrinder reached the 38th Parallel—the frontier of 1950— in six months, at an average speed of 10 miles per month, at a daily cost in death and wounds that averaged more than 1000 for U.N. and South Korean forces alone, and at a daily cost in money that could be estimated only in millions of dollars. It was very much "Back to '18", with the Chinese forces organized in vintage 1918-type formations, but with the U.N. forces elaborately mechanized to economize in human life. It was a contest between illimitable reserves of Chinese manpower, and the very best in 1945-pattern machine power that the West could produce—save for the atomic bomb. Yet the U.N. forces could push the Chinese back only very slowly, and only a few miles north of the 1950 border; in the difficult hill country there, the Chinese dug in firmly and an infantry artillery deadlock continued for nearly two years, from June 1951 to April 1953. It gave no military success to either side, but it cost China a vast loss of human life,[1] which was probably beneficial to the Chinese economy and also helped feed its Communist propaganda machine; and it also cost the U.N. a vast loss of industrial products, which was far from beneficial. U.N. loss of life was

[1] Total Chinese and North Korean casualties (killed, wounded and missing) estimated by U.S. authorities to total 2 million.

South Korean military casualties (k.w.m.)	1,312,800
U.S. military casualties (k.w.m.)	157,500
Other U.N. military casualties (k.w.m.)	17,200

by no means light, but in a generally over-populated world was of less importance than industrial products, except as it affected political elections.

The question one should ask is, if the Meatgrinder progressed so haltingly against a genuine vintage 1918 army, what on earth would it have done against an up-to-date one? Is it conceivable that it could have covered 60 miles in the face of a sophisticated defensive system holding parity in air power and machine weapons?

Korea was almost a Third World War, and significantly, it was the mobile phase that was the most memorable. The rapid north-south movements between June and December 1950 seem, in the human imagination, to encompass far more in space and time than the three and a quarter years of "clean sweeping". They produced rapid decision and were relatively cheap, and each showed up the importance of detailed advance planning in the economy of time.

But after MacArthur no Western general wished to chance his arm on mobile operations, and possibly no Western government would have backed him. Profitability did not enter the scales: they were loaded with blind faith in weapon power and fear of open flanks. And much the same was true of the Chinese, whose dictator Mao Tse Tung had earlier boasted of his mastery of mobile war. During the inter-World War years, when the growing Communist army had fought against both Chinese right-wing and Japanese forces, Mao Tse Tung sedulously avoided pitched battle, and constantly taught a theory of warfare based on economy and movement. He frequently repeated aphorisms such as: "Retreat when the enemy wishes to advance"—"Move sideways and catch him unawares"—"Dissolve one's force and reassemble it elsewhere to the enemy's bewilderment"—"Hit him hardest when he turns to follow one's imagined last movement". But when the Chinese forces in Korea became entangled in trench warfare, Mao did nothing to restore the art of mobile war he had once cultivated, but simply fed more cannon fodder into a frontal push. The vast consumption of men and material was accepted as politically necessary, and was allowed, indeed encouraged, to continue for more than two years.

A similar frontalism was exhibited by the British government and
General Staff in 1956, when the former decided to join with France
to invade Egypt and re-occupy the Canal Zone. Although the zone
to be occupied was 120 miles long, and speed of occupation was of
paramount importance, the invasion was launched at one end of
the zone and was expected to progress steadily to the other while
the Egyptians sat inactive to await their fate. But the obvious
preparations for the operation, whose massive World War II pattern
limited the choice of assembly ports, and its slow and well adver-
tized approach, gave the Egyptians ample time to prepare counter-
measures, with the result that they were able not only to stall the
invasion forces completely within the main landing zone, but to
make the Canal entirely unusable. The British commander of the
seaborne forces contributed to the confusion by losing touch with
his command through travelling in an unreliable amphibious
vehicle. Instead of neatly taking over the Canal and running it
with enhanced efficiency, the British and French found themselves
in a military stalemate, being blamed by the entire world for ruin-
ing an important trade route. And this situation was brought about
by the negativing effect of mutually destructive machine weapon
systems. Using relatively small quantities of Russian armaments,
some of them obsolescent, a nation entirely without military tradition was able to bring the armoured juggernaut of a veteran warring nation to a grinding halt in a matter of hours. Fortunately
world opinion and threats of sanctions obliged the British government to abandon the action before it could escalate to disastrous
proportions.

Last in our survey of large-scale military encounters we must
consider the recent conflict between India and Pakistan, in 1965.
An Indian government under permanent and massive threat from
China across her northern borders appeared unable to see an
invasion from impecunious Pakistan in its proper perspective, and
countered it with a direct and headlong offensive against Pakistan's
capital. Within days, the major forces of India and Pakistan were
locked in a frontal tussle, in which their most expensive and locally
irreplaceable elements wrote each other off in an orgy of mutual
destruction, while the long-term threat, China, looked on and
waited. Although it was in the interest of both India and Pakistan

to procure a speedy solution to their armed dispute, neither side had attempted to devise forces specially adapted to the role. Instead, both sides fielded armies that were in all respects imitations of Western armoured forces of the period 1942–45, and set them to work in the least profitable way possible, despite all the lessons of half a century to the effect that a machine weapon system which has battered a similar system out of its way is in no fit state to effect rapid and far-reaching military decisions. What makes the orgy of mutual destruction even more remarkable is that the mechanical equipment consisted entirely of American and British cast-offs, which could not under any circumstances have been replaced from native arsenals. Yet the actual problem was not a new one. For thousands of years, impoverished and over-populated hill tribes have periodically raided the equally over-populated but slightly less impoverished Indian plains. Hitherto, successful counters to the problem have always been strictly relevant to the problem: containment and buying off, with mutual blood-letting to ease the pressure of mass hysteria. Seen thus, the mutual destruction of mechanical equipment, accompanied by haphazard air bombardment against civilian populations, is basically irrelevant to the problem; in a twentieth-century context this can be solved in the first instance only by containment, followed by sane political bargaining free from the influence of war hysteria, and in the long term only by a mutual sub-continental approach to control of population growth and the proper use of land.

But it was war hysteria and frontalism that triumphed, and millions of pounds and dollars worth of good defensive equipment were destroyed in a few days of indecisive dog-fighting, which in turn left both sides bitter and frustrated and their governments almost incapable of negotiation, reason having been swept away by the tidal waves of emotion released by a war of stalemate. It would seem that in 1965 we were still mentally back in 1918, which means back in the Stone Age, with destruction first, and decision afterwards—perhaps. Mass hysteria and frontalism prevailed, along with the unquestioned belief that the objective, no matter how small its value in the world of peace, must be pounded into the ground before it can be gained.

The gadgetry and the obsession with formalized mass annihilation

which we have so far surveyed have been the concerns of established armies. But contemporaneously there has arisen among the
un-established armies of ambitious political parties the rationalization of guerilla techniques, sometimes aiming at similar goals and
using similar techniques to those described by Fuller and Liddell
Hart as the proper aims and means of the mechanized forces of
established governments. There is nothing new about guerilla
warfare, references to which are contained in the earliest histories
of civilization. At one end of their shabby spectrum, guerilla aims
and purposes become indistinguishable from those of bandits. At
the other, they change with political respectability into the formalized procedures of official military bodies. Guerilla warfare is
militant opportunism, and its position on the scale between the
extremes of uniformed respectability and blatant banditry is determined in part by the strength or military competence of the established government, and in part by the nature of the ideology
sustaining the guerillas and their supporters in an outlawed existence. What is remarkable about guerilla warfare in the period
since 1945 is its rationalization by South-East Asian Communist
governments along lines developed by the enemies of Germany and
Japan during 1940–45, for the encouragement of mobile resistance
centres deep in enemy-held territory. But whereas the "resistance
group" of World War II contributed to the eviction of an invader,
the Communist guerilla movements are themselves organized as
invasion forces requiring no formal declaration of war. Communist
guerillas infiltrate the territory of neighbouring states for the purposes of softening-up the government and population prior to take-
over by the Communist political party. They assassinate politicians,
weaken and demoralize the army and police, and subvert or intimi-
date the civilian population.

The most important Communist guerilla offensives have been
those directed against the governments of Malaysia and South
Vietnam, and in both, the psychologically-oriented aims and the
deep-penetration techniques bear not a little resemblance to the
paralysis theories of Fuller and Liddell Hart. In both Malaya and
Vietnam the Communist forces have used infantry-type forces with
extraordinarily high standards of mobility, skilled in avoiding
frontal conflict with the forces of the established government, and

in ambushing them in a variety of ways. In Malaya the guerilla forces were decisively checked only when all possible food supplies were sealed off, and an efficient early-warning system developed for pin-pointing Communist appearances. These precautions in themselves would not have been enough. But the British infantry forces working against the guerillas developed a superior standard of jungle mobility, and this enabled them to track down the pin-pointed and restricted Communist forces, and destroy them. It is worth noticing that this efficient three-fold system bears a strong resemblance to the technique evolved by Kitchener for ending the menace of the Boer cavalry guerillas, known as Commandos, in the final stages of the Boer War. Kitchener had all food supplies rounded up, balancing the immediate cost and inconvenience of doing so against the probably astronomical expense of a protracted guerilla war. He then strung the Veldt with wire fences and guard posts, to obtain immediate notice of any Boer movements. And he raised mounted forces (in which the cavalry featured scarcely at all!) to hunt down the starved and pin-pointed Boers.

The guerilla offensive in South Vietnam has been larger in scale than in Malaya, and the attacks have shown more variety in aims and means. Terrorization of urban civilian populations, for example, was not accomplished by the Malayan Communists, nor were the latter able to penetrate deep into "secure" territory and there demolish aircraft and other equipment under the noses of armed guards. The Vietnamese Communist forces have repeatedly taken demolition equipment, including heavy mortars and machine-guns, deep into American-dominated zones, and have there set them up and used them with great success. They have also built elaborate underground earthworks in the vicinities of towns and military centres, using them as barracks and depots from which the local population could be dominated and guerilla attacks carefully prepared. Viewed objectively, these achievements are shining examples to all professional soldiers. They represent the triumph of small, highly mobile, and flexible forces obtaining the maximum value out of the minimum of equipment. Even if these guerilla units are later trapped and largely destroyed, they show a credit balance when the probable cost of their training and equipment is balanced against that of combating them with Western-type forces using machine power to economize in human life.

The fact remains that a machine age army is an outlet for industrial products, and by the nature of its activities, it is, in the short term, a wasteful outlet. Military activities are basically opposed to productivity, and therefore any pattern of it which results in a war of material attrition or of mass destruction is a dangerous one, in that it harms the industrial economy which supports it. The Communists of South-East Asia appear to have hit upon an intelligent method of thus causing the U.S. government to defray the much greater part of the cost of their war of moral and material attrition in South Vietnam. They have found a way, through the elaboration of political communication channels, to obtain maximum effect upon a population and its government with the bare minimum of military equipment, which the Americans appear able to counter only by the simple use of disproportionately expensive firepower. As has happened so frequently in Western armies, aims and means have not been clearly related. For the war in Vietnam is twenty years old; the Americans inherited it, in modified form, from the French. It is a war which has eroded the country's economic and moral resources almost to the vanishing point, and is now a cruel drain upon the American exchequer. It has achieved nothing, by Western military standards, nothing at all. But it has provided Communist South-East Asia with a bottomless pocket of free propaganda material.

Recently, it has become evident that the American army is aware that its efforts are not as closely related to the situation as is desirable. It has believed itself to be fighting a mobile war, but the kind of mobility it has practised has been that of an elephant trying to catch a wasp.

The methods employed by the British in the Boer War and in Malaya have at last gained serious consideration, and there are signs that serious attempts are to be made to check the enemy's mobility. Herbicide chemicals have been used to defoliate great tracts of guerilla-infested jungle, and projects have been mooted for completely sealing the country's frontiers and stopping all infiltration, and for breaking down the land into controllable plots. This is the point at which military operations merge into engineering, and national and regional politics. The expense would be colossal, but perhaps less in the balance than another decade of guerilla war.

The lack of long-term success attending the U.S. Army's "seek and destroy" operations may be remedied when the disputed territory is given clearly defined shape. For that army is designed to operate under more or less formal conditions: to encounter armies, not to combat administrative and economic chaos, which are the forces shaping the present dispute. A thorough sealing and compartmentalizing process might provide an environment in which it could operate profitably.

While on the subject of operations against guerilla and terrorist forces, it is interesting to note a universal characteristic dating from at least the eighteenth century. Soldiers are smartly, and above all, conspicuously dressed: they are shown off. No doubt their gleaming appearance is intended to impress the populace and cheer the peaceful majority, who probably have no desire to be involved with terrorists. Redcoats were shining symbols of security behind which the peaceful could rally, beacons of hope for a settled future. This kind of thing was excellent in the days before firearms were mass-produced; troops then held a unique advantage in their combination of missile and shock tactics, the firelock not being very effective in the hands of the solitary terrorist. Heavy, conspicuous, clumsy to load, and inaccurate, it needed the close company of its fellows. The American Revolutionaries found that to eject the British, they had first to raise a conventional army competent to defeat the redcoat at his own game.

Mass-produced small-arms changed this. The Irish Republican Army drilled itself like the American Revolutionary Army, but did not achieve its ends by engaging the British army of occupation in conventional infantry tactics; had it done so, it would probably have put itself out of business pretty soon. The Irish war of independence inaugurated a new pattern of guerilla-terrorism that has become characteristic of our century. Mass-produced small-arms— light, inconspicuous, easily obtained and replaced, with a high rate of fire which made them effective when used by solitary agents— enabled the Irish revolutionaries to place the army of occupation in a state of siege, while they themselves remained invisible. When the

English put up barbed wire and sandbags, it was not to put down the rebels, but to defend themselves. They controlled only the ground they stood on, or pointed their guns at, and as soon as they moved elsewhere, they ceased to control it. Since the time of the "troubles", this situation has erupted wherever political ambitions have been expressed with the aid of mass-produced small-arms: Palestine, Cyprus, Malaya, Aden, Vietnam. And still the soldiers are shown off in their best uniforms. Clean, bright and shining they stand up, no longer symbols of security, but targets for the machine pistols, automatic rifles, grenades, machine-guns, mortars, and bazookas of the politically disaffected. Wherever this situation arises, the soldier, as the armed, uniformed agent of government, experiences a dramatic loss of free movement, while his unseen opponents gain proportionately, and the loyalty of the mass of the population swings accordingly.

One imagines that this eighteenth-century response to urban disturbance should have been discarded long ago, and replaced by an urban re-casting of jungle and commando techniques. The only spick and span soldiers would be the few symbolizing government power at Government House. The remainder would be invisible. Perhaps they would be plain-clothes detectives rather than soldiers. It is easy for the terrorist to be confident when his opponents are clearly labelled and conspicuous. He knows that his uncommitted neighbour, who has seen him throw the grenade, dare not denounce him. But what if, unknown among the crowds, are the observers, agents, and patrols of the counter-terrorist organization?

Our army seems curiously unwilling to attempt experiment in its petty local wars. It is unthinkable that soldiers should cease to shine their boots and badges, and try to disguise themselves as the unwashed heathen! It is totally impossible that, to counter underground organizations, our army should invent additional ones, and use them to terrorize the terrorists. But modern mini-weapons, communications equipment, and not least, hair and skin cosmetics, make it excitingly possible. The war against the city terrorist is essentially a jungle war, to which jungle rules apply: cut down the enemy's power of movement while at all costs remaining invisible and free oneself, then pin-point him and eliminate him. Troops chosen to do this kind of work could probably turn themselves into the finest kind of resourceful, inventive fighting men, and could apply their new skills to other combat situations. Security work would no longer be a sideline teaching only patience and resignation.

The armies of the industrially advanced nations in this century have evolved within a quite restricted environment shaped primarily by the need to deal with armies of their own type; in this respect, they are unlike Roman armies, which encountered forces of their own type only when they fought each other in civil war. One accepts the probability that this primary role will continue; the British army must remain prepared to encounter other technologically advanced armies, although its day to day commitments are predominantly against the semi-guerilla politico-military forces. Is it well adapted to its background role?

Can the 1945-type army with nuclear encrustation, whose basic pattern was created in the days when motor-cars had scarcely attained their majority, yet find a profitable use in the age of radar, sophisticated anti-tank defences, and transonic ground-attack aircraft? Could the modern armoured force, whose £60,000, 50-ton tank can be destroyed with ease by a couple of infantrymen in a ditch with a drainpipe rocket-projector, hope once more to emulate the capacity of the panzer division of 1940 to disorganize opposition, collapsing it swiftly and profitably?

We have seen that during the fifties, only three attempts were made to use mechanized armies in this way: by the North Koreans in June 1950; by MacArthur against the North Koreans in September 1950; and by the army of the U.S.S.R. against the Hungarian revolutionaries in November 1956. Of these three essays in mobile warfare, the first two were incomplete operations and became converted to very expensive campaigns of attrition. The third, the Russian venture, was the most modern and fully mechanized, and also the most completely successful. However, we cannot say that the success was due to the "panzer" technique. It was essentially a police operation, conducted with overwhelming strength. Fifteen Russian armoured divisions, roughly equivalent to five Western ones, were sent to restore Communist law and order to a capital city harassed by political uncertainty, whose army was scarcely organized, split by divided loyalties, and quite cut off from possible aid. The use of crack armoured divisions probably accelerated the outcome, but did not create its inevitability.

In the sixties, the use of modern mechanized forces appears to have had no accelerative effect upon the modern Thirty Years War in Vietnam; and in Pakistan the clash of armoured forces in 1965 resulted only in a holocaust of expensive tanks. But in June 1967 there occurred a ghostly echo of Rommel's springtime push of 1941 that must have made tankmen everywhere think once more of the swirling, fast moving actions in open country of the early forties. Once more there were dust plumes hanging in the air behind racing tanks; the sharp crack of high-velocity guns; the exhilaration of the successful, surprise outflanking drive; the markings and re-markings on the map that spell chaos to the traditional soldier but are charged with business-like significance for the mobile one. And the supremely exhilarating climax when the shooting stops, and the leading crews push up their goggles to see the country behind them littered with columns of prisoners and abandoned enemy vehicles, and rejoice in the knowledge that, for all the hundreds of miles traversed and the scores of swift engagements, very few of their comrades lie dead along the way.

This was the Israeli-Arab campaign, fought in three phases, of which the first two lasted eighty hours, the third thirty, and which resulted in the complete military collapse of Egypt, Syria, and Jordan, and the immediate territorial expansion, almost un-scathed, of Israel. Superficially, this little war—short in duration and ranging over lines of advance of only 150 miles on the most extensive front, and only 15 or so on the most confined one—appeared to be a neo-classical one. Thus, in the Sinai desert the Israeli average speed of advance was about 18 miles per day, a breathless rate of travel in terms of attrition warfare, and a diminished echo of Guderian's 30-plus miles per day in Russia. Again, like Guderian, the Israelis fought against heavy odds; remembering that a superiority of 3 or 4 to 1 in men and weapons is considered essential to success in set-piece actions, we note that they went to warfare with odds fairly even in men (counting the total Israeli reserve and discounting the vast U.A.R. reserves and promises of men from other Arab nations); odds adverse at 2 to 1 in tanks and self-propelled guns; and odds adverse at nearly 2 to 1 in combat aircraft. But can this semblance of the early panzer campaigns be interpreted to show that armoured forces of antique pattern still have major roles to play in maintaining European and particularly British security? Or were the Sinai campaigns and its sequel in Syria exotic happenings?

The State of Israel was at war with her Arab neighbours in 1948 and 1956, and during the years between she experienced little peace on her frontiers, particularly those bordering Egypt and Syria. The Syrian army fortified the south-western slopes of the Hermon range, where the complex limestone structure lent itself readily to the excavation of artillery and machine-gun emplacements. From these, fire was directed sporadically against the nearest Israeli settlements. On the Egyptian frontier, the more open country invited a different kind of hostility; raiding parties infiltrated the frontier to plant mines in the dust of unmetalled roads or to deliver sudden bursts of machine-gun fire against farm workers on the frontier kibbutzim. Then, during the first five months of 1967, tension built up dramatically, as Cairo and Damascus radio preached hatred and holy war against Israel. In May the Jordanian government joined a mutual defence pact with Egypt and agreed to the presence of Egyptian troops. The Egyptians moved 120,000 men in two armoured and four infantry divisions into the Sinai peninsula, with about 600 tanks and 600 SP guns; airfields were established in western Sinai, and rocket-launching units were set up. The Egyptian government requested of the U.N. that its peace-keeping missions be withdrawn forthwith from the Gaza Strip and the entrance to the Gulf of Aqaba, and then announced a blockade of the port of Eilat, Israel's only means of maritime access to the east.

Ominous military activity of the same kind took place on the Israeli frontiers with Jordan and Syria. Egyptian commando troops were air-lifted to Jordan. The Syrian government ordered some 50,000 troops with armour support into the de-populated frontier zone.

As May drew to an end, Arab broadcasting systems stepped up the intensity of their hate-mongering and incitement to violence, and on May 29, Egyptian units opened machine-gun and mortar fire on Israeli farms, and Jordanian machine-gunners fired bursts into the Jewish sector of Jerusalem. War appeared to be inevitable, and the only speculation concerned when it would commence, and how long Israel could support it. For although the Israeli government maintained regular and reserve forces amounting to almost one-ninth of the country's total population of two and a half million, it was generally conceded that these forces and their mechanized equipment would be required to operate defensively on three fronts, while the crowded Israeli cities would be subject to a rain of bombs, and the country would be in immediate danger of being cut in two by an Arab thrust from Nablus, where Israel is only 15 miles wide.

While few knowledgeable Western observers imagined that Israel could be simply overwhelmed by the forces massing against her, most believed that she had lost the opportunity to fight in the only way capable of conferring advantage—that is, outside her own borders, with a lightning mobile campaign. For her mobile forces were built to the pattern of 1944, and Western and Soviet military experts were agreed that the blitzkrieg had become a heavily out-moded concept, incapable of conferring the advantage of surprise. Israel's tanks were twenty or more years old, in design if not in manufacture, and her motor infantry rode in venerable M3 half-tracks, dating from around 1939, whereas Egypt had been supplied by the U.S.S.R. with large numbers of more modern fighting vehicles. Disadvantages also attended Israel in the matter of air power; though her air force equipment was more up-to-date, it was heavily outnumbered.

Thus, it appeared highly unlikely that the Israeli forces would be able to decide the military issue on any one front quickly enough to avoid the danger—and potential disaster—of having to contain three Arab offensives simultaneously on three separate fronts. If Israel were to attempt a swift knock-out blow against any one of the besieging forces, her antique mobile forces would be caught at once in a battle of material attrition, from which they would have to be extricated hurriedly, much depleted, to face a new threat elsewhere. Eventually they would be scurrying like a frightened hen between three foxes, and Israel would ultimately disintegrate. At the very best, they would be slowly ground away between three millstones, valuable territory would be lost, and when the U.N.

ISRAEL in SINAI
JUNE, 1967

+++++ Railways
- - - - Roads and Tracks
—··—··— International Boundary

0   50   100
MILES

finally succeeded in imposing a cease-fire, little Israel would emerge tinier than ever and ill-equipped to resume the diplomatic struggle.

Nevertheless, the armed forces of Israel did in fact achieve what appeared to be impossible, in that they opened and maintained a highly mobile war and brought it to a successful and apparently profitable conclusion in a matter of days.

The Sinai Peninsula is a waste of rock, sand, gravel, and clay pans; although it is heavily scored with the paths of ancient watercourses, today it is extremely dry, with a rainfall of less than 10 inches per year providing only scanty seasonal grazing for small numbers of gazelle and Bedouin. The coastal plain, averaging an altitude of 600 feet, is surfaced with loose shifting sand—sandstorm and dune country. The land rises as one progresses south; after 45 miles it has reached 3500 feet, and the surface offers very varied going over sand, rock, or gravel. Another 80 miles and the altitude is nearly 8600 feet—the massif of Mount Sinai (Jebel Katerina) has been reached. Here the going is very difficult for motor vehicles of all kinds. From the peak of Sinai (8664 feet) the land slopes steeply to a narrow coastal shelf running round the peninsula, at the apex of which are the settlement and fortifications of Sharm el Sheikh, from which maritime traffic in the Gulf of Aqaba can be controlled. The ancient watercourses on the southern faces of the Sinai massif are sharply incised, to depths of several thousand feet, and the going is exceedingly difficult. Thus, for all its maximum width east-west of 130 miles, and length north-south of 240 miles, it is traversed by only three main routes east-west (with interconnections), and a ring-road round the coastal shelf from Suez to Eilat, and up to the Israeli Negev frontier.

The northernmost east-west route is the coastal one, where a metalled road is paralleled by a railway line. The Egyptians relied heavily on the latter. The centre route passes eastward from Ismailia to Nitsana, 30 miles inland on the Israeli frontier. The southernmost one passes from Suez to Kuntilla, 40 miles north of Eilat. It is a difficult, hilly route. At the Egyptian end it passes through the narrow Mitla Pass, and inland it makes a detour south around the Libni mountains to Themed, before tending northeastward again to Kuntilla. A meagre network of tracks links the northern, centre, and southern routes, at El Arish—Bir Lafan—Abu Agheila—Jebel Libni—Nakhl; while at Bir Gifgafa, just east of the Mitla Pass, a fork road diverts from the southern route in the direction of Abu Agheila. The latter is thus an important focus of routes, while the quadrilateral Bir Gifgafa—Nitsana—Kuntilla—Themed—Bir Gifgafa, despite its difficult terrain, is an area over which motorized forces are relatively well served by desert tracks. It is also, however, virtually bisected by the Wadi Arish, which extends south from El Arish on the coast as far as Nakhl.

The Egyptians moved two infantry divisions along the coastal road and rail routes, concentrating them in the Gaza Strip and the El Arish areas. Another infantry division was on the central east-west route between Abu Agheila and Quseima, and a fourth on the southern route between Nakhl and Kuntilla. The Egyptian armour was concentrated in the "quadrilateral", but a large number of tanks were detailed for infantry support in the coastal area, and an armoured force was stationed in the Themed area to menace Eilat. It can be seen that the Egyptian forces were of similar size and composition to those used by the British and German-Italian forces in North Africa in World War II, but were given a very different deployment. Whereas in North Africa the contending armies used their infantry divisions to build strongly fortified lines stretching at the most some 40 miles inland, and grouped their mobile armoured forces behind these lines ready to operate around them, the Egyptians spread their infantry and armour in three widely separated blocks on a front more than 100 miles long, with the mobile forces as it were mixed up with the less mobile ones. The build-up, maintenance, and supply of these forces, particularly the infantry units, over three long, separated, and difficult routes must have constituted a major problem. To give support to the army in Sinai, to facilitate the bombing of targets in Israel, and to counter Israeli air strikes, airfields and rocket bases were constructed, one series being in the Canal Zone, and another in central Sinai, at Gifgafa, Themed, and Nakhl. Unfortunately, at the time of writing, the immediate objectives of the Egyptian forces in Sinai are not known. Were they to effect a three-pronged invasion of Israel? Were they to build up an elaborate system of frontier fortifications? Or were they, like the army of the Grand Old Duke of York, merely to march up to the top of the hill for the achievement of some political effect, preparatory to marching down again? Whatever their aim, they were not arrayed in the proper manner for its achievement at first light on June 5, 1967. For as events showed, their supply of water, among other desert essentials, was inadequate to sustain their life in battle, while they had not been in Sinai long enough to build up a strong defensive system, and their training, and hence their morale, was totally inadequate for a war of rapid movement. In North Africa, about four months were needed to create an effective system of "boxes" and minefields some 40 miles long. One imagines that six or more months would have been necessary to fortify the frontier of the Gaza Strip and the Negev. It is reasonable to assume that the Egyptians were well aware that Israel intended to defend herself with mobile actions outside her own territory, and that their long-term aim was to render this impossible by fortifying the frontier. Thus, the bargaining position of Israel could be made progressively weaker, as military confrontation would lead inevitably to attrition of her defence forces and her territory. It is also reasonable to assume that an immediate three-pronged (or five-pronged, counting Syria and Jordan) invasion of Israel was not intended in June, since, as events proved, no plan for concerted action had been made. Unfortunately for the Arabs, their propaganda campaign and military activities were not synchronized. Verbally, ideologically, and diplomatically, they were already at the Jewish throat, while the Egyptian armies were still sorting out their positions and developing their air bases. Thus, the ostentatious military preparations, the too-prompt withdrawal of the U.N. peace-keeping forces, the verbal promises of annihilation, and finally the rash direction of fire upon Jewish settlements, gave the Israelis a splendid excuse to step in with their mobile forces that did not depend upon a time-wasting preparation of positions, and to turn the Egyptian forces inside out before they could complete their elaborate manoeuvres.

The Israeli "preventive war" opened with simultaneous air, land, and sea actions. The Israeli air force succeeded in destroying the greater part of the Egyptian, Syrian, and Jordanian air forces on the ground, achieving surprise by flying "below radar" and also, one supposes, simply by opening a shooting war before the Arab governments and armed forces expected one. They knocked out Arab radar stations and destroyed almost the entire Arab air strength while it was still lined up on the ground. Arab combat air-craft which escaped the initial holocaust found themselves unaided by radar and hopelessly outnumbered when they took to the air, and swiftly fell victim to swarms of Israeli fighters. Some 450 Arab aircraft, many of the most modern Russian designs, were thus destroyed at the onset of the offensive. The Israelis also achieved superior firepower by reducing the time spent on refuelling and re-charging their aircraft, thus obtaining more sorties per aircraft per day. The Israeli navy succeeded in carrying out commando-type operations against Egyptian submarines and rocket-carrying motor boats. And on land, a small mobile armoured force attacked the centre of the southern front of the Gaza Strip to the accompaniment of a brisk rolling artillery barrage, no attempt being made to clear paths through the incomplete minefields by conventional sweeping. The Egyptian infantry and their dug-in supporting tanks were apparently surprised, and while part of the Israeli force concen-trated on mopping up the Gaza Strip, another part pressed slowly westward along the coast, meeting increasing opposition, but again surprising the Egyptians by continuing the offensive after dark. The effect of these movements was to persuade the Egyptians to face north, as they imagined the Gaza attack to be the major threat.

The next day, they were again taken by surprise when the main Israeli offensive took the form of two armoured thrusts on the general lines of the centre and southern east-west routes. Of these, the northern one made for Abu Agheila, the centre of the "quadri-lateral" communications system. Its path was prepared by para-troopers, who made a night drop late on June 5 to seize the road junction and disorganize the Egyptian command there. Arrived at Agheila, the mobile forces split in three directions: one to link up with the coastal attack; one to press on to Egypt; and one to form a defensive flank in the south-east against the main concentration of Egyptian armour at Quseima. The southern thrust came from two points near Kuntilla, and unified at Themed, where it curved north-east around the rear of the Egyptian mobile forces. These thrusts were made over extremely well chosen routes, which by-passed the incomplete Egyptian positions, in which the Egyptian tanks were commonly emplaced in gun-pits. Most of the Israeli losses were experienced when these positions were bumped. The Israelis rapidly penetrated between and behind the Egyptian lines; the Egyptian command organizations, devoid of air reconnaissance and looking to the north, were overrun or cut off from their troops; and confusion piled on confusion as the Egyptian units stationed westward along the main routes found themselves embroiled in actions for which they could see no pattern, and for dealing with which they received no useful instructions. Had the Israeli forces formed leaguer at sundown on June 6, settling down to await their second-echelon fuel and ammunition lorries and to complete and forward their documentary returns like any other bureaucratic Western army, the Egyptians might have managed to pull themselves together. But the Israelis pressed on—not regardless, but with supreme intelligence.

During the night they completed the job of turning the Egyptian army inside out, and by first light on June 7, they were virtually behind it. Those Egyptian forces which still retained coherence were now obliged to counter-attack in order to break free; harassed by ceaseless air strikes and completely lacking air or ground reconnaissance information, their tanks were destroyed by either the Israeli air force, or by the Israeli tanks and anti-tank guns against which they blindly butted themselves. Their futile counter-attacks ended at 10 p.m. local time in total defeat, and the Israeli forces then pressed on again through the night, their advance units reaching the Suez Canal by 3 a.m. on June 8.

The Egyptian forces in Sinai were now almost completely disorganized and were cut off from their main supply routes. The Israeli air force continued to attack army units that showed fight or motor movement, and an appalling shortage of water was immediately experienced by the hordes of Egyptian soldiery. In their tens of thousands they began to walk to the coast or back to Egypt—to water. Their collapse was utterly complete.

There can be no doubt that the Israeli army, like its comrades in the air force, had vastly enlarged its fighting capacity by extensions of its power to move itself around. First, it had solved the problems of coherent night movement and night fighting, long held to be nearly insoluble by Western and Soviet military leaders. Second, it had expanded its period of self-sufficiency in action by 500%. For whereas the ponderous mobile forces of Britain, the U.S.A. and the U.S.S.R. consider themselves to be doing well if they can move and fight between first and last light on one day without temporary withdrawal to refill and refuel, the Israeli forces were independent of supply for seventy-two hours. It was considered a great achievement to keep mobile forces moving and fighting for twelve hours at a stretch in days when a tank carried more than 100 rounds of cannon ammunition and fuel for more than 100 miles; today, when most tanks carry only some 60 rounds and, like the Centurion—which was the Israelis' most numerous tank—have a maximum speed of only 21 mph over a circuit of action of only 60 miles, the extension of battle endurance to seventy-two hours is a tremendous achievement. The Israelis probably made use of jettison fuel tanks, armoured fuel and ammunition carriers travelling with the forward troops, a vastly broader and more flexible administrative system which made only the minimal use of paper, and a highly sophisticated use of radio communications. Needless to say, these improvements must have contributed greatly to the possibility of nocturnal operations. And of course, the philosophy of the Israeli command, which placed a low value on static "wearing-out" actions and a high value on those leading to collapse and demoralization, was bound to result in an extension of battle endurance through a clever economy in the use of force. This philosophy was not without cost. Like the Germans between 1939 and 1941, the Israelis found that a high proportion of their casualties were formation leaders. In static war, the most dangerous situations are in the rifle section or the tank driving seat. In mobile war, it is almost as dangerous to be a brigade commander.

Contemporaneous with the Sinai operation was another against the Jordanian army, aimed at capturing the Arab-held parts of the City of Jerusalem and eliminating the Jordanian salients north and south of that city. Here, the distances involved were very small compared with Sinai, the push in Jerusalem being a matter of a few hundred yards, and the larger of the two Jordanian salients being only 40 miles north-south and 25 east-west, but the terrain is heavily folded and it was expected that many routes would be mined. The Jordanian defence forces were not very thick on the ground. An infantry brigade was concentrated in the Jerusalem region, and an armoured brigade with about 80 tanks was to the east in the Jericho plain, presumably sited to deal with a break-through into Jordan in the direction of Amman. But the Israelis did not head for Amman. A brigade force of paratroopers with infantry reservists and a brigade of armour encircled the city, starting in the unlikely direction of south-east on three lines of advance, while the Israeli air force attacked and seriously weakened the Jordanian armoured forces near Jericho. The movement started at noon, and continued throughout the night—something which quite surprised the Jordanians—and by first light on June 6, the encirclement was complete, the Jordanian forces in the Jerusalem area were surrounded, and the reserve infantry were regrouping to advance into the southern Jordanian salient. During that day, the Jordanian armour and supporting troops attempted to break the encirclement, but were held off by air strikes and by the tanks and anti-tank guns established by the Israelis on their flanks, as well as by their own reluctance to shell the Holy City. By 10 a.m., the Old City of Jerusalem was virtually occupied by the paratroopers and infantry.

This accomplished, the Israeli armour was detached to push north into the Nablus salient, and the Jerusalem Brigade pushed southward, while two fresh brigades invaded the Nablus salient from the north and west. The Jordanian forces—not of great strength—in Nablus and Hebron, the centres respectively of the north and south Jordanian settlements, were too slow in deploying against the invasion and were annihilated when they made their resistance. The bridges across the River Jordan were blown to prevent fresh Jordanian troops from entering the scene of operations. With half its force trapped and lost, its air force destroyed, its capital under the menace of air attack, and with no possibility, in view of the Egyptian collapse in Sinai, of restoring the situation, the Jordanian government agreed to a cease-fire. Once again, speed and indirectness had yielded handsome dividends.

But the third phase of the war now opened, and appeared to offer no scope for indirect operations. On Israel's northern frontier, the ground slopes steeply up into Syria across heavily folded limestone ridges. This difficult country was well prepared defensively with infantry and artillery emplacements, and offered no scope for

FOUNDATIONS OF MODERN WAR

Above: Hobart (*top left*) pioneers the radio control of armoured formations, 1930. *Courtesy: R.A.C. Tank Museum.*

Below: Guderian introduces the German Army to mechanisation—with dummy tanks, circa 1930. *Courtesy: R.A.C. Tank Museum.*

Above: Modernisation was not unopposed in the German Army. Here is a German cavalry formation still on horseback in Russia in 1941. *Courtesy: Imperial War Museum.*

COMMUNIST CONSERVATISM

Below: Russian cavalry was still partially horse-mounted as late as 1942. *Courtesy: Imperial War Museum.*

subtle outflanking drives. As soon as the Sinai collapse was assured, the Israeli command withdrew forces from that area and sent them against the Syrians, without allowing any pause for a "build-up of strength" such as we would expect from a Western army faced with a new formidable obstacle of a different kind. Units withdrawn from Sinai on June 7 and 8 were committed to the attack against Syria by noon on the 9th, being aided by engineer bulldozers which cleared paths for the hundreds of wheeled vehicles of all kinds used to rush the infantry across the fire-swept zone below the first crest. As on the Jordanian front, the initial assault was not rested at sundown. Tanks, infantry, and artillery used the hours of darkness to effect deep penetration of the Syrian network of positions, so that on the following morning the Syrian forward units were faced with the perplexing problem of fighting attackers from front, flanks, and rear simultaneously, while being cut off from their conventionally arranged command system. Syrian reinforcements found movement exceptionally difficult during the daytime, owing to incessant interference from the Israeli air force, and by mid-morning they had lost any grip on the situation. At midday, a general collapse set in, which by late afternoon had become a rout, exposing Damascus, the capital, to direct invasion. At 6.30 p.m., the Syrian government accepted a cease-fire.

This was the six-day war, 1967, in which a tiny and besieged country thoroughly trounced three aggressive neighbours whose combined strength overmatched hers alarmingly on all material counts, and won tremendous profits. For the armies of Syria, Jordan, and Egypt were emasculated, losing between them more than 127,000 men killed, wounded, and missing, 1000 tanks and self-propelled guns destroyed or captured, and more than 500 aircraft, while Israel lost only 700 dead, 2700 wounded, and a handful of captives (mostly aircraft crew), about 100 tanks destroyed or badly damaged, and fewer than 100 aircraft. Each of the three Arab nations lost heavily in territory, the future of which passes, presumably, to the diplomatic struggle. In territory, in booty of war stores, and in prestige, Israel made a colossal profit out of six days of war. How was it done?

That is to say, how was the impossible achieved? For at the time, the belief that a fast deterrent strike by Israel was impossible gained world-wide credence. On June 6, the second day of the war and the one on which the patterns of the Sinai break-through and Jordan encirclements were decisively settled, the London *Times* said, "In view of the Egyptians' minefields, their defence depth, the relative army sizes and the need to protect other frontiers, it is difficult to see how Israel can fulfil Eban's claim [Abba Eban: Foreign Minister] of the need to 'frustrate attempts of Arab armies to capture Israeli territory and break the siege which they have established against us'. It remains hard to see how such a conclusive victory could be gained in the short time which is all Israel will get."

The *Times*' attitude was a typical one, centred upon the beliefs that Egypt, Syria, and Jordan had concocted a plan to extinguish the State of Israel, and moreover, that the implementation of this plan was imminent when Israel struck. The rapid collapse of the Arab nations—geared, as they supposedly were, for all-out war— was unexpected by Western and Soviet observers, as well as the Arabs themselves, and of course had to be explained. Had religion managed to retain its hold over the Western mind, it would have been convenient to suggest partisan involvement by the hand of God, although Christian theologians might have found the point a tricky one in view of the faiths prevailing in the belligerent countries.

But today, the convenience of religion being denied them, military experts were obliged to cast about for a material instrument; almost as one man, they quickly seized upon the initial victory of the Israeli air forces as an explanation for every military event that followed it up to the cease-fire in Syria on the evening of June 10.

Now we may prudently hold some doubt in our minds concerning both of these major beliefs. Of the hostility towards Israel maintained by the Arab nations there can be no doubt. Of the imminence of an Arab invasion of Israel in June 1967 there should be considerable doubt. And of the capacity of the Israeli air force utterly to collapse and subdue three armies in six days there should be even more doubt.

It is certain that the triumph of the Israeli air force contributed significantly to the collapse of the Arab armies. The value of air power for reconnaissance and security and as flying artillery is immeasurable. Nevertheless, as events have shown in World War II,

in Korea and in Vietnam, an army devoid of air cover and cease-
lessly examined and hammered by enemy air power can be capable
of the most tenacious and prolonged resistance to greatly superior
forces. The classic examples of Germany, Japan, North Korea, and
North Vietnam, demonstrate that when the swift collapse of an
enemy is required, heavy air bombardment alone is not enough to
bring it about. Conversely, an almost complete lack of air power is
not necessarily an indication that sudden military collapse is about
to occur. If we are to look for the causes of military paralysis in
giants beset by midgets, we should look for psychological ones.

First, we should remark that in spite of the fact that there was
nothing very novel about the pattern of the Israeli offensive, complete surprise was attained. To put the matter on the plane of
individual human relationships, we might say that if we tended to
quarrel with a certain person, and if every time we quarrelled he
kicked us hard upon the shin, we would learn quite soon to deal
with his little trick. Either we would not quarrel with him, or we
would move and counter sharply as he was preparing to kick. Egypt
had already suffered two hard Israeli kicks upon the shin—it is
astounding that she permitted herself to receive a third one.

It is probable that the third kick—so violent and so damaging—
was suffered because the Egyptian government mismanaged not
just the exchange of force, but the entire encounter with Israel.

The Egyptian army had for many years received advice and
training at all levels of command from Soviet experts, and had
accepted the Russian defensive policy of absorption in depth, and
the reduction of an enemy by means of local concentrations of over-
whelmingly superior all-arms strength. The Egyptian commander
on the Sinai front was General Abdul Muhsin Mortaga, an infantryman who had long admired and studied Field Marshal Montgomery,
had spent three years in the U.S.S.R., and in the early sixties had
served as Chief of Army Training. The Egyptian army in Sinai,
1967, was probably engaged in a slow and careful build-up towards
a situation in which it could confidently contain the most mobile
enemy by local absorption, and then proceed to shatter him with
short-range sledge-hammer blows in a sort of Alamein-Stalingrad
process. This done, and with the tiny Jordanian army reinforced
until it was capable of cutting Israel in half at the narrowest point,

a really big squeeze could be put on the Jews, and the Egyptian government would be strengthened in its task of establishing Arab unity under Egyptian leadership. Unfortunately, it permitted the military forces to get out of step with the propaganda service. While the slow, methodical, Soviet-Montgomery military preparations were maturing, Cairo and Damascus radio were already conducting a verbal war of rapid movement. One imagines that the Egyptians should have shown a honeyed smile to Israel while building up her encirclement unobtrusively. Instead, they told the Israelis exactly what was in store for them, while making a great show of military strength; this gave the Jewish State excellent excuse for assuming that war had begun, before the actual military preparations made war impossible for Israel. Moshe Dayan, a believer in an offensive-defensive who was quite ready to act on the assumption of enemy aggression, was made Minister of Defence on a wave of popular feeling. An expert in mobile warfare and a firm believer in the value of paralysis, he entered office to become the political chief of soldiers already steeped in the same philosophy. The Chief of Staff of Armed Forces, Major-General Yitzhak Rabin, and the Chief of Air Force, Brigadier Mordechai Hod, had already prepared a scheme under the code name Nachonim ("daring pioneers") which would enable Israel to accept the verbal offer of hostilities by the Egyptian and Syrian propaganda services, while catching the real Arab armies unprepared. Fully aware of the importance of saving time (as much as possible had to be achieved before the Arab states could react co-operatively, or before the U.N. could negotiate a cease-fire), Hod and Rabin had taken steps to extend the mobility and endurance of their commands, primarily by cultivating a sense of urgency and immediate responsibility "at the top"—virtues which are notoriously lacking in the stiff, formal military hierarchies of Britain, France, the U.S.A., and the U.S.S.R. In the event, the philosophy and method of Dayan, Rabin, and Hod were wholly justified. The Arab propaganda services confused the issue by announcing Arab victories and advances, and the Israelis, keeping studiously quiet about the whole show, were able to achieve all their military objectives before the Arab countries could reconcile their true situation with their propaganda utterances, and help the U.N. to impose a cease-fire.

The Arabs had no sound schemes for co-operative action, and the collapse of the Egyptians and of the tiny Jordanian army undoubtedly destroyed the morale of the Syrian forces, which in any case had been unsettled by political purges.

Viewed thus, as a sudden and unexpected extension of political activity in terms of hard force, the Arab-Israel war falls into a more useful perspective. To consider it wholly in terms of pitched battles, or numbers versus numbers, is to encourage unrealistic, possibly dangerous, conclusions.

Viewing the little war as widely as possible, what conclusions regarding the evolution of mechanized armies can we draw from it?

First, the 1944-type mechanized army is dangerously obsolete as a means of achieving rapid decision. Under the most favourable political conditions yielding almost absolute surprise, with absolute air superiority, after the most drastic reorganization of its supply system, and after extending its battle endurance through the hours of darkness, the Israeli army's rate of advance was no faster than that of the panzers in 1940 and 1941. Obviously, conditions as favourable as those enjoyed by Rabin's army in Sinai are not exactly commonplace. Not every nation goes to war with its mouth while still unprepared in more vital respects. Nor can a supporting air force guarantee to achieve total elimination of its opposite number every time. Armies are designed to operate within a variety of political and military situations, some of them possibly unfavourable. It appears that the Israeli mobile forces produced a result comparable in speed and immediate effect to Rommel's desert advance of 1941; the latter took place over roughly five times the distance and lasted five times as long. But Rommel enjoyed only tactical surprise and partial air superiority, while being handicapped by a very inadequate supply system and unco-operative allies.

Since 1941, the range of tank guns has increased, the availability and variety of anti-tank weapons have increased, and the attack on armour and vehicles has become a major specialization among air forces. At the same time tanks, which constitute the main striking element in a mobile force, have become slower, bulkier, and heavier, with reduced circuit of action and ammunition storage. The design of armoured cross-country transports for infantry and other troops

has remained unimaginative and undeveloped. In Sinai, the
motorized infantry rode in half-tracks of a type introduced in the
U.S.A. before World War II.

To counter these two major factors militating against the
successful high-speed use of 1944-type mobile forces, we have only
the Israeli development of supply and night operations; these, it
would appear, serve (if used with intelligence, enthusiasm, and full
political surprise) to put mobile forces having the right philosophy
back to a 1940 level of performance. For general utility by a nation
such as Britain, one imagines that a basic reconstruction of mobile
armoured forces, starting with the vehicles and ending with Israeli-
type command and supply reforms, is long overdue. There are two
lessons from Sinai that are very important for us to understand.
First, brief operations yielding surprise and profit are possible, now
as ever, but the available means for working them are obsolete and
appear to require political co-operation from the enemy. Second,
for Britain, is a lesson fraught with danger: the Sinai campaign of
1967 warns us to beware of complacency. It may encourage less
progressive elements among the armed forces to adopt a traditionalist attitude, akin to that of the cavalryman of the twenties.
The 1944-type mechanized army may gain an unjustified reputation
for general usefulness—especially with regard to quick decisions—
and obsolescence may become a virtue.

Here, it is well to remember that superior mobility hinges as
much on military philosophy as on vehicular speed. Whatever
reforms are considered, the consideration must derive from a
fundamental sense of purpose, whose definition takes us straight
back to Fuller. What is the army's aim? To surprise the enemy's
generals at breakfast? Or to kill his private soldiers one by one?
It is with this fundamental sense of purpose or values in mind that
in the next chapter we will discuss developing trends in the distribution of firepower, and the evolution and organization of new fire
platforms.

Chapter Eight

An Aspect of Evolution

Can we predict future trends in armed conflict by the terms of man-made evolution? It should be possible, for evolution of some sort is inevitable, and if we can see the general pattern of it we should be in a position both to predict and to influence matters to make our predictions self-fulfilling. Biological evolution, often called a process of natural selection, is a kind of competition in which survival and net reproductive gain have always been accompanied in successively evolving types by improvement in organization, mobility, adaptability, and above all intelligence. A similar process can be detected in the evolution of human artifacts and ideas, as we have seen in our survey of the development of machine warfare. Trends there are. Time and again, sophisticated organizations have triumphed over more primitive ones, remaining in possession of the field until vanquished in turn by yet another advance in organization or weapons. So what does the future hold in evolutionary store for the organizations and weapons of today?

There is the conspicuous and unprofitable trend, so noticeable in the West, towards simple increase in the scale of destructive power, in terms of both local devastation and concentration of devastation within brief time limits. There is the rather more important but less conspicuous trend towards ever wider and looser distributions of small-weapons fire, which, from early machine-gun days onward, has repeatedly created a condition of impasse in which the trend towards increase in simple destruction could accelerate. Third, there is the trend towards canalization of military effort directed at straightforward attrition of the enemy, which seems to be a sort of mental straightjacket which governments and military authorities put on as soon as trends one and two become operative. Fourth is the at present purely technical trend towards common function in both air and ground forces, whereby air bombardment becomes more artillery-like and ground forces increasingly utilize air transport.

Given recognition of these trends, it would appear that any power such as Britain, which has widespread commitments but little with which to safeguard them, would do well to exploit the basic trend towards wider and looser distribution of fire. This would entail abandonment of all 1942–45 ideas on military deployment deriving from sheer weight and crushing effect, and concentration on realizing the maximum mobile firepower from the minimum force over the widest range of territory. This is something that huge continental-size armies and air forces cannot easily do; they are committed to bulk purchase and bulk consumption, and tend to standardize on the lowest common denominator.

It should be possible for research to discover the make-up of the minimal firepower needed to bring any given offensive to a check, and from there it should be possible to design the most advantageous (which means inconspicuous and highly mobile) means of mounting and commanding it. This in turn would certainly involve realistic experiment in novel command systems and ground-air vehicles. Highly mobile and widely dispersed air-ground organizations would hold a relationship to contemporary land forces among the world's major powers resembling that held by Guderian's original panzer divisions *vis-à-vis* the 1918-type armies universally regarded as valid in 1939. The advantages inherent in this relationship would in all probability give opportunities for swift and decisive counter offensives. This point needs emphasizing, because it is frequently suggested that Britain's army of today is "modernized" and "highly mobile". It is not! It is not highly mobile at all in comparison with other "advanced" armies. At present, it merely tags along with all the other forces, American, European, Russian, Israeli, Egyptian, Pakistani, Indian, and Chinese, which are belatedly modelling themselves on the panzer division of a quarter of a century ago.

The trouble is that Western armies were so late in mechanizing themselves that the relatively primitive degree of it they have so far achieved makes them appear "modern" by force of contrast. This is a subtle and dangerous illusion. We should measure modernity in our army not by contrasting tanks with horses, camouflage with red tunics, and machine weapons with muzzle loaders, but by comparing the army's degree of sophistication in organization and communications with the best contemporary civilian practice.

If we wish to enforce policies and influence thought by military means, those means consist of "local" lethal apparatus carried in vehicles. Unfortunately, this apparatus has evolved far more rapidly than the vehicles; yet the vehicles are the essential means of getting the apparatus into action with the minimum waste of time, and from the psychological point of view they are the more important, for time is the most precious thing we can have in modern armed competition. One *fait accompli* is worth a thousand ponderous, devastating checkmates, for the checkmate builds up mass hysteria, and behind fear and hysteria lies the weapon of total annihilation. As yet our army vehicles, that is to say, our first means of saving time, are pathetic hang-overs from World War II. Our army's power to move itself around has been surpassed by the civilian tourist industry. Our main battle tank is not air-portable. The majority of our supply vehicles still run on four or six road wheels. The deficiencies of these vehicles are well known, and technical journals, particularly the *U.S. Army Digest*, have for years been fond of publishing imaginative designs for military vehicles "of the future". Why the future? The need has been with us since before World War II.

Novel cross-country vehicles which have been put to military use are meagre in both variety and number. The design of track-laying vehicles appears to have passed through a prolonged phase of stagnation, wherein research has concerned itself with the solution of detail problems connected with the adaptation of slow 50-tonners to various kinds of nuclear war. Again, a comparison with civilian practice is worthwhile. Most 2-litre saloon cars are powered with about 45 to 60 bhp per gross ton weight, and can operate up to 300 miles at a cruising speed of more than 60 mph. Britain's main battle tank, the Chieftain, although powered by a huge 19-litre engine, enjoys only 14 bhp per gross ton, and cruises at less than 25 mph. As it consumes more than a gallon of fuel per mile run, it does very well to have a circuit of action of 200 miles. Its cross-country agility is inferior to that of the "Mother" tank of World War I at low speed, and to that of Christie tanks of World War II at maximum speed, and it is very destructive to all surfaces over which it is driven. Although supposedly designed for participation in mobile war, it cannot be transported by air, and is useless for the "brush fire" type of operations in which the British army has been repeatedly engaged since 1945. It might be argued that a fighting vehicle must necessarily be handicapped in respect of basic power of movement; but while recognizing the burdens of a fighting unit, one must nevertheless insist that in order to be universally viable, its basic mobility must be at least equal, and preferably superior, to the norms of society at large, and not to norms which have accidentally arisen within its own organization, whose authority derives solely from their conformity to the standards of similar organizations. This has always been so in the past, from Palaeolithic times onward, and so long as armed conflict is expressed in terms both of fire and movement, one may suppose that it will continue to be so. It is worth bearing in mind that the Roman Empire, covering the whole of the then known world, was defended and kept in order by a handful of legions whose advantage over enemies and rebels lay not in hitting power, but in co-ordination of activity and mobility of a very high degree. The legions actually created mobility by building military roads throughout the Empire.

Again, it is indisputable that warships have always possessed higher mobility than merchant ships, whether under sail or engines, except perhaps briefly in the heyday of the sailing clipper. Even the heavily armed and protected ironclad was a very fast ship. Today, light naval craft are as speedy and manoeuvrable as civilian racing motorboats and a great deal more seaworthy. The reasons for this emphasis on high mobility have never been doubted by sailors; in sea warfare, firepower derives from successful movement, and unsuccessful movement negatives firepower. It was for these reasons that Fuller drew his analogies between cross-country fast tank operations and naval warfare. In air power, likewise, no one has ever questioned the importance of basic mobility in military aircraft design; it is safe to say that since World War I, more research has been devoted to improving their flying power—and short-run take-off and landing power—than to increasing the weight of their armament and protection. An exception might be made in the case of the heavy, slow night bomber, but this, in World War II, proved the most vulnerable of all military aircraft, and the one with the most doubtful attainment. The odds were five to one that British night-bomber crews would be killed, wounded, or captured before completing a tour of thirty-two trips to Europe, and in view of the continued acceleration of German war production during the years of air bombardment, the value of their sacrifices is very difficult to estimate. Today, the importance of the fighting aircraft's mobility is such that the point is in sight where it may become a sort of returnable missile case.

If fighting ships and aircraft must have mobility far superior to the common norms of the civilian world, why not military land vehicles? What I wish to draw attention to here is that our "modern" army simply is not modern, in the vital sense of basic locomobility. Incredibly, it uses vehicles with power-weight ratios as low as 3 to 1: huge, slow vehicles which have limited route availability. It uses vehicles which destroy the surface of the ground they pass over, vehicles which cannot under any circumstances be flown to their work and which resemble more than anything else a siege train of the seventeenth century. But the difference in basic mobility between a seventeenth-century siege train and the rest of the horse-and-foot-and-sailing ship seventeenth-century world was as nothing compared to the difference between the modern army's tail and the norms of mid-twentieth-century locomobility.

This reduced locomobility is something that encourages military commanders, through the complexity of their supply systems, to remain fixed-front minded. Supply systems have become appallingly complicated, having grown since the late nineteenth century faster than the study of their manipulation. We saw how in World War I supply difficulties pre-doomed the large-scale artillery offensives largely because staffs were still railway minded, at a time when they were required to move forward over ground from which all normal means of communication had vanished. A machine army has a small fighting head, but many thick necks which, intertwined and inflated, stem from a gross and relatively immobile body. The art of moving this unwieldy organism rapidly backwards, forwards, and sideways while retaining forward control and fighting cohesion was, and is, an undeveloped one.

In Britain, there has been no original experiment in the supply, control, organization, articulation, and inter-relationship of armed forces since 1928. Although so many lessons from the wars of this century show the powerful and decisive effects of small, mobile air and ground forces neutralizing and collapsing massive resistance, the potentialities of this kind of operation remain uninvestigated. It is as though we are hypnotized into believing that in all human affairs, mass is might, and extreme specialization is always meaningful. They are not! The first mammals were very small and very generalized, but it is believed that they played a large part in making the dinosaurs extinct—by eating their eggs.

This brings us to the question of integrating air with land power. We have already noted the curious fact that from 1918 onward it has been possible to consider military power by air and land as distinct and separate, both in organization and function. This, surely, is a manifestation of adaptive and educational failure, and must provide the clue to future development. Future historians may well marvel that the British army relinquished control of its Royal Flying Corps in 1918, and agreed to the creation of an autonomous air force, failing to recognize that its main strength in the future would lie in a capacity to wield air power. And they will be astounded to learn that, having achieved administrative autonomy, the R.A.F. lusted after functional independence, and showed a great reluctance to develop army co-operation work.

Or perhaps they will not be surprised at all. For if soldiers could not then see that the day of the horse was over, how should they have been able to look ahead to the day when air and mechanized land power should be integrated? The horse has at last disappeared from military combat service, if not from military ritual. Can we hope that the integration of air and land power will follow? Already the trend towards common function is clearly to be seen, as the army places increased reliance on air power for tactical combat co-operation and strategic and tactical transportation, and as both bombers and fighters are superseded by artillery-type weapons in the form of controlled rockets and the tactical nuclear shell.

Given this situation, it becomes apparent that the first military organization to rationalize this process, accelerate it, and ruthlessly prune the dead wood from it will place itself in the forefront of military competence. It is a reorganizational problem of our times, as urgent today as was the groping, partial, unco-ordinated, 20 mph mechanization of the twenties. The goal is still paralysis of enemy resistance through the exercise of swifter reaction and superior mobility. We have yet to shake off our obsession with simple destruction. We have yet to see that our present degree of mechanization is not modern. It is elaborate but it is not sophisticated. These are the evolutionary steps we must take today, or be cursed by the next generation for neglecting. The question is, are we capable of taking them?

As already remarked, a striking phenomenon of our times is the movement of some air and land fire platforms towards common function. This movement is in some respects an extension of the evolutionary trend which brought about the tank. The latter provided a platform for artillery and small-arms which was highly mobile in two dimensions. The air platform adds the third dimension. A difference is the absence, in the air platforms, of extensive armour protection (although the Russians have armoured ground-attack aircraft in the past). Similarities of function are readily apparent; the ground-attack aircraft provides instant artillery fire, is interchangeable with the anti-tank gun in many situations, in mobile war out-ranges the fast tank in dealing with enemy transport, and of course, has long served as an assault infantry carrier, penetrating deep into enemy territory to make advance seizure of important places. None of these roles is very new; some date back to 1918. Another, and more important, similarity, is ideological. The tank was long regarded as an adjunct to the organic army structure; to judge by the behaviour of the Egyptians in Sinai, it is still so regarded in some quarters. The concept of a homogeneous, all-arms, armoured force making use of a variety of tank-derived vehicles proved to be extraordinarily difficult for the ordinary military mind to accept, and as we have seen, the capabilities of this kind of force are far from completely explored. Similar mental obstacles may beset the growth of the concept of an air army.

Yet this concept is not exactly novel. In 1919, Fuller held that air power should be held integrally by a mechanized army. Later, Christie designed airborne tanks, the tempo of whose work would be shaped by the speed of an aerial supply system. But just as the creation of armies on wheels and tracks had to await the advent of the strong, reliable cross-country track-layer, so the air army has to await the creation of a vehicle combining useful ground and air mobility. The question arises, if the possibility of such a vehicle can be envisaged, can full acceptance be made of the concept of a homogeneous ground-air army? Can military thought break free from the restrictive practice of thinking about aircraft solely as adjuncts to an existing type of military organization, as, earlier in the century, tanks were thought of only as adjuncts to horse-and-foot armies? To devise a novel type of weapon or military vehicle is one thing; to envisage the reorganization of a military society operating at a different tempo is something much more difficult. For as we have seen, it introduces profound social problems.

The U.S. Army used helicopters for reconnaissance, observation, tactical control, the evacuation of wounded, and in certain cases as a means of flying infantry and supplies directly onto their objectives in the Korean War. These ventures were quite successful, and led to an awakening interest in air-mobile operations such as Christie was never able to achieve.

Several lines of enquiry were opened up, which in the event have not united. On one hand, design work commenced on air-portable tanks, resulting in two major prototypes, the T92 Airborne and the M551 Sheridan, of which the latter was accepted for service. Although very light by comparison with a modern main battle tank, and in the case of the Sheridan being made largely of aluminium, they are nevertheless in the weight range 16–19 tons, and thus weigh as much as a fairly large road roller. Their suspension is much stiffer than Christie considered advisable for air-mobile machines, and their speed on smooth going is only about 40 mph. The T92, which was designed to be landed by parachute, was equipped with a conventional high-velocity tank cannon of 76.2mm calibre, the performance of which was inadequate for the anti-tank role. The Sheridan was given a short-barrelled gun of 152mm calibre, firing a general-purpose missile called the Shillelagh, which gives excellent results in both the anti-tank and high-explosive roles. This weapon is to replace the long-barrelled high-velocity cannon in other American tanks.

Another line of development concerned the air-mobility of unarmoured troops. In 1955 and 1957 experimental "Sky Cavalry" companies were formed and tested, and the U.S. Army Aviation School formed and tested an Aerial Reconnaissance Platoon. Their conclusion was that advanced reconnaissance would prove the prime role of air combat troops, and the term Aerial Combat Reconnaissance was retained and Sky Cavalry dropped. A first A.C.R. company was then raised at Fort Knox in 1958, and was followed shortly by a second one. The School of Armour which was closely involved with the early work of these units stressed the inadvisability of their isolation within a reconnaissance role; experience in the World Wars had shown that on the machine age battlefield reconnaissance could not be adequately carried out by lightly armed troops. As a result of these representations, the A.C.R. units became Aerial Reconnaissance and Security Troops. An A.R.S.T. was made up of Troop Headquarters in one light observation helicopter and one light cargo helicopter; one Scout Platoon in four light observation helicopters; one Rifle Platoon in four light cargo helicopters; one Weapon Platoon (MG, Mortars, etc.) in four light cargo helicopters; and a Service Platoon in one light observation helicopter and one light cargo helicopter. The total manpower consisted of 33 officers and 101 men, and thus resembled that of a British company rather than a troop. The proportion of officers was rather high, owing to the Scout Platoon consisting of thirteen officers and thirteen men.

It might be thought that the decision to give the new air-mobile units a full combat potential indicated that the creation of a new basic military structure with three-dimensional mobility was at hand; this was not so. In 1960 an A.R.S.T. was raised to experiment in reconnaissance roles with an armoured regiment; the conclusion drawn was that its best work was done as an extension of the security and reconnaissance of the parent ground formation, and in 1962 it was decided that an air troop should be made organic to each divisional armoured reconnaissance squadron. Here, the significance of the tentative naming and renaming of the new air-mobile units became apparent. Reconnaissance and security organizations can have no autonomous role. The words indicate servitude and limitation of function. As was the case with the tank, a novel military tool was to be adapted to old work carried out at the old tempo. The air-mobile power was to be put in double harness with the motor lorry, just as the tank was at first teamed up with the horse and pedestrian.

From 1955 to 1962, the development of air-mobile units was strongly influenced by armour, but in the latter years the Secretary of Defence directed that an Army Tactical Mobility Requirements Board (the Howze Board) should be convened to examine the question of air mobility on a more general basis, and in August 1962, after five months' work, the Howze Board recommended experiment on a much larger scale, involving infantry and transport organizations, without delay. Experiment was to have proceeded on two lines: an expansion of the existing A.R.S.T. to squadron and brigade strength, and a new experiment on an infantry footing, to be styled 11th Air Assault Division. These proposals were never fully implemented because the equipment needed was not forthcoming, and a compromise had to be effected; also, one suspects, a struggle probably developed for control of the new, prestige-giving organizations, analogous to that which developed in most countries earlier in the century for control of ground mechanized forces. The Air Cavalry Brigade (the armour line of development) was never raised. But the 11th A.A.D. (the infantry line of development) was raised, although only at brigade strength, in February 1966. Although ostensibly a new organization with air mobility, in fact it more closely resembled an air-portéed road infantry formation, since a special transport unit, the 10th Air Transport Brigade, was provided to supply it with the means of air mobility. The three A.R.S.T.'s were combined, together with a ground-rescue unit, to form an Air Cavalry Squadron, and this was later incorporated organically in the permanent structure derived from the evaluation of the 11th A.A.D. This process of testing and evaluation lasted two years, during which the U.S. Air Force interested itself in the work and came forward with alternative proposals, offering transportation and combat air platforms under air force control. While the army tolerated these proposals to the extent of providing a standard Road Infantry Division for experimental exercises, it refused to allow the air force to muscle in on its testing of the A.A.D. The air force competition faded, and in midsummer 1965, the Secretary of Defence approved the creation of a per-

MOBILE WAR—SPEED AND SURPRISE

A complete Italian Brigade Staff captured in January, 1941. *Courtesy: Imperial War Museum.*

The British Chieftain, the heaviest, slowest and most underpowered of today's tanks. Can a more mobile, more intelligent fighting machine replace it?

MATERIAL FOR THE FUTURE

Above: The U.S. Army's parachute-tank: M551 Sheridan. *Courtesy:* *U.S. Army.*

Below: The U.S. Army's project for a totally new air/ground fighting platform: the Ah56A. *Courtesy: U.S. Army.*

manent air-mobile division with integral organization of air vehicles, to be named the 1st Cavalry Division (Airmobile). It was raised at Fort Benning in July 1965, by an interesting device that recalls Hitler's arbitrary doubling of panzer divisions in 1941. As we know, the 11th A.A.D. was actually of only brigade strength, and even with the Air Cavalry Squadron could provide only a third of the air-trained strength of the new 1st Cavalry. The vacant places were therefore filled from sources locally available; the footsloggers of the nearby 2nd Road Infantry Division were turned overnight into air cavalrymen by a stroke of a pen. Within a month they were in Vietnam, and by October were committed to action.

Meanwhile armour had maintained its original slight hold on the evolution of air-mobile forces. More troops of the A.R.S.T. type were trained, originally to replace the aviation (liaison type) company already integral with each armoured regiment headquarters, and later to provide an air troop for each fighting squadron as well. Also, two squadrons of the 17th Cavalry were retrained as air units, and presumably will become Air Cavalry Squadrons organic to future units of Cavalry Division (Airmobile) type.

The air mobility of the U.S. Army's new formations hinges on the helicopter, which is primarily a carrying, not a fighting vehicle. Weapons can be mounted on a soft-skinned carrying vehicle such as the helicopter, but this does not turn it into an all-round fighting vehicle, for it remains vulnerable, when exposed, to every missile that can disable the unprotected human body, from the grenade fragment to the nuclear shell. Protection is essential to the machine age combat unit, human and vehicular, and protection is afforded in varying combinations by firepower, to destroy the enemy's means of making effective response; by armour, to prevent his response from taking effect; and by rapid movement, which enables the attacker to engage the enemy before he can organize an effective response. Accumulated experiences gained in the wars of the machine age seem to indicate that of these three protective measures, the first is the least useful, and the second and the last together the most useful. It would appear that the helicopter affords means of rapid movement to a high degree, but in the absence of a bullet-proof skin (and the bullet and the exploded metal fragment remain universal hazards in every type of military operation), it relies heavily for survival on the suppressive effects of supporting firepower.

It might appear that among units organized like the U.S. air-mobile forces, that is, as adjuncts to conventional ground forces, the difficulties of mounting adequate supporting firepower against a technologically advanced enemy might well negative the mobility of the helicopter. The U.S. Army soon recognized the limitations of the conventional helicopter for the role of combat vehicle, and in 1965 entrusted the Lockheed (California) Company with the development of a prototype high-speed compound helicopter, desig-nated Advanced Aerial Fire Support System. This machine is large, some 50 feet long, with stub wings, and its fixed rotor and pusher airscrew are powered by a 3400 bhp gas turbine. It has a cruising speed of 230 mph—half as fast again as other military helicopters—yet is highly manoeuvrable and stable as a fire platform. It is crewed by two or three men, and armed with selections from a variety of weapons: machine-guns, anti-tank missiles, etc. Its role, defined in its name, is to provide escort for troop-carrying heli-copters and to provide suppressive fire support in the landing zones.

The air-mobile forces of the U.S. Army have clearly shown them-selves capable of operating with great profitability. The use of helicopters rapidly increases the availability of a given force, while markedly reducing its casualties. "Difficult" terrain no longer impedes movement, and hence the choices of location and direction in making contact with the enemy are vastly enlarged. The reaction time of formation commanders is reduced. Fatigue (which has direct bearings on availability, combat success, and the incidence of casualties) is cut right down. The morale of the combat troops is enhanced by the awareness of their swift two-way communications with centres of command—something of tremendous value in diffi-cult country. In material terms, the 1st Cavalry Division (Air-mobile) uses only 434 air vehicles and 1607 land vehicles, against the Road Infantry Division's 101 and 3178. Fuel consumption is heavier on a simple time comparison, but should be more than adequately compensated by the air-mobile formation's increased work potential.

These successes gained by an early and relatively primitive form of army air mobility appear to demonstrate its existence as a superior form of military organization. If this superiority is real within a given operational context, should not the organization be given the scope, in free competition, to enlarge its sphere of effect through whatever means become available, even to the point of ultimately dominating and absorbing earlier organizations? Will this be the future of the air-ground army division?

The Commandant of the U.S. Army Armour School, Major-General A. D. Surles, states[1] that American armour is "looking forward to a Dynamic Tri-Dimensional Mobility (DTM) concept for manoeuvring and fighting mounted, from air and ground combat vehicles. Integration of air-armour manoeuvre units into armoured formations will provide a marked increase in mobility over present armoured formations. These air-armour units must live within the battle areas with other ground armour units and have a capability of seizing and holding ground. Yet while these air-armour units lift from the ground, their firepower and shock effect will remain and be enhanced.

"The key to the Armour DTM concept will remain the balance of firepower, protection and mobility. Just manoeuvring rapidly through the air without the capability to seize and hold ground will be improper. Likewise armour protection to the point of reducing mobility, and therefore losing rapid mobile reaction will be undesirable.

"The Armour DTM concept will not infringe upon the missions of the tactical air force, infantry air mobile forces, or even air cavalry forces... Neither will the DTM concept change Armour's role, but it will change its methods of operating and greatly enhance its capabilities... we face the challenge of mounting a portion of our forces in air vehicles that dart about the battlefield, very close to the ground, bringing heavy volumes of fire to bear on the enemy with great speed, surprise and shock effect."

The official U.S. view of the evolution of its air-mobile forces, as expressed by the U.S. Army's Public Information Division (July 1967), is that the Air Cavalry Division is unique among other units, and it is not designed to replace the standard infantry, armoured, or mechanized divisions. It may be used in its present form in a sophisticated war when air superiority has been obtained, to locate

[1] U.S. Army Aviation Digest, June 1967.

and maintain contact with the enemy or to maintain contact
between other friendly forces, and to counter hostile air-mobile,
airborne, and irregular forces.

How do we analyse these statements, which indicate the views,
first of an arm traditionally possessing high degrees of strategic and
tactical mobility, and second, of the General Staff of the U.S.
Army?

. Major-General Surles' view is simultaneously progressive and
retrogressive, positive and negative. He betrays anxiety to preserve
too much, to avoid treading on toes. Fuller, of course, did not care
about treading on the toes of the older arms. That is why he built
up resentment and eventually got the sack; and perhaps that is why
his greatest influence was among foreign armies. But if the capacities
of an air arm are to be thoroughly explored, the people making the
exploration simply will have to tread on certain toes; revolutions
cannot be accomplished without displacing somebody. The aim of
the progressive element should be to ensure that, whoever is jostled,
the revolution is effective in the right place. And the development
of air mobility must constitute, unavoidably, a form of revolution. A superior form of army movement is developing. It cannot develop without creating redundancy among more primitive
forms.

Again, while applauding the insistence of an air-ground machine
embodying all-round combat potential, one experiences disquiet
over its role of "dashing about the battlefield". An army favoured
with an unprecedented extension of mobility is empowered to avoid
the battlefield—to trip its enemy up and turn him inside out. The
experience of all machine age wars shows that to stand up face to
face with an enemy and slog it out is to initiate a combat not so
much between armies—which are moving forces—but between the
industries supplying them. Modern soldiers might do well to accept
the idea that the term "battlefield" is as obsolete as the musket. It
implies a confinement in both space and time, and is associated
firmly with the process of attrition and material destruction. Surely,
machine age armies should concentrate their strength and mobility
on the task of dissolving the restrictions of the battlefield, of getting
beyond it to the enemy's soft nerve-centres and belly. They should

aim at achieving a shot through his brain, instead of beating him slowly to death.

The official statement describing the roles and future of air mobility is regrettably negative. It ignores the factor of evolution. One is irresistably reminded of the French General Staff of the thirties, solemnly defining the roles and status of three categories of mobile division and their relationships to the older arms. For them, anxiety to preserve an obsolete army and bend new forces to its servitude resulted only in utter failure in the test of war. It was a high price to pay for preserving the social niceties and for avoiding treading on toes.

Throughout, the development of air-mobile forces in the U.S.A. has been ultra-cautious. Air-mobile units have been seen as adjuncts to existing ground forces, whether armour or infantry, rather than as potentially superior military forms whose capabilities will have to be emulated by existing organizations. In part this is no doubt due to the limitations of the helicopter vehicle, which at present cannot fight on the ground and, until the advent in service of the AA FSS (Lockheed Ah56A), has only moderate qualities as an aerial fighting platform. As things are now, the Air Cavalry really are not cavalry. The term itself is confusing. Of course, no mechanized army uses men on horseback for other than ceremonial occasions nowadays; when the name is retained, as is usually the case, for sentimental and associative reasons, it is taken to indicate the capacity to fight mounted. Now, although the First Cavalry (Air-mobile) may deliver fire from their helicopters to augment that given them in support by the U.S. Air Force, they fulfil their main tasks by landing, getting out, and fighting on foot. Thus, they might reasonably be termed dragoons, in the seventeenth-century sense, or Mounted Infantry in the Boer War sense, but never cavalry. Their closest relatives are Mechanized Infantry, and it might be not a bad idea to style them Three-Dimensional Mechanized Infantry, or Air Vehicle Infantry. To think of them as cavalry leads to a diminished concept of mobility, a failure to grasp the full mobility potential of the mounted soldier. Significantly, the scope of the U.S. air-mobile forces has always, since the creation of the first experimental units, been defined in conservative and restrictive terms.

There are other, social forces reinforcing the tendency to diminish the significance of mobility, which derive ultimately from the natural desire to preserve a comfortable society, the urge to maintain social security being no weaker in the military than in other professions. The deep roots of military efficiency can appear very remote from the sunlit upper branches of the vast, spreading tree that is the U.S. Army. And if the welfare of the tree should ever be doubted, the roots need not be examined; another massive dose of artificial fertilizer can be ordered from the inexhaustible national industries. These are very different circumstances from those surrounding the little Israeli military tree, clinging to difficult ground and repeatedly menaced by storm. That little tree simply has to strengthen its roots, and make the most sparing use of its rare doses of fertilizer.

Conservatism in the U.S. Army has led to an inverted view of mobility. It is a term repeatedly occurring in its utterances but is usually qualified by the adjective "tactical", and it boils down to variations of the means used for setting down infantry in set-piece battles. It is pertinent to ask whether tactical mobility is a proper preoccupation for a Supreme Command. Tools may be beautiful objects in themselves, but the craftsman—or perhaps artist—directs the greater part of his concentration to the purpose they serve. If a tool cannot serve the purpose, it is rejected, and a suitable one bought, made, or improvized. The purpose always dominates. The relations between tools and accomplishment, between tactics and military purpose, are exceedingly complex. But in general it is true to say that modern industrial societies, obsessed with scientific and technological achievement, tend to place excessive emphasis on the creation and refinement of tools, and give insufficient attention to their social purposes. This is as true of the military as of the commercial world, for armies are in many respects mirrors of the societies that own them.

Over-emphasis on tools at the expense of the study of their utility proved disastrous to Europe in World War I, in which, on the western front, a straightforward confrontation between rival tool-industries led directly to stalemate and impoverishment. Something similar seems to be happening in Vietnam today, where an astounding abundance of the products of technology appears unable to resolve a conflict, and constitutes in its provision a drain on the national economy, and in its expenditure, on national manpower, which increasing numbers of the population resent.

Army air mobility, then, is something which has been pioneered by the U.S. Army. Notable achievements are to be seen in the organization and command of formations, in the adaptation of vehicles, and in the creation of new weapon systems. But over all is a reluctance to break with the old, a desire to restrict the new to the role of adjunct and to define its scope in limited, tactical terms. We have already noted the effect which restrictiveness ultimately had on the French army of the thirties. We might end by quoting the remarks of the aged Field Marshal von Hindenburg on witnessing, in 1932, the attempts of the German Cavalry Corps to effect a compromise between the old and the new. The German cavalry, anxious to preserve their horsiness yet fearful of being left out of modernization, attempted to combine horses, motorcycles, armoured cars and lorries, with some heavy equipment horse-drawn and some motor-drawn. Von Hindenburg said, "In war, only that which is simple can succeed. I visited the Staff of the Cavalry Corps. What I saw there was not simple."

Among the major industrial powers it can scarcely be said today that organizations for machine warfare are simple. And, as we have seen, they have not been conspicuously successful: we have been obsessed with the complexity of our tools, and have failed to clarify our purposes.

The technological maturation of machine warfare took place over rather less than a human lifetime, some sixty-five years passing between the advent of the machine-gun in the 1880s and that of the nuclear weapon in the 1940s. As a form of social evolution, it reached the blind end of the cul-de-sac in 1945 and we have dwelt with it there over the past two decades, under endlessly reiterated threats of instant annihilation, surrounded by sporadic outbreaks of mass hysteria and violence, and without any real security despite fantastic expenditure on "defence". Thus, it would seem to be an evolutionary movement of little use to our species, compared, say, with gunpowder war, which facilitated the spread of many useful Western arts, or with classical war, which gave to Europe a relatively stable economy under the Roman standard. If machine war shows us anything clearly, it is that we are mentally out of step with it. This may be a poor sort of utility, or it may prove to be of great value, depending on our capacity for objective self-scrutiny, and for profiting by unwelcome self-knowledge.

The technology of machine warfare evolved at a tremendous and accelerating rate for less than a century. Having reached its logical goal of potential total destruction of life and habitat with the thermo-nuclear device, it halted its onward rush and began to proliferate laterally, as it were, in the manner of the biological evolution of a species within a newly colonized environment, into various specializations. Now, we are reaching the stage where the easily attainable goal of total destruction may be won by an ever-increasing number of rival methods—thermal, parasitic, neural, what-have-you. The nuclear weapon is only the archetypal total annihilator. Soon, it should be possible to gain the same instant effect by less noisy methods. It takes all sorts to unmake a world.

Contrasted with this, our actual warlike behaviour appears not to have changed a scrap throughout the entire period of eighty years, and as we are apprehensively aware, this has placed us in some very difficult situations—and has placed many people right out of existence—throughout the period. The reason for this breakdown of what should be unified achievement is that the growth and use of knowledge, and the development of adaptive behaviour, while complementary aspects of social evolution, unfortunately have very dissimilar metabolic rates. As Sir Julian Huxley remarked, "Concepts and beliefs gradually evolve, and may become more relevant to the changing conditions of life. On the other hand, concepts and beliefs may persist and continue to affect men's lives, even where, in the light of later experience, they can be seen as false and erroneous. . ."[2]

And it is with machine warfare that the hang-over of obsolete ideas has hit us hardest. It is in machine warfare that the development of tools, and therefore of material conditions, has run wildly ahead of our ideas about their utility.

It is only in the twentieth century—our own times—that social evolution has attained such speed and universality, and it is con-

[2] See Sir J. Huxley *Essays of a Humanist*.

ceivable that this dizzy expansion could have been almost wholly beneficial. But to our collective misfortune, the human activity first and most seriously affected was armed group competition. For all practical purposes we were still on horseback, yelling tribal slogans, when our battle-axes were exchanged for nuclear bombs. And so far we have been unable to evolve useful ideas about the aims and reorganization of machine age armed forces quickly enough. The means have run wildly ahead of the end, which should be an evolving human community. The means are twentieth-century, but our attitude to them is still Neolithic. We are still obsessed with killing, eighty years after we entered the cul-de-sac of machine warfare and made killing both irrelevant to the prosecution of war and dysgenic to our species.

Curiously, the military side of social evolution was one of the first to receive critical study. As early as the mid-nineteenth century it was noticed by a few statesmen, soldiers, and civilian observers that the British army was decidedly behind the times in ideas, organization, and some important matters of equipment, and military criticism became one of the first social studies. Of course, criticism was based on possible threats to national security (only "national", a mere century ago), and solutions were sought only within a narrow social environment. To explain increasing divergence between military ideas, attainment, and social requirements, most critics attacked the system by which officers were selected and promoted, on the grounds that it produced an unintelligent and ill-educated officer corps, which in turn elected only its most dunderous dunderheads to high office. Critics believed that a higher level of intelligence among recruits, both officers and other ranks, along with a system for promotion based on the objective measurement of abilities, would give an army modern thinking.

This is an important point. Too often, our military disasters have been laid at the door of stupidity. It is certainly true that until 1939 most armies selected their officers from a narrow social range, by means that could not measure their abilities objectively. Possibly this tended to produce officers of below-average ability, inasmuch as sons of superior ability would be encouraged to enter a professional or business career in the family interest, leaving the Army or Church to the fool of the family. But the example of the U.S. Army shows that intelligence is by no means the most important factor in shaping military behaviour. The U.S. Army was the first to introduce objective intelligence tests for the selection of officers, which it did in 1918, using Professor Binet's system. This has resulted in a high level of competence within the accepted field of military endeavour, but has had no progressive effect on the evolution of military thought, particularly in its higher social and force-to-aim relationships. Rather the reverse: the U.S.A. proved the most reluctant of nations to accept the introduction of armoured divisions, and when it did so, took steps to render them as immobile as possible, by dividing the divisional command between an infantryman and a tankman, by giving most of the tanks non-transmitting radios, and by giving the formation a cumbersome non-fighting tail that prevented it from ever attaining a high degree of flexibility. Having done this, the U.S. Army argued on the basis of its self-reduced mobility, that "long-range operations" were no longer a practical possibility. Again, the U.S. Army scorned and rejected Christie, its genius among tank designers. It failed to provide specialist armoured assault vehicles for the invasion of Europe in 1944, and in consequence suffered thousands of unnecessary casualties on the beaches. Its daylight strategic bombing policy was demonstrably unsound, by mathematical calculation or by practical experiment, yet it was pushed ahead regardless of appalling casualties in the early stages, doubtful results, and a cruel effect upon the civilian populations of enemy-occupied territory. And finally, the government and the General Staff of the U.S.A. in 1945 were prepared to place their entire strategic reliance on the atomic big stick, of which they naïvely imagined themselves holding a complete monopoly throughout the foreseeable future, and they actually disbanded a great part of their mobile forces, as if nuclear warfare were the only kind in store for humanity. It was partly due to this lopsided concept of war that no mobile armoured forces were available to scotch the invasion of South Korea in June 1950. This was an army which pioneered the use of objective tests for officers and skilled men! One does not doubt that many of the men who rejected Christie, preferred frontalism to obliquity, and suffered from nuclear myopia, were also men of superior intelligence. Objective tests measure abilities, and for a given range of activities intelligence, persistence, and emotional stability tests will be valuable guides for personnel selection. In fact, the U.S. Army may well have had the best possible human material in its officer corps ever since 1918, and may justly be proud of it. But tests of this nature do not measure attitudes and beliefs; they take the society's ideological framework as given, and only measure the individual's competence to perform tasks within it. And as we have seen, our chief difficulty with the psycho-social evolution of machine warfare is that we have not yet succeeded in re-defining its ideology with respect to its altered physical circumstances. In this situation, the most intelligent man can behave both intelligently and disastrously at the same time.

Soldiers more than any other class of society must act within tightly framed areas of behaviour, because their work is fraught with potential disaster and so hinges upon absolute inter-group confidence in rehearsed, reliable, "proven" behaviour. This makes them extremely dependent upon inherited ideas, which must, once accepted, remain unquestioned except by authority of the class leaders. As we have seen, it was the failure of the British military class leaders to authorize the overhaul of British military thought after World War I, that led to tragic confusion over mechanization, confusion which played no small part in reducing Britain as a world power. It might be thought that today armies should find relatively little difficulty in modernizing their outlook, having the example of other professions and industries to help them. Unfortunately, in machine war, which is also total war, the army in uniform is only a small part of the army that actually fights. The modernization and acceptance of ideas is a task not just for the professional soldiers of a nation, but for the nation as a whole, and this is something that presents special educational and hierarchical difficulties, which in my opinion are overdue for detailed investigation by psychologists specializing in behaviour studies.

Huxley says, with reference to the organization of religion, that an ideological framework which does not evolve and keep pace with new knowledge and social change is not able to serve its community usefully. This argument applies with even greater force to the organization of military force, for prevailing military concepts are strongly bound to the military social organization, and both together are more subject to collision—potentially disastrous collision—with new knowledge and the artifacts deriving from it than any other type of human society one can think of. And as the military society of a machine age civilization is merely the front end of a vast competitive industrial web, its collisions send shocks throughout the length and breadth of the community. Yet the hang-over of obsolete ideas on the conduct of war is a colossal one. We do not educate our young to see war as an aspect of normal inter-group competition, bearing definite relationships to economic, population, and psychological conditions. Instead, we deal with it episodically and emotionally, often taking our studies no deeper than the public utterances of politicians. As a result, each generation grows up with its ideas on war enveloped in a sort of woolly cloud, shot with spangles such as "justice", "glory" and "honour", and darkened by thunderclaps such as "enemy aggression", "evil", "grave injustice', and "atrocity". Considering the nature of our means of waging war, we really should clear our minds as to why and how we might want to wage it. Do we want to paralyse and collapse those with whom we come into political, economic, and ultimately armed conflict? Or do we want to wear them away, to "grind them into powder" as Winston Churchill said of the Japanese? If we think the grinding process might prove rather too expensive, how should we set about achieving a more economical alternative? Through mobility or massivity? With what new vehicles and with what use of machine age armour? We really should make up our minds: otherwise, we might find ourselves one day committed to an impasse like that of 1914—but infinitely more destructive.

Appendix A

Plan 1919

From Chapter XIII, *Memoirs of an Unconventional Soldier*, by
Major-General J. F. C. Fuller, C.B., C.B.E., D.S.O.
The original title of this project was:
"THE TACTICS OF THE ATTACK AS AFFECTED BY THE
SPEED AND CIRCUIT OF THE MEDIUM TANK".
It was changed later in 1918 to
"STRATEGICAL PARALYSIS AS THE OBJECT OF THE
DECISIVE ATTACK";
later still, this was changed, for brevity's sake, to
"PLAN 1919".

1. The Influence of Tanks on Tactics: Tactics, or the art of moving
armed men on the battlefield, change according to the weapons
used and the means of transportation. Each new or improved
weapon or method of movement demands a corresponding change
in the art of war, and today the introduction of the tank entirely
revolutionizes this art in that:

   i) it increases mobility by replacing muscular with mechanical
   power;

  ii) it increases security by using armour plate to cut out the
   bullet;

 iii) it increases offensive power by relieving the soldier from
   having to carry his weapons, and the horse from having to
   haul them, and it multiplies the destructive power of weapons
   by increasing ammunition supply. Consequently, petrol enables an army to obtain greater effect from its weapons, in a
   given time and with less loss to itself than an army which
   relies upon muscular energy. Whilst securing a man dynami-
   cally, it enables him to fight statically; consequently, it

superimposes naval upon land tactics: that is, it enables men to discharge their weapons from a moving platform protected by a fixed shield.

2. *The Influence of Tanks on Strategy:* Strategy is woven upon communications: hitherto upon roads, railways, rivers, and canals. Today the introduction of a cross-country petrol-driven machine, tank or tractor, has expanded communications to include at least 75% of the theatre of war over and above communications as we at present know them. The possibility today of maintaining supply and of moving weapons and munitions over the open, irrespective of roads and without the limiting factor of animal endurance, introduces an entirely new problem in the history of war. At the moment he who grasps the full meaning of this change, namely, that the earth has now become as easily traversable as the sea, multiplies his chances of victory to an almost unlimited extent. Every principle of war becomes easy to apply if movement can be accelerated, and accelerated at the expense of the opposing side. Today, to pit an overland mechanically moving army against one relying on roads, rails, and muscular energy is to pit a fleet of modern battleships against one of wind-driven three-deckers. The result of such an action is not even within the possibilities of doubt; the latter will for a certainty be destroyed, for the highest form of machinery must win because it saves time, which is the controlling factor in war.

3. *The Present Tank Tactical Theory:* Up to the present the theory of the tactical employment of tanks has been based on trying to harmonize their powers with existing methods of fighting, that is, with infantry and artillery tactics. In fact, the tank idea, which carries with it a revolution in the methods of waging war, has been grafted on to a system it is destined to destroy, instead of being given free scope to develop on its own lines. This has been unavoidable, because of the novelty of the idea, the uncertainty of the machine, and ignorance in its use.

Knowledge can best be gained by practical experience, and at first this experience is difficult to obtain unless the new idea is grafted onto the old system of war. Nevertheless, it behoves us not to forget that the tank (a weapon as different from those which preceded it as the armoured knight was from the unarmoured infantry who preceded him) will eventually, as perfection is gained and numbers are increased, demand a fundamental change in our tactical theory of battle.

The facts upon which this theory is based are now rapidly changing, and unless it changes with them, we shall not develop to the full the powers of the new machine: that is, the possibility of moving rapidly in all directions with comparative immunity to small-arm fire.

From this we can deduce the all-important fact that infantry, as at present equipped, will become first a subsidiary and later a useless arm on all ground over which tanks can move. This fact alone revolutionizes our present conception of war, and introduces a new epoch in tactics.

4. *The Strategical Objective:* Irrespective of the arm employed, the principles of strategy remain immutable, changes in weapons affecting their application only. The first of all strategical principles is "the principle of the object", the object being "the destruction of the enemy's fighting strength". This can be accomplished in several ways, the normal being the destruction of the enemy's field armies —his fighting personnel.

Now, the potential fighting strength of a body of men lies in its organization; consequently, if we can destroy this organization, we shall destroy its fighting strength and so gain our object.

There are two ways of destroying an organization:

i) by wearing it down (dissipating it);
ii) by rendering it inoperative (unhinging it).

In war the first comprises the killing, wounding, capturing, and disarming of the enemy's soldiers—body warfare. The second, the rendering inoperative of his power of command, is brain warfare. Taking a single man as an example, the first method may be compared to a succession of slight wounds which will eventually cause him to bleed to death, and the second to a shot through the brain.

The brains of an army are its staff—Army, Corps and Divisional Headquarters. Could we suddenly remove these from an extensive sector of the German front, the collapse of the personnel they control would be a mere matter of hours, even if only slight opposition were put up against it. Even if we put up no opposition at all, but in addition to the shot through the brain we fire a second shot through the stomach, that is, we dislocate the enemy's supply system behind his protective front, his men will starve to death or scatter.

Our present theory, based on our present weapons of limited range of action, has been one of attaining our strategical object by brute force; that is, the wearing away of the enemy's muscles, bone and blood. To accomplish this rapidly with tanks will demand many thousands of these machines, and there is little likelihood of our obtaining the requisite number by next year; therefore let us search for some other means, always remembering that probably at no time in the history of war has a difficulty arisen whose solution has not at the time in question existed in some man's head, and frequently in those of several. The main difficulty has nearly always lurked, not in the solution itself, but in its acceptance by those who have vested interests in the existing methods.

As our present theory is to destroy "personnel", so should our new theory be to destroy "command", not after the enemy's personnel has been disorganized, but before it has been attacked, so that it may be found in a state of complete disorganization when attacked. Here we have the highest application of the principle of surprise— surprise by novelty of action, or the impossibility of establishing security even when the unexpected has become the commonplace.

Compared to fighting men there are but a few commanders in the field; therefore the means required to destroy these commanders will be far less than those normally required to destroy the men they control.

It is no longer a question of, had Napoleon possessed a section of machine-guns at Waterloo, would he not have won that battle? The question is rather, had he been able to kidnap or kill the Duke of Wellington and his Staff at 9 a.m. on June 18, 1815, would he not have done equally well without firing a shot? Would not the sudden loss of command in the British army have reduced it to such a state of disorganization that, when he did advance, he would have been able to walk through it?

It is not my intention in this paper to deprecate the use of brute force, but to show that much brute energy and loss of brute energy may be saved and prevented if we make use of the highest brain-power at our disposal in applying it.

5. *The Suggested Solution:* In order to render inoperative the command of the German forces on any given front, what are the requirements?

From the German front line the average distance to nine of their Army Headquarters is eighteen miles; to three Army Group Head-quarters forty-five miles; and the distance away of their Western G.H.Q. is one hundred miles. For purposes of illustration the eighteen-mile belt or zone containing Army, Corps, and Divisional Headquarters will prove sufficient.

Before reaching these Headquarters, elaborate systems of trenches and wire entanglements, protected by every known type of missile-throwing weapon, have to be crossed.

To penetrate or avoid this belt of resistance, which may be compared to a shield protecting the system of command, two types of weapons suggest themselves:

   i) the aeroplane;
  ii) the tank.

The first is able to surmount all obstacles; the second, to traverse most.

The difficulties in using the first are very great, for even if land-ing-grounds can be found close to the various Headquarters, once the men are landed, they are no better armed than the men they will meet; in fact, they may be compared to dismounted cavalry facing infantry.

The difficulties of the second are merely relative. At present we do not possess a tank capable of carrying out the work satisfactorily, yet this is no reason why we should not have one nine months hence if all energies are devoted to design and production. The idea of such a tank exists, and it has already been considered by many good brains; it is known as the "Medium D Tank", and its specifications are as follows:

   i) to move at a maximum speed of 20 miles an hour;
  ii) to possess a circuit of action of 150 to 200 miles;
 iii) to be able to cross a 13- to 14-foot gap;

iv) to be sufficiently light to cross ordinary road, river, and canal
bridges.

6. *The Tactics of the Medium D Tank:* The tactics of the Medium
D tank are based on the principles of movement and surprise, its
tactical object being to accentuate surprise by movement, not so
much through rapidity as by creating unexpected situations. We
must never do what the enemy expects us to do; instead, we must
mislead him, that is, control his brain by our own. We must suggest
to him the probability of certain actions, and then, when action is
demanded, we must develop it in a way diametrically opposite to
the one we have suggested through our preparations.

Thus, in the past, when we massed men and guns opposite a
given sector, he did the same and frustrated our attack by making
his own defences so strong that we could not break through them,
or if we did, were then too exhausted to exploit our initial success.
At the battle of Cambrai, when our normal method was set aside,
our blow could not be taken advantage of, because the forces which
broke through were not powerful enough to cause more than local
disorganization. The enemy's strength was not in his front line, but
in rear of it; we could not, in the circumstances which we and not
he had created, disorganize his reserves. Reserves are the capital of
victory.

A study of Napoleon's tactics will show us that the first step he
took in battle was not to break his enemy's front, and then when
his forces were disorganized risk being hit by the enemy's reserves;
but instead to draw the enemy's reserves into the fire fight, and
directly they were drawn in, to break through them or envelop
them. Once this was done, security was gained; consequently, a
pursuit could be carried out, a pursuit being more often than not
initiated by troops disorganized by victory against troops disorganized by defeat.

Before the third battle of Ypres (Passchendaele) began, we had
drawn in large forces of the enemy's reserves; this, judged by the
Napoleonic standard, was correct. Where we failed was that once
we had drawn them in, we had no old guard at hand to smash
them. At the battle of Cambrai[1] we struck with our old guard

[1] Cambrai as fought—not Cambrai as originally projected (see
Ch. 3).

(tanks) before the German reserves were on the battlefield. It was a blow in the air, and the result was that we crashed through the enemy's front and then, when his organized reserves were brought up, having no old guard to meet them, the tactical advantage was theirs and not ours—we were repulsed.

Tactical success in war is generally gained by pitting an organized force against a disorganized one. This is the secret of Napoleon's success. At Ypres we had not the means to disorganize the enemy; at Cambrai the enemy did not offer us the opportunity to disorganize his. Both battles were conceived on fundamentally unsound tactical premises. What we want to aim at now is a combination of these two ideas:

   i) to force the enemy to mass his reserves in a given sector;
  ii) to disorganize these reserves before we break through them.

This done, pursuit, the tactical act of annihilation, becomes possible. Pursuit is the dividend of victory; the more reserves we force the enemy to mass, so long as we disorganize them, the greater will be the tactical interest on our capital. With the Medium D tank and the aeroplane there is no reason why we should not receive one hundred per cent interest upon our investments. This represents winning the war in a single battle.

7. *The Medium D Tank Battle:* A battle based on the powers of the Medium D tank may in brief be outlined as follows.

A frontage of attack of some ninety miles should be selected, and on this frontage, by the inducement of visible preparation, some four or five German armies collected. Then the area lying between the lines connecting up the German Army Headquarters and those linking their Divisional Headquarters will form the zone of the primary tactical objective. Heretofore it has been the area between the enemy's front line and his main gun positions, but this zone will now become the secondary tactical objective. The geographical position of objectives is therefore reversed: the last becomes the first and the first becomes the last. Here is the foundation of surprise.

Once preparations are well in hand, without any tactical warning whatsoever, fleets of Medium D tanks should proceed at top speed by day, or possibly by night, directly on to the various Headquarters lying in the primary tactical zone. If by day, these targets can be marked by aeroplanes dropping coloured smoke, and if by night, by dropping coloured lights, or by guns firing coloured light shells. As the longest distance to be covered may be taken as twenty miles, the Medium D tanks should reach the German Army Headquarters in about two hours.

Meanwhile every available bombing machine should concentrate on the various supply and road centres. The signal communications should not be destroyed, for it is important that the confusion resulting from the dual attack carried out by the Medium D tanks and aeroplanes should be circulated by the enemy. Bad news confuses, confusion stimulates panic.

As soon as orders and counter-orders have been given a little time to become epidemic, a carefully mounted tank, infantry, and artillery attack should be launched, the objective of which is the zone of the enemy's guns; namely, the secondary tactical zone some 10,000 yards deep.

Directly penetration has been effected, pursuit should follow, the pursuing force consisting of all Medium tanks available and lorry-carried infantry. To render this force doubly powerful, it should be preceded by squadrons of Medium D tanks, which will secure all centres of communication, break up hostile Army Group Headquarters, and disperse all formed bodies of troops met with. The German Western G.H.Q. should be dealt with by dropping several hundred tons of explosives upon it: that at least will neutralize clear thinking.

8. The Morcellated Front of Attack: A continuous front of attack of ninety miles may seem too extended to be practicable. By a simple tank manoeuvre, this front, so far as the attackers are concerned, can be reduced to fifty miles without reducing the total of ninety miles to be disorganized.

9. The Effect of the Medium D Tank on Tactics: The improvement in any one arm, especially an improvement in mobility, will affect the utility and employment of all the remaining arms in a degree proportionate to the improvement. Taking the various arms— infantry, cavalry, artillery, aircraft, engineers, and commissariat— the following deductions can be made:

i) *Infantry.* Except for gaining the secondary zone, infantry on their feet will be next to useless. They will have to be carried forward in mechanical transport if they are ever to keep up with the pursuit of the Medium D tank, which will advance to a minimum depth of twenty miles a day.

The employment of infantry should be on the following lines:

a) to assist in the tactical penetration;
b) to operate in areas unsuited to tanks;
c) to occupy the areas conquered by the tanks;
d) to protect our rear services.

After the first blow, the likelihood of infantry having to attack will be reduced; consequently, their chief duty will be to form a mobile protective line in rear of the Medium D tanks, in order to secure the administrative and engineer services from local annoyance. Therefore, their tactics will be defensive, and their chief weapon will be the machine-gun.

ii) *Cavalry.* If cavalry have sufficient endurance to keep up a pursuit of at least twenty miles a day for a period of five to seven days, their value will be considerable, for they will be able to form mounted skirmishing lines between the groups of Medium D tanks, and it may be assumed that even should the entire cavalry force by the end of the seventh day be horseless, after a pursuit of 150 miles the enemy will be reduced to a non-fighting condition.[2]

iii) *Artillery.* The heavy artillery will disappear as a mobile arm after the first day's advance, and will be relegated to its original position in the siege train. The field artillery, if still horse-drawn, will be unable to keep up with the fighting after the second or third day's advance. Field artillery horses must, therefore, be replaced by tractors; even today this is becoming a necessity on account of the difficulty of keeping horses alive on or behind the battlefield.

iv) *The Royal Air Force.* As the mobility of the tank increases,

[2] This paragraph was inserted to propitiate the horse worshippers. Tractor-drawn light infantry would have been more effective. [Fuller's own comment.]

so will it have more and more to rely on the aeroplane for its security and preservation.

The duties of the R.A.F. will be as follows:

a) to act as an advanced guard to the tanks;
b) to assist tanks in disorganizing the enemy's Headquarters;
c) to guide tanks on to their objectives;
d) to protect tanks from hostile gunfire;
e) to supply advanced squadrons of tanks with petrol, ammunition, etc.;
f) to act as messengers between tanks and their bases;
g) to carry tank brigade commanders above their sectors of operation, in order that these officers may see what their machines are doing and may handle their reserves accordingly. Aeroplanes will bear to tanks a relationship similar to that of cavalry to infantry in the old days.

v) *Royal Engineers.* The duties of Royal Engineers and Pioneer units will be considerably enlarged. Their work will be confined chiefly to the improvement of communications—road and rails and the building of bridges. All defence work will be relegated to infantry.

vi) *Army Service Corps.* The mobility of the A.S.C. will be taxed to its utmost. Horses will disappear and road lorries will have to be supplemented by field lorries if the troops are to be adequately supplied. All road lorries should easily be convertible into field lorries by some simple attachment, which will enable them to traverse grass and ploughland. The main fact is that the mobility of the Medium D tank will increase the mobility of all the other arms. Draught horses will disappear, and by degrees riding horses as well. Consequently, the more mobile arms will prove the most useful, the less mobile either disappearing from the battlefield or being brought up to the requisite standard of mobility by mechanical means.

10. *The Influence of the Medium D Tank on Grand Tactics:* The influence of the mobility of the Medium D tank on grand tactics

(the penetration or envelopment of an enemy) is almost beyond appreciation. Penetration of existing defences becomes considerably easier than the old field attack over untrenched ground, and envelopment a mere matter of leisurely manoeuvre.

Besides these advantages, frontages of attack can be exhausted out of all former proportion to the strength of the attacking forces, and surprise forms the basis of every action.

So long as the enemy is unable to meet the Medium D tank by a similar or a superior weapon, all attacks based on its powers will become methodical; that is, they will be carried out according to plan, the disorganization of the rear services will cease because the initiative will be ours, the enemy's will being subordinate to our own.

11. The Influence of the Medium D Tank on Strategy: Strategy, or the science of making the most of time for warlike ends, that is of opportunity, will practically cease for that side which pits muscular endurance against mechanical energy.

The possibility of applying naval tactics to land warfare is an entirely new application of the strategical principles, which at present endow the side which can apply them with incalculable power. Formerly strategy depended on communications; now communications will become universal, and though roads and rails will not disappear, they will become but lines of least resistance to movement in the universal vehicle which the earth's surface will be turned into by all types of cross-country machines.

Strategically the leading characteristic of the Medium D tank is that it is a time-saver, on account of its high speed, its extensive radius of action and its locomobility, or power to move in all directions on a plane surface. Compared to infantry in battle, its speed is ten times greater and its radius of action twenty-five times greater. Its protective power is beyond comparison.

The saving of time in battle means the saving of time in manufacture, and consequently, the reduction of manpower in production.

Time is, however, our enemy; for the only thing to fear now is that we shall not have sufficient time wherein to produce these machines by next year. To use a new machine in driblets is to make the enemy a patentee in the design. To fail to win the war in 1919 through lack of Medium D's is to risk being beaten by a better German machine in 1920. For it must be remembered that as yet no weapon has been produced which time has not rendered obsolete. The number of Medium D tanks required by May 1919 is 2000, and with this number there is every prospect of ending the war.

Appendix B

Strategic Paralysis

Extracts from Captain B. H. Liddell Hart's book, *Thoughts on War 1919–39*, illustrating the growth of his concept of Strategic Paralysis.

A. *A Vision*

"Thinking ahead"—into the problems of warfare—has led me to the view that military operations in the future, the exact date being still indefinite, will be carried out almost predominantly by fleets of tanks and aircraft, which will be maintained by communications based on cross-country transport vehicles with air transport as an auxiliary or secondary line of supply. Under these conditions heavy artillery and infantry will alone survive of the other arms, the former functioning again in the original defensive role of garrison artillery, whilst infantry will become a species of "land-marines" for the defence of fortified bases and to be discharged as landing parties, from the bowels of a tank fleet, for "ferret work" against suitable objectives. But to suppose that this metamorphosis from traditional armies will be accomplished as by the wave of a wizard's wand betokens an ignorance of the slow fruition of all new growths throughout history, due to the natural conservatism of the military masses even more than that of the leaders.

In past centuries the scientific development in weapons was so slow, and the military hierarchy so conservative, that comparatively few wars have been determined by the possession by one side of a superior weapon. But the majority of wars have been decided by some new development in the science of war, most frequently in means of movement or tactics. Philip's Macedonian phalanx, Hannibal's tactics of surprise, Nero's use of interior lines resulting in the Metaurus victory, Scipio's use of a reserve, the English long-bow tactics at Crecy and Poitiers, Cromwell's Ironsides, Marlborough's development of manoeuvre, Frederick's oblique order,

Napoleon's bataillon carré and swift concentrations, Moore's light infantry, Wellington's defensive-offensive tactics and line formation, Moltke's staff system, are but a few examples of how the instrument forged, or the tactics thought out, in advance have decided the fate of nations.

As changes in weapons now succeed each other so rapidly, the task of assimilating the lessons which they bring with them becomes more and more difficult. Yet the nation whose military advisers grasp most quickly the sense behind every new development has an advantage which grows more decisive with the increasingly greater effect of each successive new weapon.

The very zenith of surprise is to obtain one at the onset of a war. Research, accordingly, becomes a matter of the most vital importance to the security of a nation. An expansion of technical research and design establishments is a need so urgent as to brook no delay.

But to possess a new weapon is of little value unless we also know how to exploit its advantages to the utmost when we use it. Because of the failure to ensure that progress in tactics kept pace with progress in weapons, the Germans threw away their chance of decisive surprise on the introduction of gas, and we were similarly at fault with the tank. It would seem essential, therefore, that a tactical research department should be created to work in close co-operation with the technical branch. At the same time, we need to maintain an experimental formation, commanded and staffed by the pick of our military talent and assured of continuity of composition, in order to test out practically the application to the troops of new tactical and technical ideas.

Of all qualities in war it is speed which is dominant, speed both of mind and movement—without which hitting-power is valueless and with which it is multiplied. An acceleration of pace, only to be obtained by the full development of scientific inventions, will transform the battlefields of the future from squalid trench labyrinths into arenas wherein manoeuvre, the essence of surprise, will reign after hibernating for too long within the mausoleums of mud. Then only can the art of war, temporarily paralysed by the grip of trench warfare conditions, come into its own once more. [June 1921]

B. *The Mongols*

They [the Mongols] proved that mobility is the king-pin of tactics, as of strategy; that lightly armed troops can beat more heavily armed ones if their mobility is sufficiently superior, demonstrating that the "weight" of a force is its weapon-power multiplied by its mobility, and that this mobility is a far better protection than any form of negative defence. Is there not a lesson here for the armies of today? The development of mechanical firepower has negatived the hitting-power of cavalry against a properly equipped enemy. But on land the armoured caterpillar vehicle, or tank, appears to be the natural heir of the Mongol horseman, for the "caterpillars" are essentially mechanized cavalry.

Further, aeroplanes would seem to have the same qualities in ever higher degree, and it may be that in future they will prove the successors of the Mongol horsemen.

A study of the Mongol methods and the secrets of their success may at least serve to clear our minds of long-inherited prejudices, and reveal the unsoundness of conventional objections to a new and mobile arm which are based on its minor limitations for movement in certain localities and over occasional types of ground. The deduction from the Mongol campaigns would surely seem to be that superior general mobility when allied with hitting-power is both a more powerful and a more secure tool than the mere loco-mobility and defensive power of an army founded on infantry. [December 1923]

C. *Speed and Paralysis*

While developing means of quicker control on our own part, it is no less important to apply our minds to the problem of upsetting the enemy's control, and to apply new means to that purpose. We must not only exploit the offensive use of aircraft against the enemy's reserves and communications, but grasp the value of an air blow against the command and signal centres of the enemy—paralysing his brain and nervous system. [September 1924]

D. *Paralysis or Destruction?*

From the delusion that the armed forces themselves were the real objective in war, it was the natural sequence of ideas that the combatant troops who composed the armies should be regarded as the target to strike at.

Thus progressive butchery, politely called "attrition", becomes the essence of war. To kill, if possible, more of the enemy troops than your own side loses, is the sum total of this military creed, which attained its tragi-comic climax on the Western Front in the Great War.

The absurdity and wrong-headedness of this doctrine should have been apparent to any mind which attempted to think logically instead of blindly accepting inherited traditions. War is but a duel between two nations instead of two individuals. A moment's unprejudiced reflection on the analogy of a boxing match would be sufficient to reveal the objective dictated by common sense. Only the most stupid boxer would attempt to beat his opponent by merely battering and bruising the latter until at last he weakens and yields. Even if this method of attrition finally succeeds, it is probable that the victor himself will be exhausted and injured. The victorious boxer, however, has won his stake, and can afford not to worry over the period of convalescence, whereas the recovery of a nation is a slow and painful process.

A boxer who uses his intelligence, however, aims to strike a decisive blow as early as possible against some vital point—the jaw or the solar plexus—which will instantly paralyse his opponent's resistance. Thus he gains his objective without himself suffering seriously. Surely those responsible for the direction of war might be expected to use their intelligence as much as a professional pugilist?

The true military objective is a mental rather than a physical objective—the paralysis of the opposing command, not the bodies of the actual soldiers. For an army without orders, without co-ordination, without supplies, easily becomes a panic-stricken and famine-stricken mob, incapable of effective action. [March 1925]

E. *The Real Target*

The real target in war is the mind of the enemy command, not the bodies of his troops. If we operate against his troops, it is fundamentally for the effect that action will produce on the mind and will of the commander; indeed, the trend of warfare and the development of new weapons—aircraft and tanks—promise to give us increased and more direct opportunities of striking at this psychological target. [June 1926]

Appendix C

J. W. Christie

Mr. J. W. Christie was born in 1866 at River Edge, New Jersey, and died in 1944. He was a mechanical engineer, and gained a good reputation in the field of armament design before World War I with his very successful naval gun turrets, which were adopted by the U.S. and British navies. He entered the field of tank design during the later years of World War I, after being commissioned to build a number of self-propelled artillery mounts. He did not invent either self-propelled artillery or the tank, but his mind was so penetrating and restless that, having encountered these weapons in their earliest forms, he was impelled to improve them almost out of recognition. That was perhaps the most astonishing thing about him. He was not a soldier, nor was he greatly encouraged by soldiers or politicians to develop U.S. armaments. He was essentially an artist-engineer, a Brunel within his limited field. He entered tank design because its problems first interested and later fascinated him, and he worked out his projects to their logical end, regardless of business considerations.

Independently of Fuller and Liddell Hart, he saw that the fast cross-country armoured vehicle could transcend the limitations of position war. Through the twenties he worked to produce a land tank that could fight across country at speeds normal to motor traffic on main roads, and complementary to it, an amphibious tank that could swim from ship to shore, or across rivers, coping with a strong tideway or river current. These two vehicles were perfected by 1928, but were received with incomprehension by most U.S. military authorities, and rejected on grounds of petty unreliability or unorthodox layout. But a few discerning soldiers hailed them with acclaim.

Christie gave his ideas on mobile warfare no expression in written argument as did Fuller and Liddell Hart: his tanks expressed his ideas. It seemed to him so obvious that superior mobility, by exploiting time, must logically save cash and life expenditure, that he simply failed to appreciate the magnitude of the mental gulf stretching between his mind and the orthodox military one. He expected soldiers to regard their work as objectively as he regarded his, and could not see that military society is tied down to rules of precedent and status and to the cult of tradition, by the very nature of its activities.

In 1932 he left even the most advanced American soldiers far behind him, when he built an expendable airborne tank, and suggested that its role should be the destruction not of an enemy army, but of political, administrative, and industrial targets deep within the enemy homeland. In a way, it was Liddell Hart's "paralysis" on wings. Between 1932 and 1942 Christie built several expendable airborne tanks of various types, and demonstrated the feasibility of releasing them at low altitudes from bomber aircraft, and motoring them instantly into action. But the idea was far beyond the range of military acceptance. He was regarded as eccentric, and although some of his earlier land tanks were copied and adapted for limited forms of mobile war by the U.S.S.R. and Britain, and although his amphibious vehicles were developed by the Japanese for their seaborne offensive of 1941, both the Christie Airborne Tank and the idea of using it for ultra-deep operations are still of the future.

Appendix D

Comparative Tank Anatomy

Comparative Tank Anatomy

The question of material superiority in the desert has ever been a vexed one, and it has been alleged frequently that the German armoured forces were both more numerous than our own, and better equipped. While most British historians now admit that we had numerical advantages, some still assert that British machines were hopelessly inferior in quality and design.

Straight comparisons are not easy to make. From 1939 onward, German tank cannon were of several sizes, while up to 1942 there was only one British type. Thus, the British 2-pound missile of 40mm calibre looks very tiny against the 14-pound missile of 75mm calibre in the Panzer 4, until one remembers that the latter's gun was not an armour-piercing weapon at all, but a short-barrelled howitzer which could throw low-velocity shell accurately at ranges up to 3000 yards. The other German tank guns were dual-purpose weapons, in calibres ranging from 20mm to 50mm, firing solid shot against tanks and shell against "soft" targets; and as there is an immutable law of cannon foundry which insists that a dual-purpose gun cannot have the best of both worlds—it is dangerous to fire an explosive shell down a choke bore—it can be accepted that a 50mm German gun could hurl a 4½-pound shot which yet was less effective than a British 40mm gun's 2-pound shot, because the British gun fired solids only with a proportionately higher armour-piercing performance. If a 2-pound shot gets inside a tank it can mangle the crew, or set off the ammunition and petrol, as effectively as a bigger missile. The superiority of the British 40mm gun held good until the Germans extended their 50mm cannon from calibre-length L42 to L60, and so obtained a shot speed of 2700 feet per second, 100 feet per second faster than that of the British 2-pounder; but then one must ask, how many German tanks were so equipped?

Many firing tests were conducted on anti-tank ranges in Egypt, and these showed that in straight duelling at 1000 yards with normal impact of strike (90° to plane of surface), British tanks were in no way inferior, in either penetration power or armour defence, to the German medium tanks 3 and 4, and were definitely superior to the early Panzers 1 and 2 and to the Italian medium and light machines. Up to 1942, no German tank except the 3(J) Special with 50mm L60 cannon (and there were none of these in Africa until the summer of 1942, and only 19 then) could penetrate any British tank frontally, in hull or turret, at 1000 yards or over. But at 1000 yards the British 2-pounder could penetrate all German turret fronts. Here, one must remember that the penetrable turret front outside the area of the gun mantlet appears very small at 1000 yards, and additional complications were the slightly inferior quality of the British tank gunsights,[1] and the introduction, in 1942, on both sides of limited supplies of armour-piercing ammunition with special characteristics. These were the German "Composite" shot which flew faster at short ranges but was ineffective at long ranges, and the American-made "Piercing Cap" which had similar advantages and limitations.

Armour likewise varied considerably, not admitting of superficial comparisons. It could be single-plate, appliqué, or cast, while its hardening could be homogeneous or on the face only. Each type had its own characteristics of shot resistance. Face-hardened plate could cause striking shots of high muzzle velocity to disintegrate harmlessly even when the angle of strike was perfect, yet would fall to pieces under repeated clobbering by slower but heavier missiles, which in turn would be useless against thick cast or rolled single-plate homogeneous armour. Further, on many tanks the distribution of the different types of armour was not uniform: turrets and hulls could be of different constitution, and so could frontal and side plates.

What else remains for evaluation? Speed? The maximum road speeds of German tanks ranged from 20 to 26 mph; of British, from 15 to 35 mph. Range? It cannot be considered here, in view of the disparities in fuel supply and operational purpose. Reliability?

[1] This question is discussed at some length in *The Tanks*, Vol. 2, Ch. 3, by Capt. B. H. Liddell Hart.

Here the Germans scored markedly, although some doubt exists as to whether the mechanical unreliability of some British tanks derived from faults in design and manufacture or from poor maintenance in the field. The British tank most frequently condemned as mechanically unreliable was the Crusader cruiser, a Nuffield product. Its defective water pump became a persistent desert legend, a bogey blamed for many a tankman's death. A suddenly overheating engine stops, and a tank is held immobile upon the battlefield—a sitting duck to a hail of shot, a cripple drawing fire from every enemy quarter. But the Crusader was not uniformly unreliable. Some regiments had persistent trouble; others none at all. The inference is that it responded faithfully to sound maintenance, and broke down under neglect. Perhaps we see here a consequence of the delayed mechanization of the cavalry regiments.

We have discussed the mobility, firepower, and protection characteristics of tanks that fought in the desert. Dare we carry comparisons further in any but the most specific terms? Perhaps we should call to mind Dr. Samuel Johnson's reply to the question whether he considered men or women the more intelligent: "Pray, Sir: Which Man, and Which Woman?" To which, when we think of tanks and the desert war, we may add, "And under What Circumstances?"

Two circumstances had the effect of supporting the myth of German tank superiority. First, the technique of forward control developed by the panzer leaders enabled them to give their troops the advantage of local numerical superiority, which was quickly expanded by its victims into a myth of overall material superiority. Second, and more important from the qualitative point of view, was the panzer leaders' sword-and-shield technique with tanks and anti-tank guns. The concept of strategic paralysis required the tank crews to infiltrate forward, and never to commit suicide unprofitably. When they bumped into opposition too strong to be eliminated rapidly, they sought a way round it. If the enemy followed with a counter-attack by tanks, they retired behind mobile defences in which anti-tank guns played a very important part. Thus, in a moving tank battle a time nearly always came when the fighting machines passed into the area occupied by the German anti-tank gun screen, and as these guns were invariably well concealed, their intervention was not easily distinguished. That is to say, when British tanks were knocked out, it was very often uncertain whether panzers or anti-tank guns had done the damage.

There were three main types of German anti-tank cannon, of 37mm, 50mm long-barrel, and 88mm calibre. The first two were easily concealed, and so could strike from ambush at short range. The third was a dual-purpose anti-aircraft and anti-tank gun which, although very bulky and difficult to conceal, was still extremely effective in ambushing tanks because it could destroy them at extreme range. Its 22-pound shot, which contained a small explosive charge actuated by a graze fuse, could penetrate 92mm of armour at 1000 yards, and at 2000 yards could still get inside Matildas. Here, then, in the unseen anti-tank gun, was the real bogey of the tank-fight.

	Armour Max/Min mm		*Gun*	*Engine* bhp
		Calibre mm	Muzzle Velocity ft/sec	
A) *Germany*				
Panzer 4	85–10	75	2461	270
Panther	110–20 sloped	75	3068	690
Tiger 1	105–26	88	2657	640
Tiger 2	150–25	88	3340	700
B) *Russia*				
T34/85	110–20 sloped	85	2200	500
Josef Stalin	150–26 sloped	122	2625	600
C) *America*				
M4 Sherman	76–28	76·2	2600	425
M26 Pershing	110–30	90	2700	500
D) *Britain*				
Cromwell 7	101–10	75	2050	600
Comet	101–14	76·2	2600	600
Churchill 7	152–25	75	2050	350

1943–45

Weight tons	Power Weight	Speed mph	Mechanical Reliability
25	10·8/1	22	Good
45	15·3/1	29	Fair/Good
56	11·4/1	25	Poor
67	10·4/1	26	Very Poor
30	16·6/1	33	Good
46	13·4/1	23	Good
32	13·2/1	25	Good
38	13·1/1	20	Good
28	21·4/1	32	Good
32	15·5/1	29	Good
40	8·7/1	12	Good

Selected Bibliography

ANDRONIKOV AND MOSTOVENKO (trans. edited by von Senger und Etterlin), *Die Roten Panzer*, Lehmann 1962

BRYANT, SIR A., *The Turn of the Tide: 1939-43*, Collins 1957

ESTIENNE, *Les Chars d'Assaut*, Libraire de l'Enseignement Technique 1920
EYSENCK, H. J., *The Uses and Abuses of Psychology*, Penguin 1953

FULLER, J. F. C., *Tanks in the Great War*, Murray 1920
— *Operations between Mechanized Forces*, Sifton Praed 1932
— *Memoirs of an Unconventional Soldier*, Nicholson & Watson 1936

GARTHOFF, R. L., *Soviet Military Policy*, Faber 1966
GUDERIAN, H. (edited by Liddell Hart), *Panzer Leader*, Michael Joseph 1952, Dutton 1952

HART, B. H. LIDDELL, *Paris, or the Future of War*, Murray 1925
— *Europe in Arms*, Faber 1937
— *Strategy: the Indirect Approach*, Faber 1954
— *The Tanks: the History of the Royal Tank Regiment and its Predecessors* (2 vol.), Cassell 1959
— (editor), *The Rommel Papers*, Collins 1953, Harcourt 1953
— (editor), *The Soviet Army*, Weidenfeld & Nicolson 1956
HASHAVIA, A., *The Story of a War*, 1967 (Tel Aviv)
HEIGL, *Taschenbuch der Tanks*, Lehmann 1926
HUVIGNAC, *Histoire de l'Armée Motorisée*, Imprimerie Nationale 1947
HUXLEY, SIR J., *Essays of a Humanist*, Chatto & Windus 1964

230   *Bibliography*

LUVAAS, J., *The Education of an Army: British Military Thought, 1815–1940*, Cassell 1965

MAGNUSKI, *Wozy Bojowe*, Polish Defence Ministry 1960
MARTEL, G. LE Q., *In the Wake of the Tank*, Sifton Praed 1931
— *Our Armoured Forces*, Faber 1945
MELLENTHIN, F. W. VON (edited by L. C. F. Turner), *Panzer Battles 1939–45*, Cassell 1955

POSTAN, M. N. AND OTHERS, *Design and Development of Weapons: Studies in Government and Industrial Organization in History of Second World War*, H.M.S.O. 1964

ROYAL TANK CORPS, *A Short History of the Royal Tank Corps*, Gale & Polden 1938

SCOTT, J. D., *Vickers: a History*, Weidenfeld & Nicolson 1963
SPROTT, W. J. H., *Human Groups*, Penguin 1958
SWINTON, E. D., *Eyewitness*, Hodder & Stoughton 1932
SENGER, VON UND ETTERLIN, *Die Deutschen Panzer 1926-45*, Lehmann 1959
— *Taschenbuch der Panzer 1960*, Lehmann 1960

VERNON, M. D., *The Psychology of Perception*, Penguin 1962

YOUNG, D., *Rommel*, Collins 1950

Journals, etc.
French Army, *Notes d'instruction de l'Armée Blindée*, Saumur 1965
U.S. Army, *Army Information Digest*, Washington August 1965
— *Army Aviation Digest*, Washington June 1967
— *Ordnance Journal*, Washington July/August 1957

Index

PRINTED IN GREAT BRITAIN BY
WESTERN PRINTING SERVICES LTD., BRISTOL